'Most business books are poorly written, difficult to follow, and not worth the purchase price. This book is fun to read, exciting to apply, and profitable to implement.'

Sir John Kay, economist

'This is more than just a refreshingly honest guide to growing by acquisition – it is a common sense bible for how to run a business, written by someone who has nothing left to prove. Thoroughly recommended.'

Michael McLintock, Chair, AB Foods plc

'I started and sold a publishing company but if I'd taken advice from Charles Skinner, I could have easily built a business many times larger. As someone now involved in government and higher education, I wish more people understood how powerful and practical this route to leading business success could be.'

Lord Mendoza, HMG Commissioner for Cultural Recovery and Renewal

'This book is an excellent manual for any entrepreneur or could-be business owner. It is written by a practitioner who understands the tough realities of actually investing in and managing businesses. The book provides practical advice and fascinating case studies of all the pitfalls which can happen to anyone brave enough to embark on an enterprising journey. I strongly recommend it to anyone who has the fortitude and vision to seize the day.'

Luke Johnson, entrepreneur, former Chair of the Royal Society of Arts

'Charles Skinner is a veteran corporate turnaround specialist who is as frank about his disasters as he is modest about his triumphs. The very opposite of the boastful tech-bros who tell us how to change the world, Skinner makes a persuasive case in *Buy, Run, Build* for what he's good at – finding hidden value in unfashionable businesses – with honesty and humour. I treasure especially his image of the struggling chief executive as the embattled ambassador played by Sid James in "Carry On Up The Khyber".'

Martin vander Weyer, Business Editor, The Spectator

'Management is difficult. This book is essential for anyone who wants to do it well. Clear, insightful, and thought-provoking in equal measure. And, unlike most management books, a good read.'

Sir Alex Beard, CEO, Royal Opera House

'Charles Skinner is a businessman with vast experience of finding, acquiring, growing and (mostly) successfully selling over 100 businesses. This engaging and at times very funny book is one that I wish that I had read much earlier in my career and which I have told my children and my students is essential reading for anyone who wants to be a successful entrepreneur.'

Mungo Wilson, Professor of Financial Economics,
Said Business School, University of Oxford

BUY, RUN, BUILD

A guide to Entrepreneurship
Through Acquisition

CHARLES SKINNER

BLOOMSBURY BUSINESS
LONDON · NEW YORK · OXFORD · NEW DELHI · SYDNEY

BLOOMSBURY BUSINESS
Bloomsbury Publishing Plc, 50 Bedford Square, London, WC1B 3DP, UK
Bloomsbury Publishing Inc, 1359 Broadway, New York, NY 10018, USA
Bloomsbury Publishing Ireland, 29 Earlsfort Terrace, Dublin 2, D02 AY28, Ireland

BLOOMSBURY, BLOOMSBURY BUSINESS and the Diana logo are trademarks of Bloomsbury Publishing Plc

First published in Great Britain 2025

Copyright © Charles Skinner, 2025

Charles Skinner has asserted his right under the Copyright, Designs and Patents Act, 1988, to be identified as Author of this work.

Cover design: Amanda Keyte
Cover image © Getty Images

All rights reserved. No part of this publication may be: i) reproduced or transmitted in any form, electronic or mechanical, including photocopying, recording or by means of any information storage or retrieval system without prior permission in writing from the publishers; or ii) used or reproduced in any way for the training, development or operation of artificial intelligence (AI) technologies, including generative AI technologies. The rights holders expressly reserve this publication from the text and data mining exception as per Article 4(3) of the Digital Single Market Directive (EU) 2019/790.

Bloomsbury Publishing Plc does not have any control over, or responsibility for, any third-party websites referred to or in this book. All internet addresses given in this book were correct at the time of going to press. The author and publisher regret any inconvenience caused if addresses have changed or sites have ceased to exist, but can accept no responsibility for any such changes.

A catalogue record for this book is available from the British Library.

A catalogue record for this book is available from the Library of Congress.

ISBN: HB: 978-1-3994-2712-8
ePDF: 978-1-3994-2709-8
ePub: 978-1-3994-2710-4

Typeset by Deanta Global Publishing Services, Chennai, India
Printed and bound in Great Britain

For product safety related questions contact productsafety@bloomsbury.com.

To find out more about our authors and books visit www.bloomsbury.com and sign up for our newsletters.

To Carol

CONTENTS

Introduction 1
    I am not a 'classic' entrepreneur 1
    A builder, not a founder 2
    Entrepreneurship Through Acquisition 4

1 What Do You Really Want to Do? 7
    What suits you? 7
    Understand what's right for you 8
    The emotional side 10
    A leap of faith 11
    Don't ignore the lifestyle side 11
    What sort of business do you want to run? 12
    Understand the market dynamics 14
    Understand the cycle 15
    Finding a business 16
    Make contact 17
    If you want something, just ask for it 18
    Cultivate your contacts 19

2 Checking Out a Business 21
    Success teaches you all the wrong lessons 21
    Do your homework 23
    Lessons learned and bullets dodged 25
    Getting into the weeds 28
    Due diligence 30
    Follow the cash 31
    Property 33
    Taking a view 34
    And the people of course 36

3 Buying and Selling a Business 39
    Something I *do* know about 39
    Valuing a business 40
    The vendor's viewpoint 43
    The purchaser's viewpoint 44

The Venn diagram 46
Pursuit 46
Tactics 47
The information 49
Who are you talking to? 51
The key moment 52
The importance of momentum 56
When to walk away 57
Post-acquisition management 57

4 How Do You Get the Money? 61
Starting up 61
Early-stage funding 62
What if you don't have the money to buy a business? 63
Private equity funding 63
Small private equity funding 64
Search funds 65
Angels, family and friends 65
What size of company should you be looking to acquire? 66
An example of buying a business without any money 67
But there may still be a gap 70
What next? 71

5 Being the CEO 73
The power of one 73
The tone of the business 75
The customer isn't always right 76
Strategy vs narrative 78
Get people on board with your story 80
How I think you should CEO 81
The horrors of matrix management 83
What do you want at the centre? 83
Hands off, but... 84
Everyday CEO stuff 87
Manage your advisers 90
Big decisions 92
Being a leader 93

6 The Board 95
The chairman and the CEO 95
Good chair 96
Bad chair 97
What makes a good board? 100
The basics for an effective board meeting 102
What the board should do 104
What does 'non-executive' mean? 106

CONTENTS

7 The Business of Management 109
  Drucker said it best 109
  Power and responsibility 111
  Business clichés are often true 114
  Taking over as a new boss 114
  Age and motivation 116
  Have your people's backs 117
  Why mean is good 118

8 People and Pay 123
  The role of HR 123
  Recruitment and talent 124
  Succession management 125
  Family businesses and succession 127
  How to pay people properly 128
  Bonuses and incentives 129
  Keep it simple, stupid (KISS) 132
  What doesn't work 133

9 The Tough Side of People Management 137
  When people have got to go 137
  Getting it right and wrong 139
  Performance management in three meetings 141
  Telling people they have to leave 143
  Performance management outside business 145
  Who wields the axe? 147
  Managing bastards 148
  On the other hand 151

10 Big Money 153
  Banks in principle, and a little history 153
  What a CEO wants from banks 154
  Creative debt 155
  How to keep the banks off your back 156
  What happens when you fall out with the banks 157
  The ABCs of PE 159
  A little more history (this time on private equity) 160
  The private equity cycle 162
  So – private equity or quoted company? 164
  Why be a public company? 167
  Understanding public company investors 169
  The rules for a public CEO 171
  The Indian Rope Trick 175

11 When It All Goes Wrong 179
   Shit happens 179
   Why shit happens 180
   How to sort out a mess 181
   Some practical tips 182
   Failure is an orphan 184
   Carry on Up the Khyber 186
   What happens next? 187

Acknowledgements 189

Index 191

INTRODUCTION

We live in world that celebrates business founders. The icons of our age are people like Mark Zuckerberg, Jeff Bezos, Steve Jobs, Bill Gates and, of course, perhaps the most controversial of all, Elon Musk. The idea of starting a company at a kitchen table or in a garage has become sort of foundational myth of twenty-first-century success.

But this is a *practical* book. And its central idea is that, for the vast majority of people – even many would-be entrepreneurs – this is not the best route. Rather, it's better to go into an existing business, build on it, and improve it. Why? Because starting a business is stressful, time-consuming and you often have little idea whether it's going to work or not. The risks are huge – and not just for the business. It can take over or even ruin your life.

With an existing business you already have customers, suppliers and staff – and, from day one, you have the ability to make a positive impact on the company and the people you are working with. Compared to starting a business, this may sound like a cop-out: entrepreneurialism for wimps. But I promise you it isn't. If you can turn a £3m company into a £100m company, I'd argue you're every bit as much of an entrepreneur as someone who founds and builds a £10m company. You're probably much wealthier too.

I am not a 'classic' entrepreneur

I have only started one business from scratch in my life and it didn't last very long. This was called WePod. Cast your mind back to 2002, when people still had vast CD collections which needed to be laboriously transferred to their iPods by hand. I was given an iPod for Christmas and immediately struck by what an incredible hassle this was. Bingo. My one great, original idea for a start-up.

WePod's proposition was simple. We'd load your iPod for you. We would collect your CDs from your house and return them and your fully loaded iPod, a week or so later. We charged £1 to rip a CD and transfer it to your device. It was a pretty good business model. This was just after the dot.com bust, so we wanted to start a company with a decent, early revenue stream. This provided it. Customers paid for the service up front.

There were four shareholders: me (the guy who'd had the idea and was a CEO), my wife, Carol (who had marketing and advertising experience), Hector (the owner of a Soho post-production house who had technical knowledge and who came up with the name), and a guy who worked for Hector who was happy to design the download system. The shareholding was split four ways and we all agreed to work for free initially.

The business was an immediate success. We did £10k in revenues in the first full month and were covered by the *Evening Standard* and a glossy magazine. But then we put an advert in a day school's parents' magazine. This was one of those not-quite-business decisions. Yes, the ad would reach a wealthy demographic (private school parents), but it was as much to support the school my children attended as anything else.

Unfortunately another parent at the school was the CEO of EMI. We got a 'Cease and Desist' letter from music industry lawyers three days after the magazine was published. The next two months involved endless legal fights with the big four record companies. Their argument was this: while individuals were ripping CDs on to their iPods and this was a technical breach of contract, WePod was doing it as a commercial venture and they would pursue us in court.

Apple had been very supportive and offered us a kiosk in their new flagship store in London but they wouldn't supply us with the critical digital rights management software which the record companies required (probably because the software had taken them years and millions of dollars to develop). We tried to explain to the record company lawyers that the course they were pursuing meant they were handing a big chunk of the music market to Apple. They didn't care. I suppose it's some consolation that we were more right here than we ever imagined.

And so, a few months after we founded it, we closed WePod. It just wasn't worth the legal hassle and, besides, it was a 'side hustle' before the term existed. We all had other jobs, which was just as well. If we'd been classic entrepreneurs and bet the farm on WePod, we'd have been in real trouble.

A builder, not a founder

WePod was an interesting experience. It made me realize that I'm not an entrepreneur who starts companies, although I have the greatest respect for those who are. These include friends such as Charlie Bigham (of upmarket ready meals fame) and my frequent business partner John Laycock, who started out selling nuts and bolts from the back of a van and who I later advised on selling

INTRODUCTION

a business for an eight-figure sum. Other friends who've built great businesses from scratch include, Johnnie Boden, Nick Wheeler (Charles Tyrwhitt), Rohan Blacker (sofa.com and Pookie), Chrissie Rucker (The White Company) and the late, great Paul Tustain (BullionVault).

But if I'm not a founder-entrepreneur, then what am I?

I'm a manager who has always found it difficult to work for other people. I need to be the CEO. I like to take small, often troubled, companies and turn them into much bigger, better companies – usually via a mixture of smart acquisitions and organic growth.

The seed for this was planted early in my career. After I realized I was in the wrong place in the City (as did my employers) in the early 1980s, I spent seven years advising on buying and selling private companies with revenues ranging from £500,000 to £50m. I enjoyed it more than my first City job which I had perceived as the pointless movement of money, but while doing it, I became aware of a particular type of businessperson. These were individuals who had usually sold a business at some point and who were always on the lookout for small, private companies that might be up for sale. They generally had a reasonable idea of the broad area they liked (e.g. industrial, consumer, services) but were up for something interesting and new. They liked running businesses and had the energy, enthusiasm, funds and experience to do so, but were too shrewd to contemplate starting from scratch.

This is what I've done as a CEO. Find an established business where the owners didn't know what they had, wanted to exit or were in trouble for reasons that didn't compromise the business (or at least the entire company). Then either buy the business or buy into it. Here it's important to note that you do not need millions to buy into a business. You just need to be able to put together the financing or know people who can. Many people put none of their own money in.

The first company I did this with was Brandon Hire. John Laycock and I bought into a tiny quoted company (market cap: £3m) with half a dozen tool hire branches around Bristol. The majority owners were good operators but they wanted different things at their stage in life. Moreover a horrible accident involving a bouncy castle and the bankruptcy of their insurance company had spooked them.

From an early stage, I could see how the business could be better – to take the most obvious point, tool hire, bouncy castles and fancy dress (which the business also rented out) suggested a lack of focus. But I could also see that there were many other small, local companies like this and that there were economies of scale and synergies to be had. A decade later, having bought up dozens of small tool hire companies and grown organically, we sold the business (which had over 100 branches by this point) to Wolseley for £100m.

I'd like to say I repeated this formula at the next business I joined as CEO. But this this was far from the case. My success at Brandon led me to believe I had the Midas touch and I took over a business without doing full due diligence. It was a disaster and, by 2007, I was out on my ear and thought I was on the scrapheap. It was the lowest point of my professional life. But I picked myself up and trawled through endless businesses, eventually identifying a lovely business hiding in a bankrupt quoted company (market cap: £2m). I emailed the majority shareholder and told them that I had a cunning plan.

A month later I was the CEO. A year later, I'd sorted the group balance sheet, got rid of the disastrous businesses that were causing the company so much trouble, and was on the way to making the first acquisition in the star-performing business. Seven years later we were one of the two main operators in that space and the company's shares had gone up 40-fold since I'd joined.

Even within this business, I was wary of starting afresh in a new space. But I had spotted another opportunity. While snooping around the backs of the warehouses of a company I'd acquired (to see who was having a smoke and whether the site managers really looked after their premises) I noticed a number of metal cages full of discarded IT equipment. That company had a removal business and clearly customers wanted to ditch their old IT kit.

So we bought a small IT recycler and we tried to work out how the IT recycling market worked. There was plenty of other activity going on in the group, so I was in no rush. Once we had the hang of it and had recognized how fragmented the market was, we bought another IT recycler and we are now the biggest IT recycler in the UK.

This is what I am. I like to build companies, mainly through acquisition rather than starting them myself. I am a buy-up entrepreneur, not a start-up entrepreneur. And I'm a big fan of unsung, unfashionable sectors such as tool hire, laundries, storing / scanning / shredding paper, office removals, IT recycling, self-storage and so on.

Entrepreneurship Through Acquisition

Perhaps surprisingly, given my career, I only became aware of Entrepreneurship Through Acquisition (ETA) as a formal idea when talking to someone half my age. The 30-year-old CEO of the largest of my tool hire companies, who is herself a Harvard MBA, recently told me that this is one of the most popular courses at Harvard.

This makes good sense to me – and not just because it's easier to buy up than start up. Buying an existing company should also should give you some security in life if you're any good at business. The company will be a going concern, you can improve it and, if need be, you can sell it. None of this will necessarily be true of a start-up.

INTRODUCTION

What's more, there has also never been a better time to do this, especially in the UK. Partly this is demographic. Many baby boomers, even those running humble small-to-medium sized enterprises (SMEs), are looking for an exit. Often they don't want to pass the company on to their kids. I'm always surprised by how realistic smallbusiness owners are about their children. Most business owners are practical people and unless the kids are a chip off the old block, they don't want to burden their kids and scupper their own retirement plans by handing on the business. Often these people are tired too – they no longer have the energy or inclination to grow the business, seek new markets, raise capital to take advantage of opportunities, and so on.

On top of all this, market valuations for small companies around the world are low. In the past, I'd usually value a typical business at around six years' earnings. My experience of the current market suggests three years' earnings is now the norm. There are bargains to be had everywhere. So if you want to run a company, what are you waiting for?

1
WHAT DO YOU REALLY WANT TO DO?

'If one doesn't know to which port one is sailing, no wind is favourable.'
SENECA THE YOUNGER

Understanding the right sector for you, the sort of company you want to work in and what your skills and inclinations are. Getting to grips with markets and cycles. Finding the right sort of business. Networks, contacts and how to ask for what you want.

What suits you?

It took me 15 years and five employers to realize that I needed to be the boss. I suppose the signs were there early. I resented being pushed around as a graduate trainee at S.G. Warburg (although I dare say this is true of most graduate trainees). However, subsequent jobs slowly confirmed that I needed to be in the driving seat. As a business adviser and, later, as the editor of a business magazine, I always felt as if I was on the sidelines, rather than in the thick of things. This rankled. I wanted to be where the real decisions were being made, rather than helping people make those decisions – or analyzing their decisions afterwards.

Eventually I did become the boss – and my stints as CEO have been (mostly) the best years of my working life. Had I recognized what suited me earlier, I might have got there quicker.

This is a book which addresses how you run things. But you need to get there first – and in order to maximize your chances of getting there, you need to ask yourself two very basic questions. The first is: 'What am I good at?' And the second is: 'What do I enjoy?'

Let's take what you enjoy first – the kind of business you want to work in. Some people – such as doctors, lawyers or elite athletes – have thought long and hard about their chosen field. Most people have not.

In fact, many people – regardless of their position – fall into a career after school or university and then stick with it. If they're lucky it suits them; if they're not, it doesn't. They never step back and ask, 'Was I destined to work in events management?' and their entire careers are based on a decision they made at 22 with virtually no first-hand knowledge

This is very odd given that work takes up more of our time than any other activity. But it's not quite as odd – or as bad – as it sounds. Many jobs, especially management roles, have a great deal of commonality regardless of the sector or business you're in. Sacking an underperformer in an engineering company is much the same as sacking an underperformer in an ad agency. Being the finance director of a chemical company isn't so different to being the financial director of a book publisher.

There are also numerous factors in careers which are secondary to the job or sector itself. You might, for instance, be happier in a field which is your second choice if it is growing strongly while your first choice shrivels. The idea that we have one true calling is nonsense for most people.

Nonetheless, if you're going to run a company, found a company or move to a senior job within a company, you should take time to think about what suits you both in terms of sector and your talents. I believe you should fit your career to your personality rather than your interests. This is an important distinction and it's one many people miss.

Understand what's right for you

My own career has been pretty eclectic. I started in banking (which was my arbitrary graduate choice) and then moved to venture capital before editing a business magazine. After that I joined a tool hire company as CEO, which I left to head up a textile rental group. I was then CEO of a records and documents management company. I left and then returned to run this business again after the succession process went wrong.

This may sound like a random collection of roles. But if you look more closely, these jumps do make a kind of sense: I gradually worked out that I was more interested in business than finance and that I wanted to be part of business itself rather than advising on it or writing about it. I also recognized that I wanted to do it as much on my own terms as possible. Eventually I got to a position that suited me well, but it took a long time. So, what advice would I offer?

Let's start with the obvious. Most people move up the greasy pole in the same sector, or even in the same company. This is where you know the product and have the contacts. These are significant advantages which shouldn't be thrown away lightly.

Indeed, so significant is this 'home' advantage that it allows many people to set up their own businesses without being natural entrepreneurs. Rather, they are in the right place at the right time and they feel confident enough to take a chance. The classic example of this is the ad agency where a big customer likes you, but not the agency. You leave, set up a new agency and take the big customer with you. This model works very well in capital-light areas like consultancies and talent management where the value of companies is largely in networks and contacts, not factories.

A related strategy to this is where you outsource a chunk of your employer's business (usually non-core activities such as records management, catering, tool hire, and so on) and found a new company around this. Again, this is something you can only really do on your home turf.

A good example of the power of home advantage is Capita and Rod Aldridge. Capita was originally a division of CIPFA (the Chartered Institute of Public Finance and Accountancy), which is a non-profit organization. Having founded the division in 1984, Aldridge led a management buyout in 1987. Capita went on to become the UK's biggest business process outsourcing company and now has around a third of the market. As Aldridge never founded another company one could say he is probably not a natural, or a serial, entrepreneur.

While home advantage can be enormous, you shouldn't be constrained by it. If, for instance, you work in conventional power generation, you might move to renewables. Or, if you have considerable experience of marketing at an airline, you could found a consumer marketing agency.

Of course, this is not the only way – and this book is about getting yourself into the driving seat. I came into business from a financial and advisory background. This meant I had some 'transferable skills' – I knew how to talk to shareholders, I understood the financials, I understood the patterns in different industries and I had a broad outlook. However, I have always needed people around me who really understand how to execute the day-to-day business. This is not ideal but it is workable. It's also why my first CEO role was at a struggling company that was willing to take a chance on someone whose background was not perfect.

The way to approach any big step upwards is to take a cool, dispassionate look at the skills you have, ask yourself which are portable and then identify roles where they could be applied. The ideal new role will stretch you and expand what you know but it won't be wholly new. You will not be starting from scratch and you should be able to deploy some of your existing skills.

My very first move was a bit like this. After two years at S.G. Warburg, I knew I was not a natural banker (and I'd learned was what it's like to be unhappy in a job and badly managed). But I'd also learned a great deal there which I knew would be useful in venture capital where I thought I'd be much happier. In the longer run, it also made me feel comfortable in the City, which is really useful for the CEO of a public company

The emotional side

What about the emotional side then? What about the idea – popular among entrepreneurs – that you should follow your passion, your one true calling? I believe you need to be very careful here, whether you're buying into a business (or founding one). Trying to turn something you love into a business can leave you with a failing company and a passion you now hate. There is a very good reason why people who open restaurants and hotels with little knowledge of what working in hospitality involves are such a staple of television documentaries. It's because disasters make great TV.

However, you should also be careful about going too far in the other direction. The archetype here is the City banker who is earning six or even seven figures but has no life outside of work; many people in this position would probably be happier earning a quarter of their salary, having time for friends and family and taking full responsibility for their working lives. Be wary too of jobs and sectors that promise a certain lifestyle – travel is a good example here. The lifestyle side of work can quickly pall and when it does, what seemed to be a positive, like spending half your life in Singapore, can become a very significant negative.

Know too what sort of role you're happy in. I was far happier as CEO of a medium-sized company than I would have been as a divisional head in a larger company. Others will feel the opposite way and there is no right or wrong answer here. Similarly, some people love founding and owning companies while others are keener on managing businesses that are up-and-running already, with the need for majority ownership being less important. Again, it's about what suits your personality type.

Entire books are written on finding the right job. But for senior managers the basics can be covered pretty quickly. You want to be working in a type of business that interests and challenges you. For me, the type of business is more important than the specific sector. My checklist might include factors like: Is it B2B (business to business)? Is it multi-branch? Is there an opportunity to consolidate the market? And so on.

Hopefully it will be a sector you like, but there is no need to be in a sector you love. You should know what you're doing but not be so comfortable that you're not learning new things and finding some aspects difficult. You want to get up in the morning enthusiastic, but you also want to be able to step back and have a life outside work. And, finally, you want to be reasonably well rewarded. This may all seem very obvious but so many people get it wrong.

A leap of faith

If you are ambitious, at some point you will probably have to take a chance if you want to get on. My first job as CEO was like this – it was a big leap for both me and Brandon Hire, the company in question. But we needed each other. The company was struggling, having expanded without focus, and I was on hand, having been a non-executive director on the board for three years. Although I had no real management experience, I had worked as an adviser to several similar businesses, I had energy and ideas and I had a strong understanding of the financial side of the business. I could deal with banks and boards and I could lead teams.

All this was enough that not having hands-on experience of the tool hire business was not too much of a problem. The board and I were both prepared to take the risk that my lack of business management would be balanced by the chairman's strengths in this area. It took time to get it right and many mistakes were made (particularly by me) but it worked out well in the end. Getting the job was my lucky break – and you always need a bit of luck in your career.

Sometimes, however, you don't have that luck. By the time I started my second role as CEO, I was an experienced operator who'd run a successful public company for 10 years. Nonetheless, this job turned out to be an eight-month long, value-destroying horror show. It might have gone marginally better if I had known the sector well, as I couldn't get to grips with the immediate issues while I was finding my way around. But really I can only blame myself: I hadn't done my homework – and I was unlucky.

Don't ignore the lifestyle side

I've already touched on work-life balance, but you need to think about where you sit on the work-to-live / live-to-work spectrum – and then you need to think about it again. People often view lifestyle considerations as somehow unworthy and unimportant when it comes to choosing a job. But they're not. A huge commute, for example, can mean the difference between four hours a day with your family and no hours a day with your family. Being posted abroad can be an incredible adventure or an unpleasant wrench that disrupts children's schools and damages social ties.

Above all, recognizing what is important to you – across the board – will make identifying the right job easier. My own experience here was taking months to realize that, subconsciously, I was only properly considering working in businesses that were in areas of the UK I wanted to live in. There's nothing wrong with this and I would have saved myself considerable time and effort if I'd recognized it from the outset. As the Ancient Greeks said, 'know thyself' – it'll mean you pick a company that suits you.

What sort of business do you want to run?

OK, so you've worked out which areas suit you and you have an idea of the kind of business you might be interested in. But the self-interrogation isn't over yet. You now need to ask yourself the same questions again, but from a more technical and detailed point of view.

If you're looking for a company to run, there are essentially two types. One is a business you own yourself. There are considerable attractions to this, not least the freedom to do whatever you like, within the law. If, as an owner-manager, you want to give a huge chunk of the profits to charity or share them amongst your staff you can – and there are companies that do this. Many owner-managed companies are run successfully as lifestyle businesses, working at a pace and style dictated by the owner. But if you are going to own the business without founding it, you will probably need access to some capital. This will be a significant undertaking – and I cover it in chapter four.

The second option is running a business that is owned by other people. This may be a private company, a public company (or plc as they are known in the UK) or a division of a bigger group. My last three full-time roles have been as CEO of a public company, so I know about working for shareholders. However, with a few key differences most of what running a company is about is the same, regardless of the ownership structure. A good business is a good business no matter who owns it.

Next, you might ask yourself what sort of business you feel comfortable with – in a very broad sense. I have always worked in B2B (business to business) companies. These are companies which sell goods or services to other companies, rather than consumers. So a textile hire company (which provides staff uniforms) rather than a retail clothing chain. I feel that I understand businesses and their concerns and what motivates them. I do not have the same feel for consumers – so I would not be comfortable taking charge of a B2C (business to consumer) company. Give me a business where the customers want a regular supply of services which they don't want to look after in-house and I know exactly what I'm doing. Ask me what high-street shoppers will want next year and I won't have a clue.

For me, one of most important things a business can have is a secure income stream. This is why I like sectors such as records management and textile rental. Both have customers with a consistent business need and no desire to chop and change their suppliers. A reliable income stream means you can plan ahead. It means that, if you can make cost savings or sell additional services, the business's profitability will rise considerably. It means that you can move into an industry where you don't need personal connections and detailed product knowledge to keep the revenue up.

It's also (again) about knowing yourself. I am not a natural salesman and I never will be – so I would choose a business where the CEO can generate value by delivering efficiencies or by making acquisitions over one where the CEO's key role lies in driving sales. Looking at criteria like this can go a long way towards narrowing down the field of companies you have to choose from.

Next, ask yourself how capital intensive the business is. If you want to grow the business (and that is what shareholders will want), in many sectors access to capital will determine the rate at which you can expand. For instance, if you run a company that makes parts for wind turbines and you want to expand, you will need to build a new factory and this will require serious financial backing. Similarly, if it's a sector that you want to consolidate through buying other companies, you're going to need money to buy them. If you expect that you will be able to access capital easily, fine. I feel very comfortable raising money for the right opportunities. But if this isn't you, you should be looking for businesses that won't need external funds.

There are plenty of these. Some companies, particularly in the knowledge economy, are very capital-light. This is especially true if they use Cloud infrastructure (which can be bought incrementally like electricity) and have large numbers of remote workers. The ultimate expression of this is the 'virtual business', which may operate entirely in the online world and have no owned infrastructure at all. This is something that was becoming common before the pandemic – but the lockdowns accelerated this by massively expanding the variety of roles and work that we know can be done at home.

It's not always immediately obvious what makes a business capital intensive, though. You might look at retailers with their fitted-out shops and high stock levels and believe there must be significant capital sunk into them. This is not the case: apart from fitting the shops out, most retail properties are capital-light. The shops are rented with quarterly payments to the landlords and the industry's payment norms tend to work in the retailers' favour. Once a business is established, suppliers will usually accept delayed payment, meaning the money arrives in the till before the goods need to be paid for. So the faster you grow, the more cash you have on hand for future development. If you take clothing retail, there is rarely a need to raise any external capital, meaning that founders often retain majority shareholdings.

Similarly deceptive appearances exist right across the board. A manufacturer may have old but functioning equipment – and so not appear capital intensive. But it will usually have to stock significant amounts of material for production which will need to be paid for, like the factory workers, long before the customer gets the goods and even longer before the customer pays. Winning that big order is often the moment these companies need to speak to the bank manager or look for external funding.

Running any business will give you headaches but some involve more pressure than others. This is particularly true of companies in cyclical businesses or those with a high fixed-cost base and insecure revenues. High fixed-cost base businesses can look like great when trading is strong but are likely to face difficult decisions very quickly if revenues start dropping. Without secure revenues, they are vulnerable to ordinary downturns because sales fall but you can't stop the bills coming in. Of course, if things get really bad, as with global disasters like COVID, the government may step in, but this is not to be relied upon and few proper business people think government intervention is a good thing.

Make sure, that if you choose to go into this sort of business, you're prepared to make tough decisions, such as mass redundancies when there's a downturn. These types of business are best managed by people with a strong sense of prudence who are ready for lean times rather than those who want to grow fast without a strong balance sheet. Personally, I like high fixed-cost businesses, but as a worrier who likes to grow things, only when I'm sure the revenues are consistently solid.

All this underscores the same point – that you need to run a business that works for you. Some people are happy to make tough decisions while others thrive on taking risks. Know what sort of person you are and find a sector and company type that suits you.

Understand the market dynamics

Once you've narrowed down the sort of sectors that suit you, look at the structure of the markets you want to operate in. My first question is usually: 'What stage of maturity is the market in?' While different sectors have different dynamics there are four typical stages.

1. An immature market is exciting and dynamic and often has a Wild West feel to it. There will be an increasingly large number of operators and many of them will be small and recent start-ups. Prices will be 'uncommoditized', meaning that nobody, particularly the customers, yet knows what the right price for the service or product is. There will be big profits (and losses) to be made.

2. In a developing market, the more successful operators (who have better products, better sales skills, are more efficient, etc.) grow at the expense of the weaker operators. The pricing is becoming more commoditized but operating efficiencies are improving, so profit margins can still be high.
3. In a consolidating market, the large operators get bigger because they are more efficient and can still make money at prices which are now fully commoditized.
4. A fourth and final stage may be big corporations sweating their cash cows.

All these stages present opportunities for good managers, but some people are better suited to certain stages than others. Those with entrepreneurial flair and an appetite for risk will do well in stage 1, people with sales skills are likely to thrive in stage 2, financiers will flourish in stage 3, while big businesses will probably rule the roost in stage 4.

It's pretty straightforward to identify which stage a market is at by looking at who is operating in it. Once you've done this, you can start looking at the individual companies.

Occasionally markets don't suit such analysis, particularly in more obscure areas. These are normally the kinds of markets that outsiders won't bother entering. They're cosy niches where established operators tend to do well and will often have significant barriers to entry such as historic sunk costs that make entry for new players unattractive and costly.

However, you should still keep a weather eye on these. Fast-moving technology has a way of opening up once-closed markets, and aggressive, well-funded companies may be attracted by high margins. Finally, what used to protect these markets, more than anything is else, is simply that few people knew they existed. The ease with which any market can now be researched has changed this – and in the world of big data it's much harder to keep your high profit margins hidden away in blissful obscurity. Today's cosy niche may be tomorrow's hot opportunity.

Understand the cycle

Timing is a factor, too. Regardless of what stage a market is in, many markets are cyclical (in the sense of the economic cycle), so you need to understand if you're at the top of a cycle and times are good (but may not last) or at the bottom of a cycle (where the only way is up). I'm a huge believer in the importance of luck and timing – you can't do much about luck but you can work with timing.

We sold Brandon Hire before the 2008 financial crisis. The subsequent collapse in activity in the construction industry led to a collapse in revenues for tool hire companies. With high fixed costs, tool hire businesses and their value were mashed. It was pure luck that we sold before this. However, I reinvested in several tool hire start-ups in 2011 and 2012 when I knew the industry had a following wind in the form of the 'up' phase of the construction cycle. I also recognized that many of the surviving players in tool hire were still struggling from debts they'd incurred during the collapse and the market was ripe for nimble new entrants. This was not luck.

Finding a business

OK, you're now in a position where you have a sector or sectors which are up your street and you understand the market dynamics and the business cycle. How do you make a target list of companies to approach?

Researching companies isn't hard. The information is all out there. Years ago, when I was looking for a job, the *Yellow Pages* was still in widespread use and I would plough through the sections I was interested in by trade, working out what might be a good fit for me. This makes me sound as old as Methuselah – and that there may now be young entrepreneurs who have never ever heard of the *Yellow Pages*. But it's not a bad model. Once you're interested in a sector, look at who is operating in it.

Of course online information is both plentiful and of greatly varying quality. But googling is much faster than reading a phone book. You will quickly realize that there are sources ranging from industry lists to Glassdoor to LinkedIn and you'll soon get a feel for the businesses that come up again and again, and why. Even those that are not relevant to your search are useful in terms of your overall view and, via online communities ranging from Reddit to X (formerly Twitter), you can be privy to insider gossip from these companies, which is an interesting form of unstructured intelligence.

Perhaps the single best resource if you're looking at a private company are online databases such as the UK's Companies House. This is a remarkable and wonderful thing and it lets you search any company and download its accounts and other details – and it's free. It's not just the obvious stuff like profitability either. If you want to acquire a private company, looking at the ages of directors (which are in the CH records) is helpful for retirement sales. Back in the bad old days, you had to physically visit Companies House in London and view the accounts individually on microfiche.

With so much data to hand, you should be able to work out which companies might appeal. Even if you're just idly thinking about moving on, undertaking the exercise is helpful – and if you decide you really want to make that move, you will be far better informed.

Finally, it's worth noting that many businesses operate in multiple sectors – and there are often opportunities to be had in this. At Mavinwood (which would later become Restore), the terrible performance of the property maintenance business was masking the potential of the high-performing records management business. Selling off some parts of the maintenance arm and closing others meant we could focus on the star performer whose qualities had been camouflaged by the shambles elsewhere. Similarly, at Johnson Service Group, a number of poor divisions were hiding the fundamental strength of the industrial laundry business. Alas, I wasn't CEO long enough to huck these laggards out, but doing so was what started the company on the road to post-disaster recovery after I left.

Many of the best acquisition opportunities come up when a large company wants out of a particular business. This can be many reasons: underperformance, not fitting into a new strategy, taking up too much management time and so on. Often the underlying business is in pretty good shape and performance can be drastically improved through focus and thought.

Make contact

On one hand, approaching a business you want to be involved with is pretty straightforward – you just do it. However, on the other, letting someone know you want to buy their business or want to run it may require you to be slightly more cloak and dagger.

It requires a mixture of tact, bravado and preparation. The trick is to be polite but demonstrate that you have the right background and ideas and that you've done your homework. In my experience a carefully thought-through approach will nearly always get a hearing. People are likely to be intrigued – and, besides, almost all of them will really enjoy talking about their businesses.

There is an element of this being a numbers game and you have to reach as much of your target universe as you can. Whether you're looking to be the next boss in an existing business or to effect a change of ownership where you will be the key person, appreciate that serious management changes typically come up every five years. Where things are going well, the next CEO will often be an internal promotion. But sometimes it's not going so well and shareholders are looking for someone from outside to shake things up or are looking to get out. So the chances of your correspondence arriving at the right time are not as slender as you might think. About three-quarters of the 100 or so companies I have acquired came about through a direct approach made by me. I literally wrote to them and said, 'I'm interested in buying your company.'

Of course, you have to kiss a few frogs too. You will go to meetings where you very quickly realize nothing is going to happen. But that's OK. A few wasted days are the price of finding your prince – and even these have their memorable moments. I was particularly impressed by one elderly owner-manager whose business I wanted to buy and run, who patted me on the shoulder after less than five minutes and said kindly, 'I really don't think you're in the right place here, Charles.'

If you want something, just ask for it

When I was an out-of-work plc CEO, I would look at all the quoted companies in sectors I thought I could work in. The idea here was that I'd stumble across poorly performing businesses where the shareholders should have been considering a change of management and possibly ownership. This was pretty hard work back then and looking at the performance of public companies is much easier to do now. With a couple of keystrokes you can display a graph of how a company has performed compared to its sector, other sectors, or the market as a whole, over a week, a year or a decade.

You might think that underperforming public companies could be easily picked out and then picked off or at least have their management changed. However, historically, this has rarely been the case. Chances are the company's biggest shareholder will be a managed fund. If the shares are performing really badly the fund manager will just dump them – which is a lot easier than getting involved in improving the business and its management. This may be changing as a result of activist investors, but it's not changing fast. So the private sector is usually the place to fish.

But with Mavinwood I was in luck. There was a majority shareholder who was an individual. I sent a letter to his office. This outlined my skill set and my analysis of how to sort the company out. I also included a (reasonably) honest assessment of what had gone wrong in my previous role. It hit the right spot and a few weeks later I was the new CEO.

I've been on the receiving end of this too. During my 10 years at Restore I got three genuinely thoughtful job approaches from people out of the blue. They told me exactly what I needed and why the person was right for the job. One of these became the MD of one of our largest operating divisions and did a great job.

There's a wider point here, too. We're back to most people not thinking much about their careers. They take a very reactive approach – and only get involved when someone approaches them. By actively approaching people, you open up a new universe of opportunities. And besides, the worst that can happen is they'll say no.

Cultivate your contacts

One thing that never ceases to amaze me is the number of people who believe that a job search when you want to run something centres around registering with headhunters. The same is true of buying companies. An acquisition strategy should involve more than asking a few business brokers what they've got to offer.

Networking can often feel like a dirty word – and perhaps bad networking is. But there's no substitute for meeting people, seeing and being seen and keeping in touch. However good your research and cold approaches are, you should never neglect your contacts These are the people who can bring opportunities to you.

My first two CEO roles came via people I knew through business. With the first, I'd advised a brilliant entrepreneur several years earlier on selling his business. I later helped him in taking a stake in Brandon Hire, and he invited me on to the board, initially as a non-executive director. Finally, the board took a chance on me as the CEO. As I have said, this was a very lucky break for me and I am very grateful to him for it.

I am rather less grateful to the man who made my second introduction (with the obvious caveat that nobody forced me take this 'opportunity'). He was Johnson's largest shareholder and, having done rather well out of Brandon Hire (while I was CEO), suggested me for the Johnson CEO role. He knew the company better than I did (and so knew that it might well be a turkey). Shortly after my appointment, he sold as many shares as the market could take. I took him to task for it and he simply replied 'Charles, this may be a worse situation than you think'. But I can't hold that much of a grudge. Really, he was just looking after his own interests ahead of mine.

2
CHECKING OUT A BUSINESS

'The propensity to truck, barter and exchange one thing for another is common for all men, and to be found in no other race of animals.'
ADAM SMITH, THE WEALTH OF NATIONS

Why success is a terrible teacher – and learning the right lessons. What to really look for in companies and how to dig down to differentiate between total duds which look great and apparent basket cases masking real potential. Why you really need to follow the cash, why property is so important, how to interpret these things – and why people really do matter.

Success teaches you all the wrong lessons

Success teaches you all the wrong lessons and you should never believe your own hype. This is particularly true when parachuting into a CEO role of any scale. Here, I can offer a cautionary tale, about how I forgot all this and set myself up to fail. It's a story about how I let a mixture of flattery, breezy nonchalance and personal vanity land me a job that was unlikely to ever be a success. It's all the old clichés in action. It's how failing to prepare means you prepare to fail and how an ounce of prevention is worth a pound of cure.

It all started with the perfect job offer. I had recently stepped down as CEO of the tool hire company Brandon Hire – I'd left on a high, having sold the business to Wolseley, and was looking for a new challenge. The largest institutional shareholder in Brandon Hire was also the biggest shareholder in Johnson plc, an industrial laundry company which had several other businesses, including Sketchley, the high-street dry-cleaners. The CEO at Johnson had recently left the company and the institutional shareholders suggested I looked at the job.

It sounded right up my street. Johnson was a troubled company which seemed to have real potential. It was also a company with 10,000 employees and £400m in turnover, which made it the perfect next step up for me. That it was struggling wasn't a problem in itself. Rather it was part and parcel of the opportunity. You don't get chances like this at well-run companies.

Besides which, the problems were far from insoluble. I had a broad understanding of Johnson's various business units. The operating companies within the business looked solid and many of the issues appeared to be down to naive senior management. The shareholders gave me confidence, too. They were a combination of long-term value investors (who had presumably identified the strength of the underlying businesses) and equity income funds which were attracted by the consistent and chunky dividends the company was paying.

I was just the man for the job. Much like I'd done at Brandon, I would turn a troubled business around. True, this would involve some tough decisions, particularly in the first year or two, but after that we'd have a solid, steadily growing company with great cash flow. I'd deliver value for my value investors and even chunkier dividends for my income funds.

It appeared that others agreed with me. When my appointment was announced, the steep climb in the share price (from 260p to over 300p) suggested that the markets thought I was a good choice and were willing to support whatever plans I might have for the business. And, this, alas, is pretty much where the happy story ends. So, why did I get it so badly wrong?

First, a bit on the vanity. In the way that failure is usually a great teacher, success is not. Rather, it can teach you all the wrong lessons. Specifically, it allows you to create a causal relationship between whatever it was you did at a business and its success. You tell yourself that your actions were the reason for the success and if you do the same thing elsewhere you will be able to replicate that success. But this is often far from the case. Success may have nothing to do with you. In a heatwave, a company selling ice-cream will prosper even if the management are idiots.

So my first problem was that my success at Brandon made me believe that I'd mastered the art of management. I thought I understood what made a business work and what made people tick. I believed I could take a disengaged workforce, apply my managerial magic and they'd all love me and start delivering 110 per cent.

This is something Warren Buffett has done a lot of hard thinking about – and he is very sceptical about the ability of management to significantly change problem companies. His most famous quote here is: 'When a management with a reputation for brilliance gets hooked up with a business with a reputation for bad economics, it's the reputation of the business that remains intact.' I thought I was an exception to this. Reader, I was not.

Do your homework

My second mistake was that I didn't do my homework. When you look at a company that you are going to be running for five years, you need to do so coolly and objectively. If you are going to be the CEO of a public company this is doubly true. You will be the public face of the company externally, and the figurehead for staff internally. A lot of waffle is talked about values, but, as CEO, you really do have to believe in the business and share and embody its values and culture. It's not a role you take on with a view to seeing how it goes. You need to *be* the business.

The issue here was not so much that I approached the company like a dilettante; it's that I wanted the job too much. Having already decided that this was the job for me, I wanted to get on board as quickly as possible. There's nothing wrong with really wanting a job. But if you want it too much, you don't do your due diligence and you are setting yourself up for a fall. It's like wanting a house so badly that you don't have a proper survey done and then discover it's about to collapse.

So I went through the interview process with the board and the headhunters as part process and part salesmanship. I met the four worthy non-executive directors (NEDs), as well as the chairman (who was acting as part time CEO until the role was filled) and the finance director (CFO). I had coffee with two of the NEDs at The Athenaeum, a private members' club in Whitehall in London's West End. This would have been the ideal opportunity to quiz them over the circumstances of the previous CEO's departure. I did not.

In retrospect, this was just one of a long list of questions that I *didn't* ask. I didn't query the nature of the relationships between the board, head office and the operating companies. I knew the company had high levels of debt but I didn't look too closely at the detail of the banking covenants and the relationship with the banks (much more of which later). I even ignored the kind advice from the incumbent Chief Financial Officer (CFO) – that the business might not be quite what I was expecting. I made breezy, Panglossian assumptions about the nature of the company's internal and external relationships.

Why? Because I wanted the job and I was so busy selling myself. As it turned out I wanted the job so much, I never made sure that the job (as described by the company) was real.

I even ignored some of the warning signs I did come across. Although my due diligence may have lacked much real diligence, I did do some research. I methodically went through all the publicly available material on Johnson. This included ten years' worth of annual reports and accounts, various websites, brokers' notes, press cuttings, market intelligence, and so on.

From these I learnt that Johnson had run up huge debts in a furious acquisition spree, that it had found it easier to acquire businesses than to sell them (hardly surprising) and that its operating companies were generally sound and held good market positions, but never quite delivered the results the market was after. The cash flow was also curiously far poorer than you'd expect for a business reporting after-tax profits of £30m. Finally, there were a few cultural oddities, such as one of the subsidiaries still presenting itself on its website as being independently owned. These were not necessarily red flags but they warranted closer examination than I gave them.

So what should I have done? As ever in business, it's about relationships and talking to people. Here, I had to be discreet so that the fact I was looking at the job did not come to the attention of the wrong people, but I had considerable scope to do far better reconnaissance than I did.

The key issues that needed addressing were the debt (here I should have talked to the banks), the external perceptions of the company (City advisers and the major shareholder who had introduced me to the business but had been somewhat cagey subsequently) and the internal relationships (the operating company managers).

A chat with the auditors wouldn't have gone amiss either, in order to understand the nuances of the figures. While auditors check that accounts are accurate, the use of provisions, one-off small sales, capitalization of costs and exceptional items can massage the figures up and down to meet investors' expectations. Everyone does this to some extent but I should have ascertained the extent to which it was going on here. I should also have asked for an explanation of the surprisingly poor cash flow as this was meant to be a cash-rich business.

But I didn't. Again, a cliché. I married in haste and repented at leisure. My hubris and my desire to create a shining company out of Johnson meant I dispensed with the tiresome best practices which were there to protect me. In a public company this has wider ramifications. Certain investors trusted that I had found a good opportunity and followed my share-purchasing, without any recommendation from me. This enabled the better-informed existing shareholders to offload their stock while 'Team Skinner' subsequently got mashed.

Speaking of which, there is one further question I should have asked. Part of my agreement was that I would buy £200,000 worth of Johnson shares before becoming CEO. This figure was more than the shareholding of the rest of the board and the senior management team combined. I suppose at the time I told myself this was part of aligning my interests with those of the shareholders. It was part of the culture of the new, forward-thinking Johnson that I was going to build.

So, the big question: Knowing all this, would I have walked away? Probably not. There was some genuine potential in the company and if I'd known where the pitfalls were I might have been able find a way through. But this is entirely moot. I didn't know any of it because I didn't want to. So I walked straight into a minefield, having blithely ignored all the signs screaming 'Danger, Mines'.

Lessons learned and bullets dodged

OK, so we've looked at what I did (and what I didn't do). Now, let's have a look at what I actually learned from my Johnson debacle. First, it made me a lot more cautious and savvy. Again, we're back to clichés – once bitten, twice shy, fool me once, shame on you and so on… These sound obvious. But, after leaving Johnson only eight months after starting, I was not in a good place. I was under considerable pressure from myself not to let my world slide and mentally I was far from my usual self. I was depressed and had been medicated. I felt pretty wobbly. And I wasn't popular with banks or investors. I was in the kind of place where you follow one bad decision with another.

I really needed a job. But nonetheless, I managed to resist the siren call of further bad bets. It's instructive here to look at a few examples of businesses to whom I said no when I should have said no.

The first CEO job offer after Johnson was from a company which supplied specialist plant and equipment to the rail industry. At the time we were courting each other, it was a private equity (PE) backed business which had recently changed hands for the fourth time. Each time it had been flipped (sold for a quick profit), the managing director had picked up a very nice cheque and the company had taken on more debt even though it was growing slowly.

The new owners were smart operators and they had a good non-executive chairman. The CEO (who was younger than me) had been there while the company went through several changes of ownership, pocketing handsome rewards on each change of ownership, and apparently felt it was time to step back from the front line. I was interested. But this time I interrogated the company and myself properly. For starters, I didn't really know the sector. Yes, I knew plant and equipment. But this was a very specialist, very niche area.

The company had one major customer who could be tricky and the volume of business was highly dependent on this customer's maintenance programme. Thus, it was largely at the mercy of external factors it could not control. It had a strong trading history and was making a healthy 40 per cent EBITDA (earnings before interest, taxes, depreciation and amortization) margin, but high maintenance and equipment replacement costs meant much of the supposed free cash flow of £20m a year was going to be spent on kit. Furthermore, any drop in revenue would come straight off this free cash flow. Finally, the company had a lot of debt. This totalled 2.5 times those healthy revenues and, moreover, some of it was very expensive debt (borrowed at high interest rates).

In the end, the debt was the killer for me. The salary looked attractive but I would have been required to invest cash in the equity based on the existing valuation of the business. I could never see a way that the business could be worth more than the £125m of debt it was operating under. Thus, I was being asked to invest money in equity that would never be worth anything.

I put it to the board that the company was hopelessly overvalued and couldn't sustain its debt burden unless the revenue grew dramatically – and that was unlikely because the specialist nature of the niche it operated in meant opportunities were limited. The board responded I'd lost my nerve and was wasting their time. I shrugged and left. Within a year, the revenues had fallen and the business had collapsed.

The next bullet dodged was a long-established quoted uniform supplier which had made some poor acquisitions and facility investments. The long-standing and well-paid CEO and CFO had recently left the mess (taking chunky contractual payouts) and some ineffective Non-Executive Directors were picking up the pieces. There was also a large underfunded defined benefit (DB) pension scheme. DB schemes are always a risk, especially if not fully funded, because the pension fund trustees can insist that the company pays in real money to ensure that the fund is able to fulfil its commitment to current and future pensioners – huge sums can be involved given the length of the obligation.

I was asked by the chairman to take it on. He felt that the business was sound and could easily be sorted out by improving the working capital; here there were significant sums tied up in stock. With my former CFO from Brandon, I spent a couple of days in the company. It was breaking even but the cash position (the level of cash on hand minus pending liabilities) was very weak.

Having been told that money was tied up in stock stored in warehouses, we reviewed on paper the stock the business actually held. We then visited one of the warehouses which was deserted and looked as if nobody had been there for months. It took a while to get in but when we did we found it was bulging with stock. We opened a bundle on the nearest pallet and hundreds of polo shirts spilled out, all bearing the logo of a supermarket that had gone out of business 10 years earlier. The stock that was supporting the company's balance sheet was worthless.

We reported back to the company's NEDs that there was no Aladdin's cave of valuable stock and this meant the business was probably bust. I also called the professional pension trustee who took a while to appreciate that the underfunded pension fund was unlikely to ever honour its obligations. The business went into receivership shortly afterwards.

CHECKING OUT A BUSINESS

Despite the pressure on me to get a job, I walked away from a third opportunity. This was a portable building provider which offered temporary kitchens, operating theatres and even field hospitals. It had been floated on the Alternative Investment Market (AIM - the UK's junior stock market) but was subsequently taken back into private ownership by the original shareholders (who had made a tidy profit on the flotation). The plan was now to sell a majority stake to a PE company which would bring in a CEO (potentially me) to replace the founders and then sell the business or re-float it.

The business made decent profits but its cash flow fluctuated wildly. Highly profitable contracts, ranging from temporary hospital kitchens (used when hospitals were being renovated) to temporary operating theatres for use in overseas military locations like Afghanistan, were signed irregularly. Once these contracts were in place, the money rolled in. However, despite this, there had never been much long-term cash generation and the shareholders had only really taken out money when the business was floated. Still, it seemed well run and the management team were a nice group.

I had been approached to take on the role by the PE company. They were pretty sensible and had plans to develop the business more aggressively. Negotiations were at an advanced stage and significant due diligence had been carried out by a large team of expensive professionals. But I couldn't quite understand why such a profitable company had never generated much cash.

It was only on my third visit to the business (and shortly before the completion of the PE deal) that I worked it out. Poking around the business's beautiful countryside location, I found a field full of Portakabin-type accommodation units, many looking dilapidated from years of non-use. This was where the cash had gone! Highly specialist accommodation units would be hired out but were frequently returned long before the units had paid for themselves. Often they were too specialist or well used to be recycled on to the next job and so they ended up in the field where their value slowly depreciated. This meant they were being counted as assets while earning no money and slowly mouldering away into worthlessness.

As long as new contracts were being signed, company profits would rise as the early years of the contracts yielded great returns but, once the contract ended, the initial cash cost might never be recovered. It was like spending £20,000 on a car, renting it out for three years at £6,000 a year and then leaving the high-mileage car to rot in a field, possibly writing it off at some stage. Net effect? Reported profits of £4,000 a year for the first three years (after depreciation of £2,000 a year) but you've actually turned £20,000 into £18,000 in real money.

Reporting this to the private equity company and their advisers was not popular as the deal had considerable momentum. But, with the supposed new CEO concluding that the cash profitability was nothing like the accounts, the transaction had to fall apart. The business was eventually sold many years later for a trivial amount compared to what had been mooted at the time.

Getting into the weeds

When you're looking to become CEO of a company, it's rare that you get to pore over the business to the extent you'd like to. But usually when you're buying a company, you can get into the detail – and if the money is coming from outside investors or bankers, there is often a requirement from the funders that you involve professional advisers to conduct due diligence into the company as part of the process.

Clearly this is at your or your company's cost, and, unsurprisingly, the accountants and the funders, particularly the debt providers, will know one another rather well on the hospitality circuit. It won't be cheap either – the accounting fees on a formal due diligence (DD) report are unlikely to be less than six figures. I'll leave you to draw your conclusions about conflicts of interest.

One of the reasons it is so expensive is that the accountants often only get paid their full fee when the deal is done, particularly when the buyer is a private equity purchaser or an individual. This means the deals that happen bear the cost of the deals that don't. Still, you might think that at least you're paying the professionals well so that they can check everything is in order while you plan and dream what you're going to do when you own the business.

Er… no. Formal DD is often rarely more than a box-ticking, arse-covering exercise. Thumping great reports from experts frequently give you nothing but complacency and can never be used as an excuse for your own lack of oversight. The financial DD in particular is often little more than the accountants writing down what they are being told by the target's financial people. It is much more useful, and much, much cheaper, for you to do this yourself.

To return to our house-buying analogy, much of the formal DD process is like the survey you get done so that the bank will give you a mortgage. It won't tell you the most important things about whether you should buy the house, which you should have worked out before making an offer and be checking again once the offer is accepted.

Even in its area of expertise – checking out the structure – there are a lot of things the house survey won't cover (or won't cover very well) and it will have endless caveats. So it is with your costly DD. In fact, before the accountants start, they require that you send them 'Hold Harmless' letters which mean their necks are not on the line if the deal turns out to be a complete turkey. So while you may have to have the DD done professionally, you also *have* to do it yourself.

CHECKING OUT A BUSINESS

This reliance on external advisers with nobody taking full responsibility often reaches absurd levels. When buying a subsidiary off a struggling parent company, our management questioning involved just the group CFO and me. I learnt subsequently that a private equity buyer brought along 17 people, including five different sets of advisers. Who was taking full responsibility there?

If you know the sector well, you'll know which key elements you need to check and understand: the security of the revenues, the typical cost base, the operating margins, the amount of equipment needed, and so on. There may be areas outside your knowledge, such as the robustness and sophistication of the target's IT systems, where bringing in a specialist will give you the necessary comfort, but generally it's your responsibility to ensure you're buying what you think you're buying. You're the person handing over the money, you're going to be responsible for the business once you own it and you're going to be judged on whether you wasted or created money for your company. The due diligence professionals (like the surveyors) will have banked their fees and be long gone by the time you realize you've bought a pup.

Where professional DD is valuable is making sure there aren't any nasty surprises – or 'outliers' lurking in the places where you wouldn't expect them. This is where the lawyers' checklist comes in. Generally your lawyers' list will not tell you much about the business – but it will tell you which outliers merit further examination. These might include tax liabilities (usually covered by a tax indemnity), pension obligations, ongoing legal cases, intellectual property rights and licences (where these are not a key element in the deal), employee terms and conditions, leasing and service contracts, and bad debts.

These can be quite serious. I once worked on a deal where, at a late stage, the lawyers discovered that the company being bought did not own the trademark for one of its biggest selling products. For obscure and historical reasons, the trademark was in fact owned by a second company which, several years before, had acquired part of the business from the first company. This was likely an accident as the second company did not know that it owned the trademark.

So what do you do, when you find an outlier like this? Well, it's a pain in the neck and it often involves renegotiation. However, it rarely destroys the deal unless the amounts of money involved are huge and both sides think it's the other's problem. So you find a reasonable solution. In the case of the trademark, we agreed that, if a problem arose within three years of the deal, the vendor would pay up for any related losses but the purchaser would assume the risk after that.

You should be wary of getting too hung up on esoteric outliers. The lawyers like to bring these up because they can sound dramatic and exciting (and it shows you that they're doing their job) but the chances of them actually impacting you are very remote. An example of this might be an old contractual dispute where there has been no correspondence for several years. Here the side with the deeper pockets should cover the remote liability and you should move on.

The lawyers will also review the significant contracts. But really this is your job, not theirs. If you are taking over or buying a company or business unit, you should understand the normal structure of contracts in your industry and be able to pick up anything which is amiss. You should also fully understand the detail of major contracts, particularly the termination terms.

If you can't understand a contract to your satisfaction, be very wary. This is something we've seen a lot of recently in complex, long-term contracts such as PPPs (public-private partnerships). The lessons of the disasters with big outsourcers such as Carillion, Serco and Capita are that the people who supposedly understood and signed the contracts are long gone. They basked in the early years' profits these contracts delivered, and their successors (often more than a decade later) were left to deal with the huge liabilities incurred when the contracts finally started to unravel.

In the case of Carillion, these liabilities bankrupted the company. For some (including many inside the company) it came as a bolt from the blue. It did not, however, come as much of a surprise to some of the smarter City investors who had worked out what was going on. They had been betting against the company for months in the run-up to January 2018 when it announced its liquidation. Hedge funds which shorted Carillion's stock are thought to have made £200m from its eventual collapse.

Due diligence

Due diligence relies on the buyer understanding the nature of the target company and the variables that they won't be able to subsequently control. At Brandon, I acquired more than 30 businesses, many of which were very small. Here the key elements of my DD were checking that the turnover was real and the equipment was physically present.

The turnover meant that, as long as there were no onerous ongoing costs (such as over-rented property or excessive service contracts) I knew that we could expect a certain level of profit. The physical presence of the equipment meant that the turnover itself was supportable – and that I wasn't going to have to invest significantly more in the business to achieve the turnover. It's that simple – or should be.

However, DD often doesn't cover this very basic stuff. When Wolseley (now Ferguson, the plumbing company) acquired Brandon, the reams of due diligence didn't include a physical stock count. Fortunately for Wolseley, Brandon's systems were sufficiently robust for the print-out of the equipment to be broadly accurate. This is not always the case – I know one acquirer of a £100m business which subsequently found 25 per cent of the equipment was missing.

The other part of my due diligence was to chat to the business owners about their staff and customers to get a feel for how best to manage and hold on to them. I would also often try to purchase the assets of the business, leaving what happened in the past to the vendors This was to make sure we did not require endlessly complicated legal agreements which would have significantly increased the acquisition cost.

It was a similar story at Restore. Knowing the industry well, we only really needed to check the physical presence of the document boxes and how they matched up to the system, the average price to the customer of each box, the cost of storing a box and the monthly consistency of revenues by type. This was what we wanted to know and the lawyers' checklist would pick up anything untoward in the business's history. The basic legal agreement would protect us if something odd had gone on in the past and not been disclosed or if fraudulent information had been provided (neither of which ever surfaced later in over 20 transactions).

Follow the cash

The cash movements in a company are the key to working out what's going on. By looking at the cash at the corporate clothing business, I was able to identify that the balance sheet was being propped up by worthless stock; that many of the 'operating' assets at the portable accommodation company were knackered cabins which would never operate again; and that the chunky 'free cash flow' at the plant hire company was headed straight into replacement equipment rather than paying down the overbearing debt. In all three examples, the company's profit and loss accounts and balance sheet suggested the business was in good shape.

When you're looking at a company's figures, the numbers you first get will invariably be in the form of the statutory or management accounts – and these will usually inform your initial views on a company's financial strengths and weaknesses. However, you need to move on beyond them. Your first port of call should be the cash. This tells the real story. If you can't follow the cash – or don't like it when you do – walk away.

With cash, the easiest place to start is the bank balance. Look at the dividends paid and the directors' drawings over the previous years. I once bought a business from a great operator where the bank balance had gone from zero to £5m in five years, slightly better than the reported profits. No issues that time as the business was clearly generating the cash its profit numbers were implying, but you need to look at these things in detail in every instance.

Profitable businesses may not generate cash when they're growing (because they will be reinvesting in order to expand) but stable businesses should be turning profit into cash. The reason for this is that there's nowhere else that the cash should be going if the business is mature – it will not need additional working capital, new salespeople, new factories and so on.

You should ask yourself questions such as: 'Why is this supposedly profitable private company carrying debt?' There are many acceptable reasons (bought a freehold, the owner living beyond their means, a young company paying off its original funding, a business that needs external money to fund growth and doesn't want external shareholders, etc.) but you must understand what they are. You need to sit down with the vendor and their finance people and work through all this

Here there is an important difference between public and private companies. Sensible private companies will not be playing the public company game of showing ever-rising profit growth. They don't have stock markets and analysts to impress and they want to keep their tax bills down by showing less profit rather than more. They won't customarily deploy the expansionary listed companies' financial reporting armoury, where up-front costs are capitalized, any unusual costs are exceptionalized and provisions are released to order. But they might look to massage their profits upwards when they're planning a sale. And it's your job to understand how they're doing it. There is an art to balance sheets and it is one you need to appreciate.

Often to get to the bottom of the cash you have to drill right down into the weird world of working capital and understand it properly. You may not thank me when you're doing this but you will if it reveals something important that you hadn't previously noticed – as it often does. You'll also thank me when you understand the working capital better than the other side at the end of the deal when the final amount to be paid is calculated.

So, why do so few people really get to grips with working capital? Because it's really difficult to understand. And it's difficult to understand because few businesses are good at cash-flow forecasting. Cash fluctuates considerably with debtors paying unpredictably, inventory bulk buys, capital investment payments, and so forth.

Even regular cash movements operate on timings that the accounts don't reflect. You have daily movements (paying bills, receiving payments); weekly cash movements (cash-banking and weekly paid staff still exist); four-weekly movements (many companies run 13 four-week accounts), monthly (payroll), quarterly (rent-roll) and even annual movements (insurance payments).

Understanding working capital is particularly important when you're buying a company. If you can take a snapshot of the balance sheet and the cash balance when it most favours you (as a buyer, this would be when big payments have gone out, but not come in), you can present this to the other side as an objective assessment of what cash or debt you think you're getting.

Sharing these snapshots can reveal major misunderstandings. An example of this was the sale of an employment agency I worked on. Every month, the company borrowed money in order to pay its agency staff before the client (who were using the staff) paid the agency. This was a big number, more than a year's profit, but did it constitute debt when calculating the purchase price? That is to say, is a short-term loan that gets repaid every single month debt or not? This transaction fell apart at the last minute as both sides had interpreted this debt differently (and in their own favour).

You find smaller versions of this problem in most deals. Are vehicle leases and hire purchase obligations debts to be deducted from a purchase price? There's no clear answer here. But if you know the facts you will be better placed to negotiate. And if you know them better than the other side, there's a good chance your interpretation of the finances will carry the day. Your time spent getting to the bottom of the working capital will not only reveal any unpleasant surprises and help you understand the business, it will also repay your time investment many times over.

Property

Property is important because it's a long-term thing. Whether it's manufacturing plants, distribution centres or retail outlets, you need to know that property is fit for purpose. You also need to know with freehold properties whether the book value lines up with market valuations. Often, particularly in private companies, there may be a property worth far more than it is valued at in the books, something which the old-fashioned asset-strippers were always alert to.

On leasehold properties you need to know that the rents are in line with market. You don't want them too high, but you don't want them too low either. Too high means that if you want to break the lease in the future, it could cost you a fortune, particularly on a long-term lease. But if they're too low, you could soon be whacked with a savage rent review. I like to drive around the industrial estates on which key buildings are located to see how many 'To Let' signs are up in case we might want to get out or expand at some point.

Be wary too of the dreaded 'dilapidations' clauses. These require a tenant to pay the cost of returning the property to the state it was originally rented in at the end of a lease. I once bought a business with very little time left on the 25-year lease. When the lease ended, the landlord gouged us for the cost of returning it to its original state and pocketed the money, which was far more than we'd paid for the business itself. All entirely legal and very, very painful.

Even when acquiring a company, there's no real need for a huge, exhaustive document on properties from an expensive, big-name surveying company, although this is often required by financiers. Generally some opinion, and possibly a survey, from a knowledgeable local agent will give you what you need to know at a fraction of the cost from the big players.

Nonetheless, property is frequently a pain when acquiring companies. The paperwork is often not in the right place and landlords (assuming the property is leased) can be unhelpful as they're being asked to do something like transfer leases for which they are often get no benefit. This may be simply because they cannot be bothered to provide you with the documents you need or it may be because they're savvy (or perhaps unscrupulous) and realize that they are a key part of the transaction and there could be an angle for them. Occasionally, by doing nothing, they force the deal-doers to assume that they will be helpful in due course, which further strengthens their hand.

Property can also be prone to very random, almost comic, twists of fate. I worked on a major deal where only one man could sign a key lease – and he couldn't be found anywhere. The financing was due to expire at midnight. The man was eventually located – he was at a funeral in Ireland. He signed the lease at 3am and the financiers were willing to grant us the extra three hours.

Years after the Sale and Purchase Agreement on the deal has been forgotten about, the legal documentation for the property will be still be relevant, so you can't treat an onerous lease lightly.

Taking a view

Once you've understood the company's financial position and structure, you should put your interpretative hat on. You need to ask yourself what the current position means, how likely things are to stay that way and what factors could cause them to change.

You should normally have a feel for the sort of profit margin a business ought to be making, particularly if you're operating in the same sector already. This will be based on industry norms. You also need to take into account where you are in the economic cycle and adjust for any particular quirks you've found in the company such as oddly priced contracts or particularly cheap or expensive rents. Thus, once you know what the revenue is, you should have a decent idea of what profits the business will make in the future if revenue remains steady.

But you need to ensure that it will stay steady. Start by checking the predictability of the revenue, going back several years. My preferred method of doing this is to look at the monthly revenues received from the top 30 customers for at least the past three years. You'll soon see a pattern (or not).

In records management, where customers tend not to move and pay monthly, the comfort of seeing a solid table with almost all customers paying a regular monthly amount was enough. Shredding was broadly similar (contracted customers paying monthly with occasional spikes when a lot of old paperwork was ditched in one go). However, scanning was more erratic. We had many one-off projects for one-off customers, alongside the regulars who sent their paperwork through to be scanned every month, and the long-term contracts where clients like hospitals wanted all their records digitized over a period of time.

Not all types of revenue are equal either – and some are much more valuable than others. At the top of the tree would be regular payments on high-margin contracts such as software licensing, while a one-off sale of equipment bought in and sold on is worth little more than the cash profit made at the time.

A good example of this is Hewlett Packard's 2011 acquisition of the UK software business Autonomy for $11bn. When HP bought the company, it believed, among other things, that much of Autonomy's revenue was generated by high-margin software licences, when a sizeable chunk of it came from low or no margin hardware. A year on from the purchase, and HP wrote down the value of the acquisition by an astonishing $8.8bn.

HP later took Autonomy's founder and CEO Mike Lynch and his finance director to court in the UK's biggest ever civil fraud trial. Lynch was, of course, extradited to the US in 2023, where he faced criminal charges. He was tried in 2024 and found not guilty on all counts. While celebrating his acquittal on his super yacht off the coast of Sicily, a storm capsized the boat. Lynch, his daughter and five others drowned, a freakish tragedy that inevitably led to endless conspiracy theories.

Regardless of this, the revelation in court (in the UK civil case) that HP had carried out only six hours' due diligence before paying $11bn for Autonomy suggests that HP hadn't bothered to understand the business properly. In 2012, an unnamed Oracle executive told *The New York Times*, 'We looked at Autonomy. After doing the math, we couldn't make it work. We couldn't figure out where the numbers came from. And taking the numbers at face value, even at $6 billion it was overvalued.'

Getting to grips with a business isn't rocket science – and if it seems like that to you, you shouldn't be buying it. You should also ask yourself basic questions such as: 'Is the business reliant on a few big customers?' Obviously, this is a potential problem – if a big customer leaves, they might take 30 per cent of the revenues with them. But it's not an insurmountable problem. If you're a large company buying a smaller company, the big customer will be less critical to your overall revenues. Or you may be set up to generate new customers for their products so the big customer should be less of a risk to you in due course.

Once you've worked out what the elements in the revenues are and whether they are as reliable as you'd like, you can look further into areas such as pricing. This can be sensitive if you're already in the same sector. B2B pricing is very different from its B2C counterpart. Customers are often charged different amounts for similar products and nobody wants to share their pricing structure for individual customers with a competitor.

You may find that there are some really profitable elements in the business – these may feel like a great thing, but can you be sure they will last and are they really as good as they look? Sleeping dogs (customers paying more than they should) can wake up and be pretty sore when they figure out that they've been paying above market rates for years. Likewise, products without IP protection (usually patents) can be vulnerable – competitors may sniff out the high margin and launch something similar and cheaper.

Be wary too of buying a business which is operating in the same area as you but charging different rates for similar products or services. This can create a kind of in-house competition. Here, savvy customers will often identify the misaligned pricing and demand the lower rate. You effectively undercut yourself. Swift and smart integration can help prevent this. You also need to keep an eye on your customers' mergers and acquisitions. One of my companies has two global banks as customers. The banks merged and, a year afterwards, they realized than one of the banks was paying four times as much as the other for the same service. Inevitably, this led to awkward questions.

Other features can be picked up from the management accounts. For instance, a high number of credit notes may reflect customers being regularly compensated for poor service or product. This is a problem, but also, potentially, an opportunity to improve matters and make money. Higher levels of customer bad debt than normal may imply another problem – customers are using this company as a supplier because they cannot get credit elsewhere.

Make sure you understand any capital expenditure. Work out what is 'maintenance' (i.e. keeping the assets repaired and regularly replaced) rather than investment in future capacity. The line between the two may be blurred and sometimes deliberately.

All of this will mean getting close to the business, its people and its culture – and this is what you need to be doing before you buy a company or join it as a member of the senior management team.

And the people of course

An awful lot of guff is talked about businesses being about people. But the principle is sound. If you're buying a business or looking to become its CEO,

CHECKING OUT A BUSINESS   **37**

people really do matter – and time spent with people in a business before you take the plunge is rarely wasted.

Here, you need to become a kind of corporate anthropologist. Go into the company and observe as much as you can. The little things are really important. These are often as simple as how long people take to get back to you, the level of buzz in the workplace, whether standard procedural notices are in place and whether they bother to keep the visitors' records in order in out-of-the-way facilities. Individually, these things may not mean much, but together they paint a telling picture of the kind of company it is.

That said, you aren't necessarily looking for a business where all the systems are perfectly polished. First, a weakly run business could give you the opportunity to improve its performance. And second, a polished-looking business may indicate the team focus on getting all the processes right, irrespective of cost. I have bought businesses from big companies where doing things in the approved way has been more important to its management than making money. This is often the way in large, bureaucratic organizations. But for you, it's a mixed bag. On one hand, there is an obvious scope to make savings. But on the other hand, people won't be culturally attuned to making these savings. And a culture of slightly pernickety perfection can be very hard to change.

Look at language and jargon too. Listen to the words and phrases people use, particularly those that are peculiar to the company. But don't let jargon obfuscate meaning. If someone is a using a phrase you don't understand, ask them to explain. Don't worry about looking stupid. Far better to look a little stupid before you buy the business than very stupid afterwards.

If possible, try to form opinions about people's capabilities. Incompetent managers may be holding the business back – and you can change this, but they may also be a symptom of a wider malaise. Conversely, finding a real star in the business, particularly one who might have been overlooked, is a source of great encouragement. Similarly, you may get the feeling that people are being held back and could be far more productive with better management.

Look, too, at the people around the business – speak to customers and suppliers and contractors. Are they happy? Are they good people? People you'd like to work with?

Comparing the pay levels to the market or what you're used to elsewhere is also important. If people are paid less than the market rate, either there's a reason for this or it's going to cost you more to make sure you keep them. If they're overpaid without good reason, you're carrying more cost unnecessarily than your competitors and it can foul up the pay scales in other parts of your organization when you integrate the business.

You also need to understand the attitudes of the people at the top. If you're taking a job, make sure you appreciate the aspirations of the shareholders and the board. These have to match reality. If they believe they are getting you in to a run a good business but you suspect it isn't, walk away if you can't get them to acknowledge your concerns. If you don't, when your fears come true you are likely to be blamed rather than thanked. By contrast, some of the best turnarounds are companies that have hidden potential but which all the stakeholders have given up on. Here you are likely to have a lot of leeway and if you deliver even a modest improvement, you'll be hailed as a hero.

Finally, look particularly hard at the entrepreneur who is selling, or 'stepping back' from the business they founded. Many ambitious managers are appointed to their first MD role by entrepreneurs who want to do less or focus on the area of the business they enjoy most. Frequently they will say it's time their business was run by someone more professional than themselves.

Coming in from the outside to take on such a role is fraught with risk and the incomer must be absolutely sure that they will have the authority to act as a CEO. When you visit, look at how their teams react to them – is the owner the person everyone goes to for answers? Are they the only person who holds vital information? Can only they make decisions? You must be able to step into their shoes without interference from them and without the rest of the team constantly referring back to them. Too often the founder won't be ready to give up his or her baby and the new arrival ends up with responsibility without power and becomes the scapegoat if things go wrong,

If you buy such a business, you need to understand the impact of the founder on the company too. Most entrepreneurs who are selling understand that the business needs to look like it can function without them – so the question you have to ask is: Can it? I once bought a recycling business from an entrepreneur. I knew he was a critical part of the business but he had genuine personal reasons for selling, the price was low and we had a similar customer base.

I thought it was worth taking a chance, but it turned out to be a very bad deal for us. The entrepreneur had intimate market knowledge and trading skills that were impossible for us to replicate. There was no way we could ever run the business as well as he did – and a huge chunk of the value walked out of the door along with him. He was literally irreplaceable.

3
BUYING AND SELLING A BUSINESS

'The greatest victory is that which requires no battle.'
SUN TZU, *THE ART OF WAR*

Mergers & Acquisitions – valuing a business as a buyer and what to look out for as a buyer and as a seller. Finding the Venn Diagram sweet spot where a deal that leaves you both happy can be found. Identifying targets, pursuing them, tactics and negotiation, and knowing when to walk away. And last, but not least, the importance of post-acquisition management.

Something I *do* know about

Mergers and acquisitions (M&A) is the more glamorous side of financial activity. When it involves big acquisitions, it can be a pretty macho area with lots of chest-beating and gung-ho language drawn from the battlefield. You're better off leaving this stuff to the professionals as it's all a game they play with each other.

I spent seven years doing small company M&A. This is rather less appealing – the fees are much smaller because M&A advisors tend to be paid a percentage of the deal. I did this early on in my career – and it was great fun in my 20s and early 30s. You get a lot more responsibility on smaller deals; you get an insight into entrepreneurs' minds at a crucial point; and you really get to understand the companies that you're dealing with.

In all, I've advised on 40 deals, mostly acting for the vendor. I've also bought 100 companies during my 20-plus years as a CEO. I can legitimately claim to have done my Malcolm Gladwell 10,000 hours here. If I had three key takeaways, they are these.

Much as I harp on about how I dislike expensive professionals, if you're selling a company, it's a really good idea to have an adviser. Most business owners will only do this once or twice in their working lives. You want someone who has done it dozens of times and who knows what to look out for to hold your hand.

It's an obvious (but often missed) point that the buyer wants to be the only buyer whereas the seller wants to have several potential buyers. The seller should seek to establish competition. This is particularly true if they're an owner-manager and this will be the single most important deal they do. It's amazing how often vendors speak to just one buyer and a sensible adviser will rarely let this happen, whatever threats about walking away the solo buyer makes.

If you're the buyer, my key takeaway is that the post-acquisition management planning is at least as important as the deal itself. Don't just buy the thing and then expect it to run itself.

Valuing a business

If you're buying a business, the big question is how much it's worth. The bad news here is that there is no decent or consistent valuation methodology because there are too many variables. However, there are some factors you should consider.

1. Return on investment (ROI) is your starting point. Acquisitions often go wrong, so buyers normally look to get at least a 15 per cent return on their money to reflect this risk. ROI feeds back into businesses being valued on a multiple of their earnings.
2. The smaller the company, the lower the value, even as a multiple of earnings (or via other standard valuation methods). There are a number of reasons for this:

    Let's take three companies. One is a small businesses making less than £250k in profits a year. This might sell for two to three years' earnings. The second is a steady small company making £1m per year. It might go for five to seven times the earnings. The third is a large private company. This might go for a public market equity (stock market based) valuation, less 10–20 per cent.

    What this reflects is that Company 1 is very small and is likely to be a lot of hassle for a minor boost to the acquirer's bottom line. Company 2 represents a bigger boost, but still a bit of pain and its effective 16 per cent return reflects this. Company 3 is big enough to be acquired by a plc and could enhance its earnings significantly or help it develop new markets. Price-earnings ratios in public companies typically range from

10x to 30x, so a sizeable private company could be sold for these sorts of numbers (minus the aforementioned 10–20 per cent).

If this sounds like a simplification and a generalization, it's because it is. There are always exceptions. Take Company 1. There might be nobody interested in taking on a small lifestyle business with its own quirks. In this case it could only be worth what its assets are worth – so no more than £100k.

Conversely, it might come to the attention of a larger player who sees something they very much like. Or they could integrate it into their business and take out swathes of costs including the costs of the owner, comfortably turning the £250k of profit into £500k. In this case, a £3m purchase price could make sense. Now, the valuation is between £100k and £3m.

3. Valuations also usually involve looking at future prospects. So fast-growing companies or very high potential companies may be worth higher multiples of today's profits than mature businesses. You see extreme examples of this in the tech world.

4. Sometimes industries develop their own rules of thumb: for example cleaning companies are felt to be worth 50 per cent of revenues. This reflects the underlying economics in mature sectors: a cleaning business should achieve operating margins of 7 per cent, so a £10m revenue business will make £700k pa, meaning a price of £5m results in a mid-teen ROI.

Occasionally these rules of thumb can be wrong. This often happens in markets where there are few transactions. At one point in the records management industry, I was effectively the only interested buyer and established a market rule of thumb that private 'box' businesses were usually worth 1x their revenues. This was not particularly unfair as operating margins were often around 15 per cent, meaning I'd get a return of around 15 per cent, and recover my initial investment over seven years.

In fact, the post-acquisition cost savings and efficiency improvements available to my company (as a large operator) meant that we could boost the margins to 30 per cent. Given the steadiness of these types of business, these transactions were providing stunning returns. This couldn't last forever but I managed to do many transactions until, several years later, an aggressive competitor entered the acquisition markets and started offering 3x revenue for similar businesses, meaning returns on deals dropped from a stunning 30 per cent to a marginal 10 per cent. A buyer's market became a seller's market.

5. Turnover is often more important than profit – a larger purchaser may have higher operating margins than the target and may believe that its management skill and scale will boost the target's margins, which should be the case. In records management we knew what operating margins could be achieved and that's why we would value businesses largely on multiples of revenue.

6. Generally the balance sheet takes a back seat in valuations. This is because the assets (in whatever form) are usually seen to be worth what they can generate in terms of earnings. However, old equipment at a target company may have to be replaced, which will require further investment on top of the purchase price. This will lower the ROI.

7. Freehold properties owned by the business create their own issues. In terms of valuation, it is best to deduct the market rent payable from the profits, value the business on this basis and add the property value back in on top.

   I've seen many mature businesses which own property where the property valuation is higher than the value of the business as a going concern. This happens because property values tend to compound over time. Owning freeholds (meaning no rent is payable) also enables poorly run businesses to soldier on. This means that some businesses are actually worth more if you break them up, particularly if there is significant working capital. This is why the 1960s and 1970s 'asset strippers' pounced on asset-rich but under-managed businesses.

   In a related vein, owner-managers need to look at their businesses coldly to check that the returns they are generating on their assets are worthwhile. Sadly this sort of calculation is often done too late and the assets have been eroded by borrowing to the point where both the company's net assets and the value of the business don't add up to much.

8. Working capital in a company valuation throws up tricky questions. There is no fair answer here and frequently no established practice on whether the working capital is an asset to be paid for. This is one of the reasons why working capital arguments destroy deals. A canny operator sets out and seeks to establish their most favourable interpretation of the status of the working capital early on in negotiations.

9. Timing is critical as sector valuations go up and down. There may also be consolidators in the market who can see synergies and are happy to share the 'marriage value' of the earnings uplift with the vendors by

paying more for a company. Companies in a sector where trading is strong are likely to have more cash available for acquisitions.

The vendor's viewpoint

Turning an earnings stream into capital is the underlying economics of selling a business. In corporate disposals, the driver tends to be the realization that the capital and effort involved in managing a business are better deployed elsewhere.

For individual owners, the sale of a business is often triggered by the recognition that the generation of the earnings stream involves too much time, energy and hassle. Here, the owner may be better off with the capital even if the revenue stream from it is lower than when they owned the business. That is, it may be better to earn £100k a year from investments than £180k a year from a business if the latter means you're working 80-hour weeks.

In both cases timing is important – and many people get it wrong. Corporates often discover that a business is non-core only when it is performing poorly – and, as a result, they end up selling it at a low valuation point. Similarly, for individuals, the idea of getting out of a business often becomes attractive when times are tough, which is not when they're going to get the best price.

Vendors should try to avoid selling a business from a position of weakness. Rather they need to ensure the company is in good shape and the market is right. This is why, for example, retirement sales require preparation and patience, rather than just selling because you want to move to Spain and play golf at a particular moment in time.

In my experience, the smartest entrepreneurs always have an eye on the big picture in case the right time to sell comes up. They are also constantly looking ahead at macro pitfalls (such as a change of government) and micro pitfalls (like sector cycles) to see if they should get out while the going is good. Often the best time to sell is when the sale will be viewed by many as a surprise.

It's key to understand that the company market (like many markets) is usually open for buyers prepared to pay up but not so open for sellers looking for a half-sensible price. If the buyers ain't buying more generally, you'll be selling to the bottom-fishers, if you can find anyone at all.

Moreover, personal 'liquidity moments' (the polite term for cashing your chips in) are rare and need to be well-planned. Selling your private company is an event that will happen for most people only once. Where there are other shareholders, these investors won't like to see a manager taking out cash in exchange for their shares unless they can join in.

With public companies, this is even more true. Hence the rather convoluted explanations in UK public companies when an announcement is put out (a legal requirement) that a director has sold shares. The normal version is that the market needs more shares to increase liquidity in the stock, but most professional investors still see through it and become wary of the company – why is she selling?

That said, when 'personal reasons' are actually a divorce, this is viewed as acceptable. Divorces are not uncommon for entrepreneurs who've recently crystallized their assets. This may be because the entrepreneur's spouse can crystallize their contribution to the marriage, or the entrepreneur has decided that the marriage has run its course and they can afford it.

Regardless, always remember that it is far easier to put money into a company than to take it out.

My main personal liquidity events have come at the sale of a business on leaving or after I've left a company. Only once was I able to generate cash from share capital in a company which I continued to run and that was only because I'd spent many years working there on a below-average salary and hadn't cashed in previously.

The upshot of all this is that too many vendors wind up with an unsatisfactory outcome because they don't think their exit through. They sell a business when the market is in the wrong place with valuations at a low level and there are few if any buyers around.

The purchaser's viewpoint

The key point here is that value is very different for each purchaser.

Where there are easy synergy benefits, a company should be worth most to a well-financed and decently rated trade buyer. Typically this value will be around synergies for trade buyers where identical functions are being performed in both the target and the purchaser. This means the duplicate functions can be rationalized and savings made.

There are other reasons for targets to have high values. FMCG (fast-moving consumer goods) businesses are often happy to pay eye-watering prices for companies (even loss-making ones) with an up-and-coming brand which can be promoted and pumped through their distribution networks. I once advised on the sale of a break-even additive-free soap company which had hit a rich consumer vein. The buyer was a huge FMCG company. The agreed price thrilled the vendor but still turned out to be an excellent investment for the buyer. Trebles all round.

You see similar things in the drinks sector (niche alcohol brands can often be rolled out more widely), the restaurant trade (a small chain can be rolled out with a more experienced buyer's expertise and cash and management skills) and the pharmaceutical industry (where a research-based entity has done the R&D, and then Big Pharma – with its battery of lawyers and an established distribution chain – takes on the resultant drug or product).

These transactions are difficult to price and generally rely on the vendor being in the right place at the right time, although clever entrepreneurs often will set themselves up to wait for this moment. The entrepreneur Martin Miller set up a gin business, built the brand and ate the losses until major drinks companies decided they wanted a new spirits brand. Some small tech companies use a similar model, which is to build something and hope that a tech giant like Google notices it.

Valuations often go up considerably when there is a lot of cheap debt around. Businesses can be acquired by private equity with most of the consideration paid using borrowed money. The comparatively small amount of equity invested then increases very dramatically if the company becomes worth more, just like property owners with a big mortgage. This is the game many private equity companies have played (helped by interest payments being tax-deductible, which always feels rather unfair).

Where the purchaser is a private equity company rather than a trade buyer, their likely valuation is easier to estimate as everyone involved relies on a similar financing model and their sole interest is usually in five-year financial returns. So variations in value come down to their house view on factors such the attractiveness of different sectors, individual companies, management teams, and companies' overall growth prospects.

Other pricing quirks arise when an aggressive high-growth consolidator is playing the Indian Rope Trick (see Chapter 10). Here the consolidator has to keep acquiring businesses on a price / earnings ratio lower than their own to maintain EPS (earnings per share) growth and will pay a price that is earnings-enhancing even if the ROI is nonsensical. Occasionally, out-of-control acquirers will also overpay to buy something which will obfuscate weak underlying trading in their own business or get them out of a hole.

I was close to the CEO of a quoted financial services business which had some awkward litigation on the horizon. They overpaid for a large company operating in a rather dull part of the financial services sector, with the deal doubling their size. A year later, I asked the CEO about the rationale for the deal. He was disarmingly honest: 'We thought the balloon was going to go up on our original business and needed another business if that happened.'

For the buyer, timing is also key. Buying distressed, unwanted or even bust businesses, or acquiring when a sector is out of favour, usually generates far better ROI and thus creates significant shareholder value. Most businesses fail to realize this or are too stretched and stressed themselves when these opportunities arise.

It's another reason to have a strong balance sheet which is ready for tough times and not to get too carried away in a strong market. 'Never confuse brains with a bull market', as the sign on a grizzled investment manager's desk said when I started as a graduate trainee.

What all this tells you is that, while there are plenty of pointers to what a business should be worth, the actual valuation, like beauty, is in the eye of the beholder. Whether you are a buyer or a seller, it's about what you think it is worth to you (and whether there is an overlap in these valuations with the person on the other side).

The Venn diagram

Deals only happen where there is an area of commonality in which it makes sense for the buyer to buy and the seller to sell. Think of it as a Venn diagram. If there's overlap between what the buyer wants and what the seller wants, both sides can be happy.

Of course, this is a best-case scenario. A deal may well take place where one side is pretty unhappy (for example a distressed seller) but nonetheless they get something they want or need. Sometimes what they need may be their only option.

But deals are not a zero sum game. Good deals (with both sides happy) often happen when there is asymmetry of what each party wants. An example of this might be where an owner has had enough of the stress of ownership and wants a steady income as an employee of a larger group.

There is also often a 'marriage value' where the target is more valuable to the acquirer (e.g. a consolidator who can generate synergies, or a brand with distribution reach) than to the vendor. The Venn diagrams on valuation will then overlap and the final price will be determined by the relative negotiating skills of the two parties.

Deals are harder when there is symmetry of requirement – typically this is where both parties' only concern is wanting to maximize their returns. But even in the most extreme versions of this – such as private equity firms selling a company to one another – there may be asymmetries around areas like timing, with a fund in a run-off (which needs to liquidate assets) selling to a recently established fund (which needs to get its cash invested).

Pursuit

As an active acquirer, I was always keen to understand the universe of potential targets and ensure they knew I was interested. This was partly to generate transactions but also so that I had options. Vendors knew there were (theoretically, at least) other targets I was interested in and that they were not the only show in town. This strengthened my hand.

I'd regularly send out speculative letters to all targets, particularly the smaller ones who didn't need a bespoke letter, every six months or so. I'd time these for when I thought their owners might be in a reflective frame of mind and have the space to think about bigger issues – just before Christmas, for example. In these circumstances, you'd never know whether the timing was right but had the best chance of catching someone at the right moment by always being in front of them.

With larger transactions, I would constantly be in contact with my competitors, particularly those for whom the business in question seemed to be non-core, letting them know that I was around as a buyer.

Persistence is often the name of the game. Once it took several years of sending letters to different people in a large multi-national; at one point I wrote to eight different people at the same time (including the CEO running the $50bn business) to try to find someone with the authority to consider a sale. There was usually no reply but occasionally I got something back expressing a lack of interest. I kept at it and eventually got an expression of interest from one part of the organization, which culminated in us acquiring the business.

On another occasion, I thought the logic of a UK corporate selling us their non-core business was compelling for both sides. I knew the company's management well but they consistently responded that there was a plausible internal reason for them not wanting to sell. So I had to put my full hand on the table and make an unsolicited offer with a price attached to their board. Again, this culminated in us buying the business, at a price which suited both sides.

My biggest concern during both these transactions, and many others, was that, particularly before (but even after) an exclusivity agreement had been signed, another buyer would hear of the transaction and outbid us. This means that as a buyer, once you've identified your target, you need to hug it close so that its owners don't start looking around for other offers.

Tactics

Let's say we have identified the business we want to acquire or found our buyer and we are now engaged with them. What next?

This section is written primarily from the viewpoint of the buyer but it will work for vendors too as they are two sides of the same coin. And while some of it is about how to get the best deal, it is not really about winning at any cost, which is highly damaging when trying to get a deal done. Always remember that most good deals tend to work for both sides. I am somebody who likes to do deals and believes that getting a good deal done is more important than trying to extract every penny for my side.

As a buyer, you should have a pretty clear idea of the price you are prepared to pay. Generally buyers will be thinking in terms of long-term financial returns and can work out what level of consideration delivers the return they are after, given the scale of the deal, its risks and its strategic benefits.

As a vendor, the desired price may be equally straightforward, but will often reflect very different calculations. Private vendors will be looking at what suits their needs – a retiring business owner may calculate what is wanted on the basis of their retirement plans.

Likely valuations will normally be more transparent for non-private owners. A corporate may know the price at which the capital can be deployed elsewhere more effectively. A private equity company will be looking to see if the internal rates of return (IRRs) generated from a sale stack up for this particular asset.

The key, particularly with private vendors, is to understand the other side's position. This is why I want to be in front of a potential vendor at the earliest opportunity and ask them why they are thinking about selling to me. At this stage, I am only interested in what they want (as I already know what I want). So I need to understand what it is like to be in their shoes.

Here I'm all ears and I want to listen. Most private vendors will tell you most of what you want to know. Frequently this will require interpretation which tends to come from experience (anyone who says, 'It's not about the money' generally gives the game away as that almost always means it is about the money). Their answers – which may well include details from their business and personal lives – will frame how a deal might be approached and its chances of success.

Here's how I would view some common responses:

- They want to retire. Great – there's a good chance a deal that works for both sides can be done.
- They have run the company for a while, but would be happy to be part of something bigger, especially as the market's getting tough. Good – they're capable and realistic. Assuming other factors stack up, you'll probably be able to agree a sensible price.
- They have owned this business for a few years but would like to invest more in their property interests as they get older. OK – this is a common trajectory for entrepreneurs looking for a less stressful life but it's important to ascertain they have not been more involved in the business than they are letting on. And they'll be acutely aware of value.
- They've had enough, they've put their heart and soul into it and are young enough to try something else. Not good – they will want to

maximize exit value, are probably running the business in their own way and effectively, and could easily start up again if the 'something else' doesn't work out, meaning you'll have a highly effective competitor who knows the business you've just bought inside out.

Vendors should take a similarly strategic approach, but from the other side. They should be trying to establish what the buyer sees in their business. If there appear to be strong synergies or strategic gains, the size of the buyer's Venn diagram circle might be bigger and there might be a chance of grabbing a chunky slice of the 'marriage value' in the overlap. Putting yourself in the buyer's shoes gives the vendor a feel for what they might pay.

All this may seem obvious but it's surprisingly poorly understood. I remember once being about a year into the role of CEO. I was looking at how we could grow the business by consolidating a fragmented market and a larger competitor made an unwanted approach.

My chairman and I visited their CEO who immediately produced maps of our branch networks and showed how easily our network could be integrated into his and how, by paying a small premium to our market value, he would significantly enhance his company's worth. None of this had any appeal to me or my chairman despite our shareholdings in our company and our fiduciary duties as directors (ahem). The pitch was entirely about what he wanted and his personal vision. At no point had he considered that, in order to get us to sell, he would need to offer us something we wanted.

The information

Vendors are rightly wary about revealing too much about their business early on. However, as a buyer, you can get a feel for roughly what you should be prepared to pay for a business from pretty basic information, particularly if you know the sector well and especially if you are operating in it.

The last three years' management accounts, the current management accounts and any budgets and forecasts should give you a pretty good idea of historic, current and future profits. You can use these to start making ROI calculations. The company's balance sheet will give you the position on assets such as freehold properties.

The breakdown of revenues into different types will give you an idea of which of these are attractive to you. For example, based on your own knowledge of the industry, you may believe the business has the prospect of greater profitability or you might see the opportunity for economies of scale. A list of employees (anonymized is fine), their roles and salaries is also important in understanding both how the business works and what it could look like under your ownership.

The next step is to look at what differences a change of ownership would make to the profitability. The obvious place to start here is to adjust the profits to reflect costs related to the current owners. An example of this might be adjusting the directors' remuneration to what a professional manager would be paid rather than what the owners have decided to pay themselves.

Also, look out for one-offs going both ways, such as a spike in revenue / profits caused by a one-off transaction (like a property sale) or a one-off cost (like a major refurbishment). Adjust your calculation of the underlying profitability to reflect these. If you are a trade purchaser looking to integrate the business, most synergies should be quite easy to estimate and you can build a back-of-an-envelope calculation of what the ongoing costs will be under your ownership.

The synergies (aka cost savings) are the costs of staff who will no longer be needed if there is replication of roles in the acquirer and the target (typically management, sales and administration) and the costs of properties which will no longer be needed where the leases can be moved on or the property sold. Other savings will vary by sector: such as the reduction of drivers and vehicles if it's a route density business, or reduced material costs in a manufacturing business where more volume equals lower prices from suppliers.

But you also need to get a feel for the business and to get that you need to go there or speak to people. Sometimes it's obvious. I was about to start negotiating a deal and my divisional MD undertook a drive-by of a target I had asked his opinion on. 'I don't care what the returns on this looks like to you, Charles. I'm never going to run that shithole.'

He could tell from the outside of the building that the business was bad news. But it's not always that clear. Wherever and whenever possible, try to visit the vendor on site so you can start getting a feel for the business and meet as many people who work there as possible. Often, however, access to those other than the majority shareholder is impossible, which makes it much harder to understand what makes the business tick.

There are other routes to seeing value though. One is your knowledge of your industry and your own position in it. In the records management business, a target company might have been storing too many boxes and renting expensive overflow premises for boxes that we knew we could easily store in our own spare capacity. Or, conversely, acquiring a business with spare capacity in the right area might enable us to save on the costs of a new facility. You should also able to assess basic key performance indicators (KPIs). In the box business, I would want to know the average cost of storing a box and the average price a customer is paying to store a box. And I'd want to know the rate of customer churn. I should be able to get all of this from basic information supplied by the target and it will give me an idea of some of the potential value I could unlock if I bought the business.

A key tip to vendors: get this information right before asking what the valuation is. Most forms of due diligence will get to the real numbers and your hand is much weaker at that stage. If you understate the performance early on, deliberately or not, you will struggle to get an acquirer to increase their valuation once they have a figure in their head. Similarly, if you overstate performance or fail to disclose a negative up front, the buyer will likely insist on a price reduction at a point when your negotiation position is weak.

Who are you talking to?

Often – too often – deals go wrong when either or both of the negotiating parties don't have the authority to execute. Sometimes this is inevitable – my offers for businesses were usually 'subject to board approval' as acquisitions were subject to an authority level beyond my remit, but I could honestly say that this was technical and that I was speaking for the company.

But some parties, particularly buyers, view it as an advantage to hold cards up their sleeve. They may do this by letting those without authority undertake negotiations so that those with authority can nix the deal or change its terms without reason at later stages.

At a major private equity house, the deal-doers were expected to get a transaction into its near-final form before seeking investment committee approval. Yet it was far from a given that this would be granted. The deal-doers had to conceal this from the other side, who would be negotiating in good faith. This frequently resulted in terms being changed at the last minute on a 'take it or leave it basis' or occasionally deals being revoked, leaving the vendor fuming and their plans in tatters.

Sometimes powerful individuals will let their minions do the legwork and then come up with their own views in the final stages, to chip away at the price or to make fundamental changes to the transaction. Unfortunately this may be effective when a vendor cannot face re-starting the sales process or abandoning a sale which they are emotionally committed to. Even worse, I have come across people who consistently use this approach, just to show everyone who's boss.

A gentler version of this sometimes takes place with large corporates. Here, due to convoluted internal structures, the ultimate decision maker only gets to review the transaction at a very late stage (and after many others have raised their own doubts about issues that affect them). In dealing with corporates like this, I dread the unexpected phone call starting with 'I'm afraid head office...' and feel like a nervous trainee midwife until the baby is safely delivered without complications.

Recently, a small company I had invested in had spent three months of due diligence and tens of thousands of pounds in legal fees ahead of a sale to the UK subsidiary of a US subsidiary of a Fortune 100 company. I had checked from the outset that the US subsidiary was on board with the transaction and that the huge parent was not in the decision-making chain. And yet... somehow the final documents found their way to the CFO of the parent company. After a cursory flick through, he apparently said that he didn't like the deal. And that was that.

Personally, I find these sort of 'not dealing with the man' structures, whether deliberate or not, unhelpful in negotiating and delivering deals. Any benefits accruing to the party employing them gained from last-minute changes tend to be worth less than the illwill created by messing the other party around and the broader market perception that you are a back-slider.

When undertaking a transaction myself, I try to ensure that I have pretty much full authority and can give genuine personal commitment to that. And if I subcontract the negotiating role, I will stay close to the transaction so that the negotiator is always acting with my authority, even if on occasions they have offered something without my consent or support.

I strongly believe that dealing directly with the key decision-maker is an attraction for the other side and thus has appreciable value in negotiations.

The key point is to establish exactly the authority of the person you are negotiating with, and poke away until you are clear on this. This is also highly relevant when dealing with a lead shareholder who may not ultimately have authority over the other shareholdings. If the other side's internal structure does not allow you to ascertain whether or not authority is held by the team or person you are dealing with, proceed cautiously and try to establish where you are in terms of the other side's authority at every stage of the transaction.

The key moment

As a buyer, after an initial exchange of information and an exploratory meeting or two you should know what represents a good price for you. It's possible that you will know it much earlier. This price will include an assessment of all the elements mentioned so far and may include additional quirks such as being prepared to overpay for an asset to stop a competitor getting hold of it.

You should also have marshalled your arguments on why the vendor should sell the business and why they should sell to you. There are numerous elements here. Ideally you want to explain to them:

- This is the best option for your shareholders (which may include you) and your business.

- My company is the most logical buyer for your business and this is reflected in the value of my offer.
- I have the money to hand and a deal with me will be fast and simple.
- I am alive to your specific interests and will be highly flexible in accommodating them.

To me, the format of this key meeting where valuation is to be discussed for the first time is very important. By far the best is face-to-face between principals so that you can see the immediate reaction to your vague indicative offer. Generally I prefer it to be on their territory so that they are most comfortable, even if this means me travelling a considerable distance for what can be a very short meeting.

The opposite of this is submitting an offer letter to an agent by a certain time having had limited access to the principals. I will squirm endlessly to avoid this format.

Assuming the format is face-to-face, my job as a buyer is, after the initial pleasantries, to listen. I know my position and want to know as much as possible about the vendor's position. Unfortunately, the vendor, who is probably less sure of their position than I am of mine, should want to do the same. Often this leads to a very awkward silence with both sides willing the other to speak first.

If we're at an impasse here, I would eventually feel it incumbent upon me as the buyer to open up first. I would then set out my arguments as to why the vendor should be selling to me. As part of this, I will highlight every advantage to the vendor that I can think of. A typical pitch would be:

- The market is a good market but it is consolidating and the larger players have structural advantages that will ultimately squeeze out the smaller operators. Your business is currently at optimal value before this happens.
- You have certain large customers, who are increasingly moving to fewer, larger suppliers. If you lost one or two of these, the fixed cost nature of your business means that your profitability would decline rapidly.
- *As a larger operator, I am more likely to benefit from large customers moving to fewer, larger suppliers. And, given our scale, I am not that worried about acquiring a business where the biggest customer might leave as it's not very damaging for us to lose one customer
- You own your property. If we take it on with a lengthy lease it will automatically increase significantly in value as our covenant is much more valuable than that of your business. With us as a tenant, you will have a reliable income and an asset which is not only more valuable but also easier to sell should you wish to.

- You have cash in the balance sheet which I will pay you for, enabling you to receive that cash at a 10 per cent tax cost under Business Asset Disposal Relief rather than paying income tax.
- I might add in a few more rueful observations, such as: your geographical area is highly suitable for me at present and I would very much like to acquire your business but I need to be here; if you reject me, I will either acquire another business nearby or open a new operation which will increase the local market capacity (bad thing) and mean I will no longer be interested in acquiring your business; if your business struggles, your property will have a poor tenant and that means the property will be worth appreciably less, too.

I would be happy to ramble on in this way so that it feels as like I have put most of my hand on the table. Doing this also starts a narrative in the vendor's head as to what their world might look like after a deal and, once *this* has started, deals usually start to flow. But I won't mention price.

If the vendor then wishes to expand on their position, possibly picking up on something related such as the sort of lease we might be happy to sign, I will garner a better idea of their position and may even pick up some indication of their expectation on price. Failing this, there may then be another extended silence, which hangs around interminably but is usually broken by the seller who was originally contacted by the buyer asking outright what the price is.

An example of this was when I had chased down a multinational to consider selling me a division. My interest had finally been acknowledged and the necessary information exchanged and I was sitting with the savvy European M&A director of the multinational in our boardroom. After the second lengthy silence, which had gone on for five minutes but felt like five hours, he leaned forward. 'You know the rules, Charles. You approached us, you've got the information, what's the price?'

This is the moment. Somebody has to provide the anchor price and whoever goes first has the disadvantage of setting it and revealing part of their circle in the Venn diagram.

So I said, 'OK. Understood. I have a number but I'm not sure of the currency. It's not sterling ($1.35 at the time), it's highly unlikely to be euros ($1.17), but I'd be pretty comfortable if it's dollars. And the number is 100m.'

He leaned back. 'Well Charles, it would be very nice if it was sterling.' We had our range – he was very happy at £100m (sterling) and I was very happy at £75m (dollars) and we were both going to be fairly happy at the final price of £87m. I knew I would have paid £100m and suspect $100m was his lower limit.

Being there is very important because the response is nearly as revealing as the offer, as in this instance. For you, as the buyer, it is vital that you say nothing once you have given your indication Instead, you must listen hard to the response and the language used. Even the firmest rejection will normally be accompanied by some commentary and you are looking for remarks such as 'I wouldn't sell for less than x' (basically this means – I'd be very happy at x). These will give you an idea about whether the Venn diagram circles could ever overlap.

Other ways of setting a range include saying, 'I think I could get it to begin with an x.' Where this number is a two or a three, you are setting out a reasonable range where the answer again can be very helpful, such as, 'It would have to be in the high twos.'

Some very skilled and experienced vendors know that how they manage their initial response can translate into a significantly higher price. One well-known UK entrepreneur listened to an offer made by the buyer's minion for one of his largest businesses. When the minion was finished, the entrepreneur asked him to leave immediately, saying that his time was better spent looking after his children.

However, he did give him a 'take it or leave it' price-tag. This was 50 per cent more than what the minion offered and was close to what the seller got eventually.

Making the offer rather than eliciting a price from the vendor is obviously to be avoided by the buyer at all costs. However, it is the buyer who usually has to show some of their cards first.

In many situations, particularly when I'm buying a number of similar businesses in a buy-and-build scenario, I have a very clear idea of what the valuation should be. Quite often, the vendor will also know the sort of multiples that I am paying. In these case, I will front up at quite an early stage with a pricing range along the lines of 'I'm accustomed to paying between one and 1.5 times revenues and never step outside this'. If there is no immediate demurral, I can be pretty clear that there is a deal available at the top end of the stated range, and perhaps lower.

I have occasionally come across situations where most of the owners in a specific sector have convinced themselves that their businesses are worth more than they are, generally on the back of a rogue buyer overpaying for businesses in the past. In one sector, which I had expected to consolidate, this meant there were no deals to be done for several years.

But over time, as the owners got older and their priorities moved on from achieving a price based on the rogue transactions to recognizing they had to sell out at some point, they recalibrated their expectations. When I approached a potential seller, I mentioned early on that pricing expectations had been out of control for many years. When the seller acknowledged this immediately, I knew we could get to a sensible deal, as we did a month later. This transaction was noted by other sellers and I was able finally to start consolidating the industry at a sensible price, after a 10-year wait.

The importance of momentum

Once Heads of Terms (the main terms of a commercial agreement) have been agreed, the deal moves on to the next phase. This is where detailed information is provided to check that what has been provided thus far is accurate, that the assumptions made by the vendor to date are correct, and to uncover any issues in the company of which the buyer was unaware.

This is done in conjunction with the preparation of the legal documentation and, in this stage, the vendor will be revealing almost everything about the business to the buyer. Particularly when the buyer is a competitor, some of the information can be sensitive. There must be commitment on both sides. That said, there are nearly always bumps along the way as unexpected information is revealed or the business's performance improves or deteriorates during the course of the negotiations. This may require further interrogation or even adjustments to the terms. The vendor is most vulnerable to changes here as the price is unlikely go up with good news but may well go down with bad news.

The sale process is time consuming and a distraction from day-to-day business and a long, drawn-out process is more prone to failure – for reasons ranging from changing external factors to psychological weariness on either side. So there needs to be a sense of momentum and pragmatism on both sides. Points worth bearing in mind include:

- The vendor should endeavour to have the necessary information to hand – and also reveal any warts at an early stage. Nasty, late-stage surprises are the most common reason deals fall apart – although, in fairness, these sometimes come as a surprise to the vendor too.

- Both sides should devote energy and resources to the deal. However, they should not become overly emotionally involved – stay objective, set boundaries, don't fall in love with the deal.

- It's always a good idea to concede a few unimportant points. It makes you look reasonable and strengthens your hand. Look out for areas where you can be flexible and accommodating at little cost to yourself.

- Watch out for those who want to chip away at your side of the deal and capture any upsides for themselves. If you're the vendor, the best remedy for this is to have another buyer waiting in the wings.

- It's worth remembering that things can go right down to the wire. I once had to reject a deal (the disposal of a subsidiary) in its final stages as the buyer applied more and more pressure to the terms. I was leaving the lawyers' building disconsolately in the early morning after a desperate night of negotiation when a member of the vendor's team ran after me to concede the key point that had triggered my departure. This was particularly gratifying as, had the transaction not happened, my entire business could well have gone under.

- You can push people too far. A partner and I once established a knock-down price of £500k for a cleaning products business whose conglomerate parent wanted to get rid of it. After discovering the business was in worse shape than we thought, my partner offered to take it off their hands for nothing to see how low they'd go. They told us that not only would they not move, they wouldn't sell to us on any terms. I admire this – but you have to be in a strong position to do it.

When to walk away

What if the Venn diagrams don't overlap?

If you've been outbid by another interested party and have put everything into it, then that's it. Walk away. Don't be tempted to get into a bidding war. You knew your maximum and someone else offered more that's that – you don't want get emotional.

Similarly, when you're the only bidder but can't offer what the vendor wants, you should also walk away. This is a good thing to do because it puts the onus on the vendor to let the deal go. Should they re-approach you in the future, they will do so from a position of weakness. Unless their business has performed beyond expectations, you will be able to start with a lower offer than the one they rejected. Particularly when a business is struggling or something unexpected has come to light, this is almost a negotiating tactic. They're confused and unhappy but with a few weeks to reflect, they get there.

On one occasion, I was rejected by the proud owner of what had been a successful and valuable business. The market sector had been badly affected by the financial crisis and they had diversified into other areas which they had managed badly. The business was haemorrhaging cash and the owner could not be convinced that the alternative to our offer was probably receivership. When the penny dropped a few weeks later, we were able to buy the business very cheaply. We could probably have bought it even more cheaply off the receiver but the receivership process would have damaged the business significantly and might have attracted other purchasers.

Post-acquisition management

Despite all of this, deals do get done – and sometimes they even leave both sides happy. But that's not the end of it: post-acquisition management is very important.

Often (for reasons of confidentiality) very few people involved in the business will have been aware of the deal until it's actually done. Out of necessity they have it sprung upon them. So you need to follow General MacArthur's strategy: 'Have a plan. Execute it violently. Do it today'.

Key customers need to be contacted by the target's team immediately to explain the rationale of the deal and how it will improve the products or service they receive. The target's staff should be briefed by their senior management along with those of the buyer. Any assurances they can be given about the security of their employment should be spelled out, as should the possibility of redundancies. This is a time of great uncertainty for the target's staff and you owe it to them to be as frank as possible – even if the news is bad.

My experience has been that when people are agitated about what an acquisition means for the business and themselves, this is a good sign. It suggests that they understand that change may be coming. This is more constructive than the assumption that post-acquisition life will be business as usual. If and when changes do come, you will find that the people who have stuck their heads in the sand are less likely to understand or embrace it.

You should have a very clear idea of whether there will be changes to the operating structure and reporting lines and what the combined business will look like. You will need to familiarize yourself with the skills and capabilities of those in the target business. While you should have talked to the vendor and their team about individuals, you are unlikely to have had much access to the middle, and even senior, management during due diligence to assess which roles in the combined business will be carried out and by whom.

You will also be getting stuck into the detail on the customers and their pricing structures. Although these are unlikely to change in the short term you should be aware of who the outliers are. And you should have clear ideas on areas such as branding and marketing with a view to integrating everything from product names to websites. IT, too, is a huge area.

I've worked for some very slick acquirers. In one company, our acquisition integration team would arrive on day one. They'd install the IT system immediately and start training the acquired staff on it. Debtor and creditor ledgers would be transferred to head office and customer lists and details moved on to our systems. Hire equipment would be checked over, with poor equipment disposed of and the rest transferred to our system and re-badged. Health & Safety standards would be audited and raised if necessary to our standard procedures.

Within a week the acquired branches would look like our own branches, with the staff in new uniforms and newer vehicles having their livery changed. One member of the acquisition team would stay in each new branch for a month to help the team there with the glitches and educating them in the new systems.

Longer-term issues such as the consolidation of properties in the records management business would take more time. But we would know all the property details long before the acquisition had gone through and know when and which leases we might be planning to come out of long before the sales and purchase agreement (SPA) was signed.

When integrating a business, there were often many moving parts, but we would have a clear plan as to what we intended to do long before completion. We would have estimated short-term double-running costs, property provisions and any redundancy costs. We would then have fed these, along with the transaction costs, into the overall capital we were deploying – so as to work out what we could pay for the business to achieve our required return on investment.

Finally, we would monitor our performance against our projections to see whether the acquisition had lived up to our expectations and generated the returns we had expected, using the results to work out whether our valuations should be increased or decreased for the next deal.

4
HOW DO YOU GET THE MONEY?

'The first million is by far the hardest.'

ANON

Why you don't need much (or any) of your own money to buy a business – and a run-through of where the money can come from, how you can access it and what this means for you as the buyer. Private equity, search funds, family and friends – and how all these can work for you. The type and size of businesses you should be looking for. How to bridge gaps and what next?

Starting up

You can often start a business with little or no funding. There are endless examples of companies started from kitchen tables (like The Body Shop) and garages (such as Apple).

In fact, a bigger issue than funding is being able to support yourself before you start generating revenues. Look into a lot of successful, entrepreneur-led businesses and you often discover that the key ingredient, apart from entrepreneurial zeal, was simply the ability to operate without a pay packet for an extended period of time due to some degree of personal or familial wealth.

For this reason, many businesses are started after someone is made redundant (and so has a payment they can live on for a while). Figures vary but a recent report from AXA suggests that 40 per cent of UK start-ups (an example is the shoe brand Calla) are a result of redundancy.

There are other low-finance starting models too. Rag traders often started from market stalls (Mike Ashley, Monsoon, etc.), established supply chains with credit, then moved into more permanent shops using the extraordinarily positive cash-flow nature of that business to fund expansion without external capital.

Other entrepreneurs perfect one branch. Under Julian Metcalfe and Sinclair Beecham, Pret A Manger had a single outlet in London's Victoria district for three years. It later rolled-out rapidly with preserved cash and a clear business model. This is a common model in the restaurant business and you often see small chains of half a dozen branches, particularly in wealthy cities like London.

Less ambitious entrepreneurs can build patiently and fund growth internally. But most businesses need some cash early on for day-to-day survival, life-sustaining income for the founders and any form of expansion or growth.

Early-stage funding

We've already seen that a significant redundancy payout can be one form of early-stage funding. It's also not uncommon for would-be entrepreneurs to work in high-paid jobs for a few years to build up cash resources to fund start-ups. There's a well-trodden path from the City to entrepreneurship – examples here include Deliveroo and Innocent. Friends and family are a third common source for would-be entrepreneurs, with connections or family money.

All of these have benefits. For example if you're tapping your family up for funding you often won't have to give them any equity in return. Similarly, a friend of mine who built a world-class mail order business would brazenly and persistently ring round his well-to-do friends to fund the payroll if trading had been weak that month and there were no funds available to pay staff.

Beyond friends and family, there other common sources. *Dragons' Den* (or *Shark Tank*) types can be good, especially serial entrepreneurs who feel they have a nose for something but are past the point of wanting to do it themselves. They're particularly good if they know the business. Some private investors are happy to take on extreme risk where they think there may be extraordinary returns One start-up I was involved in received a seven-figure sum from one individual on the basis of the entrepreneur, his track record and his short business plan with hardly any follow-up questions.

Private individuals of any type usually mean less hassle and paperwork. But there are downsides too – many expect a significant chunk of equity for such an early investment, leaving less for the entrepreneur. And it can get more personal when things don't go well.

Government grants can also help to provide early funding but often have too many strings attached for the amount of money provided. A friend with a hospitality business at his stately home ended up returning the money as he felt he was losing control of the enterprise for a £5,000 grant. Regional development agencies and the like rarely get the money into the right places. They also run the risk of subsidizing a company, which can then distort the market for its competitors. I've often come across businesses with some form of soft state-aided loan on their books; most often it's there because it was available rather than needed.

Personally, I back people I've worked with who are starting up in an industry we both know well, particularly where we know the customers who will use us. I'm generally very wary of anything I don't fully understand, particularly at the pre-revenue stage. This may seem rather cowardly but early stage investment is a pretty scary environment.

What if you don't have the money to buy a business?

It's pretty easy to dismiss the idea of buying a company to run on the grounds that you haven't got the money. That buying a business is for those who have made their pile selling their previous business. That it's for scions of wealthy families who could never face working for someone else. That you may get to run a business owned by external shareholders such as private equity (PE) fund managers but it's never going to be majority owned, or even significantly minority-owned, by you. If that's what you think, I hope to convince you otherwise.

Private equity funding

The idea of new management coming in to run an existing business under new ownership has been around for a long time. At its simplest, this could just be a shopkeeper retiring and handing the shop on to someone they know locally. That person might then repay them by taking on the rental of the property (if it's owned by the retiree) and paying them for the stock as and when it's sold. Or perhaps just taking on the existing lease liability is all that's required.

The term 'management buy-in' (MBI) is generally believed to have been coined in the 1980s as a variant on the management buy-out (MBO). The MBO had become an increasingly popular way for owners to cash in their chips on their business, or for corporates to dispose of their unwanted businesses. The continuation of the existing management meant that there was limited risk around their capability to manage the business. Often the management team knew more about the business than the owners.

When a retiring owner was looking to pass the business on to the management, he or she may have been prepared to accept a lower price as a reward to the management they'd worked with. The early management buy-outs were not the competitive auctions which are common nowadays. Those putting up the money found it very rewarding, particularly when they could borrow heavily against the business so that their investment was leveraged.

Once the MBO was established as a great investment vehicle, the question was what to do about a business where the retiring owner didn't have a team waiting in place to take it on. This was fairly common. The managers may not have wanted the responsibility of running a business themselves. Or the management team may not have been up to much, so nobody wanted to back them. Couldn't an experienced manager and her colleagues be brought in to run it? And so the MBI started to become a private equity product.

Nowadays, large private equity firms have detailed databases of potential managers, together with extensive relationships with headhunters. This means they can access the people they need to run the businesses they control, both before and after they get their hands on a company. While they will generally prefer to keep a high-quality management team in place for their experience and knowledge of the business, the opportunity they often spot is to shake up an existing business by bringing in new management.

Small private equity funding

While the original MBIs tended to focus on larger deals and heavyweight teams, there are now plenty of smaller private equity firms who can see the opportunities MBIs present. A talented manager can have a much larger impact on a small business than a larger one.

What these operators are looking for is to be brought opportunities. Given the small scale of their investment, there simply isn't enough time for them to research large numbers of opportunities. While their door is open for ambitious managers with successful track records who want to run something, they are not like the large PE businesses who will find and negotiate opportunities while lining up who will manage them. These smaller outfits respect deal-doers with imagination, rather than managers who wait for calls from headhunters.

The other advantage in bringing a transaction to smaller PE houses is that you have more leverage in sorting out your terms of engagement. If there is no transaction without your involvement, the PE house is more likely to be generous in terms of sharing the equity with you. If you've got a deal, have the relationship with the vendor, have done your homework, have a plausible argument as to why you are the best person to manage the business, you'll be in the driving seat. You may even be able to get PE houses competing to fund your venture.

Search funds

A colleague, Steve, from my 3i days set up one of the first these in the 1990s back before the term 'search funds' existed. It wasn't particularly successful – sometimes it's as bad to have an idea too early as too late. He set up a company to incubate talented managers. The people he worked with received a small salary to enable them to spend time researching potential transactions. Once they'd identified decent opportunities, Steve would work with them on negotiating the deals and on lining up financing in exchange for equity in the businesses once acquired.

There are now a burgeoning number of search funds in the US, the UK and other financially sophisticated markets. Their approach is very similar to what Steve was doing 30 years ago. Many are very small – a tiny office and a website with would-be owner-managers scouring the smaller company market for opportunities. Most have relationships with potential funders of debt (there are several specialist funds who will provide debt much more flexibly than the larger banks) and with equity providers who may be small PE funds, family offices or wealthy angel investors. With a smart transaction where the business subsequently thrives, the entrepreneurs behind the search funds can end up as majority shareholders despite putting up only a slither of the funding to buy the company.

But how do those working in search funds survive before they actually buy something? Unless they have access to funds, they often do it part time. I know a pair of MBAs who did highly-paid consultancy work two days a week. This enabled them to support themselves and spend three days a week (and any weekends) on their searches.

Holding down a full-time job is pretty difficult when you're looking to buy a company, particularly when you are working on an actual transaction. But when you're considering this, weigh up the huge advantages you have over someone undertaking a start-up, where profitable revenues (and pay) may take a long time to come through.

If you're doing a full-time job and an opportunity to acquire a business falls into your lap, consider yourself very lucky – and pursue it.

Angels, family and friends

Many start-ups are established with very little capital investment. But some require a bit of money – and they may also take considerable time to start generating revenues, during which the entrepreneur has to survive. Often the solution here is backing from angel investors at the pre-revenue stage.

Any serious business angel is, of course, looking to make money as well as encouraging entrepreneurship. They are well aware that most start-ups get through the cash more quickly than expected, and most angels will have more than one investment on the grounds that their success rate will be fairly low and they need several to spread their risk. So don't expect them to live up to their title of angels when it comes to sharing out the rewards of your success. They need to recover their anticipated losses on the ones that don't go so well.

If you're lucky enough to have family money to back you, this is generally the cheapest investment you'll find, and family are hopefully the most forgiving of investors. Friends are also a helpful source of funding, although there is a lot that can go wrong: misunderstandings around these have ruined many relationships.

Nonetheless, all three of these sources are welcome when you're buying a company. The key when it comes to raising money from them for buying a company (rather than starting one) is that you have a far better roadmap for what's going to happen next. Subject to how the financing is structured, you can have a proper, credible business plan which shows how you intend to return their investment and generate capital growth for them. The chances of you blowing their money is far smaller than a start-up.

My preferred method of investing in small entities is a straightforward loan. The equity base can be tiny and I want a decent chunk of it if I'm putting up the money which is funding the show. Only when the loan is repaid does the equity, notably the entrepreneur's equity, come into play. It's nice when the loan is repaid and I'm thereafter in for free.

I will back start-ups, but only where I know the industry well and the people I back have immediate access to revenues from customers who will come over to them. Even then, there is usually a hairy moment when more funding is needed to support early losses and supply cash for the growing business.

What size of company should you be looking to acquire?

A highly successful professional private company investor who I know well often has a wineglass in his hand. This is helpful when he explains where you do well in private company investing.

The broad base of the wineglass represents the number of buyers for very small companies. If I'm looking to sell my hairdressing salon, I am highly likely to find someone who will take it on for a cash consideration within their means. Indeed, if I'm selling an owner-managed business with profits of up to £200,000 and am prepared to take some element of deferred payment and the buyer is prepared to offer a personal guarantee to a bank, there's normally a deal to be done. So the market in buying and selling a small business is actually quite liquid as there are many acquirers who can find the funds. But the base of the wine glass gets smaller the higher up you go – and quite quickly.

The stem of my friend's wine glass is long and very narrow indeed. This represents companies making profits of, say, £200,000 to £750,000. There are a lot of these around: owner-managed, decent businesses, which have provided a nice lifestyle for their shareholders. But who are the buyers out there with £1m to £4m to acquire them?

It's too much for a well-off individual but not worth the hassle for professional investors whose rewards depend on the scale of their investment. There's almost as much effort involved in doing and managing a £3m deal as there is a £300m one, and the fees for investment funds are often the same percentage of the investment value. So there's no sensible return for a professional investor in sub-£5m transactions. My experience is that there are several gentle PE funds who are in it more for the enjoyment of small companies than the rapacity of most financial operators. But even they can't justify being in this space.

After the stem ends (let's call it at £750k profit), the number of potential buyers starts to balloon like the wineglass. More corporates will be paying attention, as these profits move their dials, although I've always fished in 'the stem' for bolt-on acquisitions. Private equity firms start looking at whether the target might become a platform for growth with a bit of ambition and better management. And the glass of buyers gets bigger as the targets become bigger, before eventually tapering at the very top where only the really big operators can play.

So, as a would-be entrepreneur through acquisition who wants control of the company, target the stem, especially the higher end of it where you get more critical mass.

An example of buying a business without any money

You're already in quite a good place, but it's worth running through this again.

You're hoping to buy a company in a market where there are more sellers than buyers. Tick. Many of the vendors are looking for a way out rather than to extract as much money as possible. Tick. You have the skill set to grow a possibly sleepy business. Tick. You have the drive to work hard, take tough decisions and make things work as well as possible. Tick.

So let's look at a typical example of how this is done.

I noted earlier that when I came in to run Restore (or Mavinwood as it was then called), we had many underperforming businesses, lots of debt and one real gem, the records management business, which is why I was there. Over the following year, I managed to sell off a fairly chunky business (£30m revenues) to a competitor. I also closed a huge loss-making business despite onerous contracts with a couple of customers. I explained to them that, if I did not do so, the whole company would go under and they would have no supplier, and I steadily wound down the operation while providing some support to them.

I also had the UK's largest timber treatment and damp-proofing businesses. It was just about breaking even, had no logical buyers and wasn't a huge hassle but it clearly didn't fit with the rest of the company and I didn't have the management or cash resources to sort it out.

Six months after I had gone in, I was called by a smart Mancunian who was a highly effective CFO for a buccaneering entrepreneur. He had seen his boss make a lot of money while he did most of the work. He'd correctly identified the orphaned status of the timber and damp business. Would I sell it to him? I replied that the revenues of £10m and the possibility that one day it might make money enabled me to put in some aggressive projections which would buy me time from our bankers. So would he pay me enough to keep them off my back? As I expected, he said that he'd take it off my hands for free. So there was no deal.

He rang back a couple of weeks later. He'd noticed I didn't have a CFO – I couldn't afford one but was very stretched and this was putting unfair pressure on our group financial controller. He would be happy to join as a part-time CFO. I admired him and this became a very happy arrangement for the next couple of years as we got out of the trenches and started to build something, in no small part thanks to his commercial practicality.

After that couple of years, he said I could now afford a full-time CFO and he still wanted to buy the outlier business. Sad as I was to lose him, I recognized that (a) I needed a full-time CFO, (b) he wanted to have his own business, and (c) the business, now making £400k per annum in profits (helped by his attention to it as it was based in Manchester) was still an outlier. So we agreed on a price of £4m.

At the time, I didn't get involved in how he was going to fund it. He asked me to defer £1.5m to be paid off at £0.5m a year. I trusted that I'd get the money and was happy with this. With revenues of £12m, the debtor book stood at £3m. So he borrowed £2m against that through invoice discounting. There was a shabby freehold in there which he borrowed £0.3m against. I'm pretty sure that the rest came from improving the working capital, aggressively chasing debtors and stringing out payments to the chemical suppliers. I've never asked him but I don't think he put up a penny.

The story ends very happily for all concerned. This was the last step in the turnaround of Restore / Mavinwood and our investors recognized that we were now a focused and effective business. Our share price moved up 30 per cent over the next few months. And the deferred payments were met.

Four years and eight months later, my former CFO rang me. I'd put in a 'no embarrassment' clause on the sale of the business such that Restore would receive a payment from him if he sold it within five years. This was on a sliding scale, with our percentage of sale proceeds declining as time went on. So in year 5 we were entitled to 10 per cent of the value over £4m. The company was now firing on all cylinders and he had received an offer of £14m from a corporate who saw significant synergies in acquiring it.

He could easily delay the deal by four months and pay us nothing, or we could compromise. I'd honestly forgotten about the clause so thanked him and said £500k, rather than £1m, for us would be marvellous. The deal was done, he cleaned up and we got £500k out of nowhere. Subsequently he rang me: 'Delighted to send you the cheque. Thanks for compromising on the fee. I was in a difficult position as, actually, for a different reason I'd changed the ownership of the company. Legally I knew I didn't have to pay you but thought it was in the spirit of our relationship.' And that from one of the toughest CFOs I've come across.

Lessons from this example

There were four elements that this CFO brought into play which are relevant to would-be ETAs:

- If a vendor trusts the buyer and their capabilities, deferred payment often works.
- Much of the banking for small companies is not real banking. They can lend money secured on the debtors, knowing that they are first in the queue if things go wrong – and they are going to get paid by collecting the moneys owed by the people who have secured the goods or services.
- If there are capital assets such as freeholds, you can borrow against them.
- We weren't that sloppy but the CFO made sure all debtors paid promptly and some creditors were asked to hold off a bit. A good CFO understands how to get idle working capital to work.

If you worry about the obligations that these create, and that any money you put up will disappear if you fail to sort out these undertakings, ETA probably isn't for you. This would be a shame – as all the models suggest that a half-decent effort will generate stunning returns. You're in a market where sellers exceed buyers, and the rewards of owning your own business rarely come without a degree of risk.

There is another element to be added in here, which is particularly relevant to the UK. Many business owners are not enthusiastic tax payers (this is not unique to businesspeople: pop stars, successful artists and sportspeople often live lives without 'normal' jobs where the taxman will eventually turn up to take a significant chunk of what they earn). As a result they just don't understand that tax is a big part of life.

In businesses there are two elements to minimizing tax. The most obvious is running a few personal costs through the business. I was always impressed by a former chairman of mine. When we were looking at buying a business, the vendor told him that profits were understated due to personal costs being run through the business and that many cash transaction weren't in the books. The vendor wanted the multiple of earnings to be applied to a higher number. My chairman simply replied that the vendor couldn't have it both ways. To be fair, there probably is something to the vendor's argument – but most vendors will take the chairman's point on board.

The second area is cash in the business's bank balance. In the UK, capital gains tax is currently (as of November 2024) 24 per cent, whereas the highest rate of income tax is 45 per cent. So to sell a company pregnant with cash (which the buyer will add on to the purchase price) means 19 per cent less for the taxman. The business owner, who knows that the state could not survive for 10 minutes in the private sector with its absence of cost control and no understanding of customer service, relishes this. So a vendor with cash on their balance sheet is very happy to accept a discounted price to the disbenefit of the taxman.

But there may still be a gap

This is where the small PE companies may come in. But this is also a space for angels and family and friends (if you're lucky enough to have wealthy ones). Once you've used up all the sources where you don't have to give away equity, you may need a bit more. But at least you've built in the leverage which gives these extra cash suppliers the opportunity to make great returns.

Personally, I also like to see the entrepreneur putting up something. Going to the casino with other people's money but none of your own is nice but unedifying for the other people. It doesn't have to be huge but should be meaningful to them. If they're not on the hook for something, I want bigger returns as an investor.

On this note, an excellent and thoughtful search fund approached me recently with an investment proposal. This was theoretically a safe bet in terms of me getting my money back – and if things went well, I'd get three times my money back – but no more, with any further upside going to them to them. No thanks – if I back a winner I want to share in a lot of the upside.

What next?

So you've finally got your hands on the business. Hopefully, it's currently (or after a few tweaks) profitable so that you can make your interest payments, pay down debt over time and pay yourself. If you need to get cracking on your expansion plans, you have several options:

- Capital investment through hire purchase (if required)
- Working capital through your debt factoring (if required)
- You've shown your bank lenders that you have / can repay, so they want to lend you more
- You may have external investors who are happy to support again
- The company is fabulously cash-generative and you don't need to worry about the above unless your master plan involves acquiring other companies.

But you've also got to run the bloody thing.

5
BEING THE CEO

'Uneasy lies the head that wears a crown.'
SHAKESPEARE, *HENRY IV PART II*

Why you have to embody the business, set the tone and craft the narrative. Making big decisions and empowering good people to make smaller decisions. Being a CEO and being a leader, why matrix management is a horrorshow and everyday CEO stuff.

The power of one

My route to being a CEO was an unconventional one: despite never having run a business or even a division, I moved from being a non-executive director of a public company to being its CEO. This was a huge risk for all involved but I'd like to think it worked.

Recently, I brought a management consultant in her late 20s into a private company (in which I'm a significant shareholder) as CEO. After a tricky first year, her intellectual capability and management training won through and turned a plodding business into something much more exciting. I've seen this strategy fail too with a new, inexperienced CEO flailing around without ever gaining traction until it was agreed they were not the right person. Nonetheless, a left-field CEO appointment can often transform a company.

Those buying into unambitious existing companies can reap huge rewards if they get it right as CEOs. They really do have the power to effect change.

More than anyone else, the CEO embodies the business. We can all think of businesses which are extreme cases of this and are absolutely synonymous with their figureheads or founders – Amazon and Jeff Bezos, Apple and Steve Jobs, and so on. Over a decade after he had stepped down as CEO, Bill Gates was still thought of as Mr Microsoft.

Partly due to the cult of Silicon Valley, we are in a phase where CEOs are, if anything, too important (we've been here several times before with the likes of Henry Ford and Jack Welch). Power is currently concentrated in the board in general and one figure in particular. This is reflected in the re-emergence of shares carrying differential voting capabilities. And, interestingly, it echoes the era a century before when powerful individuals often sought control in a similar way.

The nineteenth century was the age of the 'Robber Barons'. By contrast, in the 1950s, 60s and 70s the CEO was often just another man in a suit and power was more diffuse (although the poor quality of management then resulted in the asset stripping of the late 1960s which contributed to the financial crisis in 1973).

At one level we are now back in the era of charismatic, high-profile founders running household-name companies. But while the Mark Zuckerbergs and Tim Cooks of this world hog the limelight, the CEOs of small businesses definitely have a greater impact on the companies they run (Elon Musk is perhaps an exception here). Huge multinationals with tens of thousands of employees have their own inertia. They also often have a set of economic advantages deriving from their size – they are, as Warren Buffett said, 'economic castles, protected by moats'. They have cultures and brands and reputations.

But smaller companies are different. In a small business the right CEO can make the difference between the business succeeding and failing. As Michael Green, former Chair and CEO of British Broadcasting company ITV, once said to me, you don't need to be Napoleon to understand the 'Power of One'. And this is particularly true of smaller companies.

This is even more true in tough times such as COVID and recessions. When the economy is strong and the sun is shining, poor and average managers often get a pass. When the tide goes out (as Warren Buffett once famously said) you see who's been swimming naked. Here I could point to two companies in which I am a major shareholder. In the first, the CEO and his team were back in the office two weeks after they left as COVID struck. During the first COVID year they managed two fundraisings and 10 acquisitions. The second company talked a good game but did little. Company A's shares rose 50 per cent during this period. Company B's fell by 20 per cent.

Of course, to exercise the Power of One, you need to live the business. And there's no way round this. It's a 24/7 thing and can be a real burden, not necessarily in terms of hours worked but in terms of constant preoccupation A friend who runs a lifestyle business (a company that fits around his life, not a clothing or interiors brand) describes being CEO as having a heavy bag which you can occasionally choose to pick up and run forward with. In a non-lifestyle business, you have to carry this burden all the time.

So heavy is this burden that, at the age of 58, with scars and medals in equal measure, I stopped looking to be a CEO again. I had 'lived' three businesses and did not want to live another for five years – but five years later, after my replacement manifestly failed, I went back in again.

This is part of the thrill of being a CEO – you really can have huge impact on a business and, if it's properly managed, have ideas and make them happen. But it's a huge commitment – as a CEO, there is no 'they'. There's only you.

The tone of the business

The CEO sets the tone of the business. Again, we can all think of companies where the style of doing business is synonymous with the top person – Facebook's 'move fast and break things' springs to mind as a not entirely positive example.

But this needn't be some big, overarching philosophy. It can be the little things too. My own 'thing' is getting back to people immediately – no matter how grave or trivial the matter. I feel this sets the standard for everyone in the company. I'm currently CEO of a service business and I want people to know that it's important that everyone is prepared to do everything they can for customers, as well as for their colleagues and other stakeholders – and that this includes me. I don't sit on requests for a week and I don't expect you to either.

I have occasionally taken this thinking quite far. When I worked at Brandon Hire, I had my mobile number printed in the front pages of the catalogues we provided to customers (the print run was over 300,000). Why would I do this in a world where CEOs often guard their privacy and are protected by layers of gatekeepers? My thinking was that it showed I believed in what I was doing – to the extent that anyone could call me with a problem. It was also a message to our people: I'm there for the customer just like you are or should be. It wasn't just customers either – to my PR advisers' occasional chagrin, I would always respond to calls from private investors. Of course, I wouldn't give them insider hints – I'd just reiterate the company line. Nonetheless, the feedback was always positive – people love it when the CEO answers their call.

Lest you imagine this would create an incredible amount of work for me, it didn't. On the rare occasions my phone rang, it tended to be well-to-do individuals on weekends doing a bit of DIY. Our core business's customers knew the number of their Brandon contact – and would phone them, not me.

Possibly the only customer I genuinely helped was a rail contractor working late on a Friday night who was in desperate need of a poker-vibrator (which is used to eliminate air bubbles from poured concrete) when his delayed concrete shipment arrived unexpectedly. Despite my repeatedly calling it a vibrator-poker, it was easy for me to locate one of our team who could sort him out. Result:

a customer who would never leave us and a workforce who felt the CEO was down in the trenches with them and not afraid to muck in.

The customer isn't always right

Of course, I sometimes get customers with grievances. But this is good too. In these cases, we've usually done everything we can – but at some point you know the customer is simply a moaner. It's been escalated to the CEO and there is nowhere higher they can take it unless they want to go legal or pester the local Citizen's Advice Bureau or equivalent (they never do). On those occasions the job of the CEO is to politely explain to the customer that nothing more could be done. And if they aren't satisfied with this, my job was to tell them to get lost. It's a myth that the customer is always right. Some customers are a vexatious pain in the arse and you're better off without them. And it's not something anyone else in the organization is similarly empowered to do.

Tone isn't just about communications though. It applies to how you conduct yourself. In one CEO role I had, a company car was provided. Much to the displeasure of the fleet manager and senior management who liked their luxury cars, I chose a low-grade Ford to set the tone – we were cutting costs and the CEO was not exempt from this belt tightening. This was exactly right for three or four years but when we started flying I was slow to pimp my ride. As I was continuing to pat myself on the back for my thriftiness, a non-executive director pointed out to me that a five-year-old Ford was now sending out the wrong message. Our workforce was mostly blue collar and male and, for them, cars were potent status symbols. In my ageing Mondeo, I looked like a loser in the eyes of many of those who mattered. And even customers wondered about whether our business was as solid as we were suggesting.

Other examples were more straightforward. At another company which I joined as CEO, it was well known that that my predecessor had a 'driver' who was actually his gardener. His expenses were running at £130,000 a year, including many overnight stays in London at a top hotel when he lived a 40-minute train journey away. In this environment it was not surprising that other senior managers viewed the spectacular box we leased at Liverpool Football Club as an executive perk rather than a marketing tool and genuine business expense.

A culture of extravagance and nest-feathering is hard to change – and when you come in as a new CEO you have to fight hard against it. In this company I found myself being booked into the best suites when travelling on business. This was clearly wrong – as the company was in major financial difficulties. I made a point of letting as many people as possible know that a basic room was all I needed – and all the company could afford.

When it comes to integrity, you have to lead from the top. Otherwise, the message you send out is that the company is to be milked at every level. You really cannot argue with someone who says, 'The CEO fiddles his expenses so why shouldn't I do it, too?' As they say, the fish rots from the head – and this applies everywhere – to companies, organizations and even to nations.

The tone set by the CEO is not just important in your own business either – it's also important in companies you are looking to do business with or acquire. The CEO of a large facilities management company was a motor-racing enthusiast and his son was a wannabe professional driver. Over the years, this led to a situation where the company's suppliers were aware that a bit of racing sponsorship might not go amiss when tendering for contracts. It was no real surprise when, a few years down the line, the company blew up like an over-tuned racing engine.

Other examples litter business history. At the height of the fashion for conglomerates in the early 90s, Hanson launched an audacious hostile takeover bid for ICI, which was then the UK's largest manufacturer. The ICI defence team caused considerable embarrassment for Gordon White and James Hanson when they revealed that not only was White not on Hanson's board but he'd also 'invested' millions of pounds' worth of company money in racehorses, his main hobby. This was a key part of killing the bid and marked a turning point in the pair's fortunes.

For me, don't waste shareholders' money is an obvious rule. But what about the moral side of things? Do I care that quite a few CEOs sleep around or otherwise misbehave? Americans, in particular, seem quite keen on canning chief executives for extra-marital affairs. Here I'm less sure – and I think the two questions have to be 'Does it affect the business?' and 'Is it an abuse of power?' If not, maybe not. Intel's performance under Brian Krzanich (who resigned in 2018 after an undisclosed affair came to light) was pretty good, as was Priceline's under Darren Huston.

However, when a CEO's behaviour brings the company into disrepute, then they should resign. Of course, it's not just affairs. Paul Flowers could not have stayed on at the Co-Op after his fondness for drug use and male sex workers became known. Took on a new CEO role and asked a broker's analyst what he attributed the previous management's failings to. He simply mimed raising a glass to his mouth.

Even so it's an odd and rather grey area. According to a paper from Stanford University entitled *Scoundrels In the C-Suite*: 'Shareholder reactions to CEO misbehaviour are not uniformly negative. Of the 38 companies in our sample, 11 exhibited positive stock price returns when CEO misbehaviour made the news.' We can all think of companies where 'character' CEOs are given leeway that less flamboyant CEOs aren't.

Overall though, I don't think this area should be that complicated. As CEO, in all areas pertaining to the business, you have to be straight, honest and act according to the best interests of the company at all times. The only possible exception to this is when you're cutting your own deal with the company – but even it should be based around you sharing in success and upsides, meaning other stakeholders will not begrudge you your spoils.

Strategy vs narrative

To be an effective CEO you need a plan and you need to communicate it to your people, including how you expect them to execute their part of it. But a lot of leaders get bogged down in strategy, narrative, plans, visions and so on. Here I'm going to focus on the difference between strategy and narrative.

Many people love talking about strategy, perhaps because it's a buzzword with military connotations. But I'm quite wary of strategy. Too much 'strategy' is platitudinous waffle – and dressing up simple ideas in elaborate obfuscatory language.

When I briefly worked as the divisional MD of a FTSE-100 company, I received an invitation to attend a group strategy meeting. The invite was worded in a way that suggested I should consider it a great honour, even if the meeting started at 7am. I sat down in a room with 20 senior managers and we started throwing out ideas. Pretty soon, it became clear that this much-vaunted, mystical strategy boiled down to 'sell more product without lowering prices'.

Strategy is rarely rocket science, much as its proponents would like it to be – and it is even more rarely worth getting out bed at 4.30am for. The well-known quote from the nineteenth-century German Field Marshal, Helmuth von Moltke the Elder, 'No plan survives contact with enemy' (perhaps equally well-expressed by boxer Mike Tyson: 'Everyone has a plan until they get punched in the mouth') actually refers to strategy not planning.

Plans are good, though. If a strategy is a kind of overarching idea, a plan is a concrete set of arrangements designed to accomplish a specific goal (for example increase our widget production by 20 per cent by buying a new machine and employing more staff). Plans should be compulsory – and you've got to act on them. As another military man, General George S. Patton, said, 'A good plan violently executed now is better than a perfect plan next week.' (it is noteworthy here how close General Patton's quote is to General MacArthur's).

So, if strategy is a lot of waffle, why is narrative (which sounds like another dreadful buzzword) any better? Well, narrative is the story you tell people. Strategy is dry and top down, narrative is inspirational and helps you take people along to a destination. Ideally your narrative should have a few numbers attached too – so it doesn't get too woolly.

Your starting point with narrative should be understanding where your business is – and where you want to take it. At Brandon, there were two main parts to our narrative. One was 'Create a £100m tool hire company with a branch within 20 minutes of every 10,000 people apart from very remote areas.' The other was, 'Achieve industry-leading Returns on Capital Employed', which was critical in a capital intensive business.

These hardly changed over the years, they could be understood by everyone and they were probably instrumental in the decision to sell the company once the goals had been achieved – not least because no obvious further narrative suggested itself.

At Johnson, by contrast, one of my many failings was not finding a workable narrative quickly enough. My idea for the narrative was something along the lines of: 'Pull together to sort out the current dysfunctionality and the strengths of our best businesses will take us through to a growth phase.' Not exactly pithy or inspirational. But it was also weak, wrong and ultimately unachievable.

A better narrative might have been: 'Our balance sheet is shot. We need to sweat our good businesses, get out of our bad businesses and get the banks off our backs by whatever means possible – if necessary, by persuading our shareholders to put in more cash.' It took too long for me to get to the right narrative – and by the time I did I was no longer the right person to deliver on it.

Still, I managed to learn from this. At Restore, which came after Johnson, the early narrative was: 'We're basically bust but have one really good business in here. Get out of all the rubbish businesses and try to survive.' That worked and then we could move on to the more positive: 'Consolidate the market in our star business through acquisitions to become a leader and then move into other sectors with the same sort of customer base.'

Another narrative I'm currently deploying is: 'Achieve industry leading margins by charging more for a differentiated service which customers will pay for, then roll out the model.' This encapsulates both what we need to do – and the perils of not doing it. If we can't get customers to pay enough, we will be another me-too operator in a tough business.

Underpinning whatever narrative you've chosen should be the general axiom: 'We're going to build a great business if you're up for it – and this is the way we're going to do it.' This is perhaps the single most important point. Narrative is both very simple and very hard. If you know what you're doing with the business, the narrative follows. If you don't, finding the right narrative may be impossible.

Get people on board with your story

OK, so you've got a narrative. Next, you have to communicate it. The ability to explain your narrative and your plans to your people simply and effectively is a crucial part of being a leader (here it's worth looking at good political speeches). A well-crafted narrative should be understood by everyone the first time they read or hear it. So, how do you do this?

The critical KISS (Keep it Simple Stupid) principle is something that's much easier to sign up to than actually deploy. You should spend time analyzing what it is you want to communicate and thinking about how you are going to say it and then condensing it into something clear, concise and actionable.

The philosopher Wittgenstein would spend months trying to extract the pith (not a malapropism for 'taking the piss') to condense complex thoughts into what look like cheap aphorisms but are actually both precise and profound. This is nicely summed up in a quote popularly attributed to Mark Twain (but probably originally from the philosopher Blaise Pascal): 'If I had more time, I would have written a shorter letter.'

The point here is that concision is both difficult and worthwhile. The ability to summarize an idea briefly is both a skill in itself and a test of the quality of the idea. To this end, I would never send out a company-wide email of more than two paragraphs. You should be able to say anything important in a few hundred words – and besides, many people won't read more. You ask people to do something simple, obvious and achievable.

In practice this means you have to draw the plan from the narrative and then work out how to achieve the plan. You communicate this to people, ensure they understand what they are being asked to do and agree they're capable of doing it and then you nail them to the plan.

Sometimes the behaviour needed to achieve the plan is most clearly explained in other terms which are easier to understand and action. At Brandon, the local tool-hire branches didn't want or need to know that my shareholders would judge me and the company on return on capital employed (ROCE). But I needed them to work on this basis.

So I charged them a monthly fee on the amount of capital they were deploying (2 per cent of the assets they were operating). This meant they made sure that they only held assets which they were actually going to deploy. The result was the branch managers didn't want to hold on to any equipment that they weren't going to use or only used rarely and my shareholders could see a healthy ROCE on the overall group.

So far, much of what I've talked about is quite one-sided – me telling people what I want them to do and what is expected of them. But what about meetings?

BEING THE CEO

These are often a way of communicating plans and narratives – but are more discursive and often lend themselves to greater ambiguity over what is expected.

Here, my own solution is to do something very few CEOs do. Where I can, I offer to take the minutes of meetings myself (you will find you rarely have much competition for this). But I find it invaluable. Too many meetings end up with a lack clarity over what has been agreed. By taking the minutes you have a record of what the goals are, how they are to be achieved and who is responsible. I still do this at smaller companies I chair. Hopefully the minutes will always have a confirmation of the current plan and next actions to deliver the plan.

Once you've agreed goals with people, your job is then to monitor performance against them. The person who doesn't deliver or comes up with unexpected surprises (these are rarely good) must be removed quickly unless there are mitigating circumstances. Those who don't do what they are asked to do are sand in the corporate gearbox. This is why you need clearly agreed goals. If goals are ambiguous or vague, people can often wriggle off the hook on the basis of a misunderstanding. Clearly communicated plans and goals, by contrast, make discussions about non-performance much easier.

How I think you should CEO

In *The Mirror of the Sea* Joseph Conrad speaks of a type of captain who at the start of a voyage might retreat to his cabin, possibly morose in the knowledge that he was leaving his family and home for a long time. For the first few days, running the ship would be left to his senior officers: 'Such a complete retirement served to imply a satisfactory amount of trust in their officers and to be trusted displeases no seaman worthy of the name.'

This is a beautifully expressed understanding of the idea that a CEO must establish the principle of locking power and responsibility together and driving this thinking down through the organization. Once people are aware of exactly what they are expected to do, the good ones will take responsibility as long as they have the power to achieve their goals. And putting trust in people is a great motivator. It is empowerment, 1900s style.

In a similar vein, a large diversified FTSE-100 company describes its management style as 'Hands Off, Eyes On'. This is a clear expression of how its management want to run their business. It's a great style and can be applied to almost all businesses apart from very small SMEs where the CEO will usually be involved in all areas of the day-to-day operations. However, running a company this way requires clarity around what is being asked and precise managerial reporting to monitor what is going on.

There are other advantages to this style of management, too. It means the CEO can focus on what he or she feels are their strengths. My own strengths lie in managing investors (e.g. raising money), communicating goals and doing deals, typically acquisitions. I'm not a salesman and so have always limited my exposure to customers beyond trying to establish what they want and being available if needed. This approach also gives you time. The best CEOs create time for themselves – so that they can perform their role properly.

This hands-off approach means a high level of devolution in many larger companies. I like to create 'baronies' for individual operating units where divisional MDs have the power and responsibility to deliver what's asked of them. These barons are the CEO's direct reports (so you can't really have more than four) and the CEO should not interfere in their operations, focusing on outcomes rather than processes within a structure of clear governance principles around areas such as Health & Safety and correct behaviour.

With correct behaviour, I found a surprisingly large amount of time being taken up by what appeared to be comparatively minor issues. But perhaps the point here is that (in a quasi-legal way) you're effectively creating precedents where the correct corporate approach needs to be confirmed. Next time round, you can refer back to these.

Examples of these varied from the serious to the ridiculous. With the former, we had unfair dismissal claims, where we were clearly in the right but the effort to defend them and publicity implications meant we had to take a pragmatic view. With the latter we had a sales director who wanted to front his wife's presentation to *Dragons' Den*. I got this one badly wrong by letting him do it. The editor's cut suggested he was going to give up his day job and revealed his salary. My fault and the outcome was he had to grovel to retain his job and had his annual bonus distributed to his cohort to apologise. I'm pleased to report he remained at the company doing a great job and after enough time had passed people could joke about it.

Communication lines with your barons need to be short and permanently open, particularly when, as is usually the case, they are not based at head office. The biggest no-no for a baron is to present the CEO with a surprise barring an exceptional circumstance. And the biggest no-no for a CEO is not responding immediately and reaching a decision as quickly as possible when asked.

Similarly, the CEO needs to be in total alignment with their CFO. I once worked remotely with my CFO when I was the CEO in a single-stream business. This was because I was spending most of my time in the field and it was OK, if not ideal. But in multi-stream business, I usually find myself talking in person to the CFO many times a day. This, I believe, is an example of why many office roles do not lend themselves to being done remotely and routine WFH (work from home) can be a recipe for disaster.

The horrors of matrix management

The worst drag for a CEO is matrix management (where individuals report to more than one boss). This should be avoided at all costs. I want to have one person I can thank or kick rather than have to track down who is responsible for a good or bad performance.

However, in many types of business, matrix management is inevitable. Does a falling top line reflect on the sales team or the production team? The sales team will say the product is weak or late while production will say the sales team is ineffectual, selling too cheaply or making promises about delivery times that can't possibly be kept. There is no correct solution and the broken link between power and responsibility causes endless headaches. You should try to avoid it wherever possible.

It is most obvious in global businesses where there is both a regional structure and a product structure. If a certain line of confectionery is failing in, say, China, is this the fault of the person in charge of the chocolate division or the person in charge of South-East Asia?

When I was editing the business magazine *Management Today*, we profiled a global FMCG company and it became clear that, over the years, different CEOs had tried different structures, flip-flopping from regional responsibilities to product responsibilities and generally ending up with a fudge which suited no one. Fortunately, the strength of their global brands meant that this was not as deleterious as it would have been for a business with a weaker 'moat'.

What do you want at the centre?

The problem with matrix management extends beyond production vs sales and regional vs product. I have always resisted having central marketing, HR or similar functions for as long as possible. I want these to be dealt with at the local level so that the barons have no one else to hand responsibility over to. But this gets tricky when closely related businesses will benefit from a unifying brand or policies on pay vary wildly across the group.

Having as few centralized functions as possible also enables you to have a tiny head office. When I left Restore we employed over 3,000 people but got by with a head office of seven people, including covering M&A deal-doing. When I returned five years later, there were 54 people on the head office payroll – and within months we were down to nine.

A side of effect of this clear-out was that the numbers of administrative roles in the divisions also fell. Head office no longer required endless reams of information to justify its own existence. Nor was it launching new initiatives that rarely achieved traction and usually involved pretty pointless activity in the various companies.

Keeping down the number of people reporting to me, means head office costs don't make much of an impact on the outposts of the operation as a percentage of revenue (apart from, ahem, share-related bonuses) and enables short lines of communication. It also means that there is less managing to do at head office so that I can be free to respond immediately to anything bubbling out of the businesses or elsewhere.

Hands off, but...

An issue with the 'barony' style of management is how you (as CEO) know what is going on inside the businesses. You may be 'hands off' but even the best reporting systems tend to revolve around numbers rather than the equally important softer stuff. If you've told the barons to get on with it, and you're not going to get in their way, are you not undermining them by snooping around in their businesses? How do you empower people properly while still keeping tabs on what's happening?

One of the best things you can do is get around the business as an observer. At both Brandon and Restore, I made a point of getting round to every site we operated once every six months, and still do now I'm back at Restore.. Even with over a hundred sites, this can be done in less time than might be expected, with visits often taking no more than 40 minutes. Whenever in an area for other reasons, I will always try to tie in branch visits. I will also dedicate at least 10 per cent of my time solely to branch visits. This, incidentally, is another good reason for the CEO to make sure they have time and are not bogged down in the day-to-day stuff (although admittedly, all this travel is easier if you are running a UK-only business).

Because I visit every branch, no individual branch feels like it's being singled out. When I arrive at a site, I will usually tell the local manager that this is an indulgence of mine and that I have no authority over their work. I'm only there to say hi to as many people as possible, to have a chat with the manager and to poke around the premises. The last of these – the looking into the nooks and crannies – is always fun, and revealing as to how the operation is being run. Whether it's a graveyard of old kit, a neglected corner of the warehouse, or toilets which no one is bothering to clean, all give an indication of how the particular branch, and hence the overall business, is being managed.

Sometimes, my lack of understanding of the real nuts and bolts of the business has resulted in comedy. Trying to stimulate conversation with a notoriously grouchy but brilliant fitter, I touched something as I asked a question about how the machine worked. The component was white hot and the flesh on my finger started sizzling, much to the amusement of the fitter. By the time I got back to the office that afternoon, it was clear that few in the company were unaware that the CEO's finger had been burnt in a spectacular display of ignorance.

I like to think that the group-wide bonding that my burned finger engendered was worth my being unable to type for a week. Perhaps my colleagues also found it slightly endearing and it helped me to promote the idea across the business that the people who were doing the work needed me to be good at the head office and financial stuff, not the stuff they were good at. We all had our roles, we all had different skills and we all needed each other to succeed.

Other advantages gained from touring include the ability to visualize people and sites when they are being discussed. Sometimes it gives me an awareness of options available. Can we take on a unit next door or build in the car park if we are expecting revenues in that area to grow over time? Or can an acquisition be rolled into an existing site? All these questions are easier to answer if you know the site rather than relying on dry details such as its technical dimensions.

On other occasions, it leads to lightbulb moments like my seeing the stacks of old IT equipment were sitting out the back of our removals sites after customers had asked us to chuck them out. As mentioned earlier, this suggested that we should have a go at IT recycling at Restore – and the company is now the UK market leader in this area.

It's also great meeting the people and realizing how fired up they are (or not) and they really do appreciate it. Once, visiting a three-man branch in the snow in Scotland in February, they were astonished that I'd stuck to the schedule, slogging from the local railway station by foot in a blizzard. The message that 'I'm nothing special' rarely goes down badly.

Relatedly, do not underestimate how important it is for the people to see the 'Head Man / Woman'. Occasionally I've arrived at sites, where the managers and their colleagues tell me that that they'd never seen anyone from head office before. Occasionally, they haven't even seen their baron or his cohort. If this is the case, I make sure relevant people know – you neglect remote outposts at your peril.

For this reason, I try to be driven around by any of our team who can be spared, sometimes taking lifts from several different people in a day. The idea is to meet as many people as possible. When being driven, the absence of eye contact and the driver's part-focus on where they are going enables conversation to flow freely and in interesting, often revealing, directions.

Attending the divisional board meetings on an occasional basis (say one in three) is also critical. Good barons relish the opportunity for the CEO to witness the quality of their operation and people. It's also an opportunity for the CEO to promote the group's values and narrative, and to chip in their thoughts. All of these are ways of keeping tabs on what's going on without treading on toes.

Tellingly, one business where I didn't manage to visit even half the sites was Johnson. There, after the initial meetings with key people and stakeholders, I knew how much firefighting needed doing and I simply didn't have time to get out. But this led to a catch-22: without a feel for what was going on in the operations I couldn't find the narrative to help me deal with the chaos.

Only once the game was clearly lost did I visit some of the key sites in a desperate attempt to construct a narrative. There I discovered a great deal that would have helped earlier, such as a strong but demotivated team in a remote part of our most dysfunctional division whose members couldn't wait to tell me what was going wrong and where the bodies were buried.

One of the most shocking moments I had at Johnson was when I noted that I wished to attend the board meetings of this dysfunctional division. The reply came: 'That's not how it works.' So I insisted that I would be attending. The response from the divisional MD was chilling: 'OK, you can come to a meeting. But we'll hold the real board meeting before or after that one.'

When I attended the board meeting, it was clear that those attending had been briefed not to engage with me. As I returned from the 'board meeting' to a desolate, rubbish-strewn Midlands railway station, I was in such a muddle that I became quite paranoid. I was actually worried that my pre-booked taxi was being driven by someone who was spying for the local baron. I genuinely thought the driver might be about to report to the baron the contents of the call that I had made to the chairman in the back of his car. At this point, I already knew that we were in trouble, but this was particularly depressing and difficult to work out how to handle.

I'm also a big fan of asking disarmingly simple and probably stupid questions, which is something the CEO is well placed to do. Asking basic questions is often the best way to get people thinking about their assumptions, even if the price is looking as if you don't have a clue.

Another benefit of getting round all the branches is that when you send a 'herogram' for exceptional performance you may actually have met the person you send it to. Some of my most enjoyable moments as a CEO were ringing people to congratulate them on star performance. When you have met the person and have a context in which you can place your congratulations, the motivational impact of a call from the CEO is enhanced.

Conversely, on these travels you should always be listening out to sense what jars and then investigating further. I've been to branches where the mood is odd and you have to find excuses to stay longer to get to the bottom of it, or at least gather as much info as you can. The smell that something is not right can be intuitional or analytical. But it needs to be acted upon.

And as a CEO, a big part of your job us 'to run towards the gunfire'. Lest, this sounds like another dumb martial metaphor, I have been under fire in real life exactly once and it's worth a short digression. I was on 'holiday' with a friend who was a journalist in Nicaragua when the civil war was raging in the 1980s. As we arrived close to Yali, a town under siege from the US-backed Contras, it was clear that we were in the wrong place. I was desperate to get out of there by whatever means. The photographer who was with us took in the situation, put on his flak jacket and, with a nonchalance born of experience in Vietnam, slung his camera over his shoulder, got out of the car, said, 'Here we go again', and ran towards the gunfire.

That was his job, and so it should be with the CEO. Run towards the gunfire and keep going until you've worked out whether it is somebody chucking firecrackers or whether it's something you've got to deal with properly. Too often CEOs get the sense that something isn't quite right and simply walk away, hoping that it's nothing of importance. The Post Office scandal in the UK, where honest post office managers were accused and pursued for non-existent crimes on the back of an error-strewn IT system, and their extensive protestations were ignored by the Post Office leadership is up there as one of the worst examples of this. Another UK example was decades of the National Health Service and senior politicians ignoring the evidence that haemophiliacs were receiving contaminated blood transfusions. But this is not unique to the UK; Volkswagen's emissions scandal should have been picked up and dealt with at the top.

Indeed, a key characteristic of any CEO or good manager is that you should never be afraid of confronting problems. This doesn't mean you have to model your management style on disgraced UK retailer Philip Green or any other mindlessly aggressive CEO. Just don't funk the straight questioning, whether you're dealing with unexplained poor sales, a clueless manager or an unhappy customer. If you have a suspicion the s*** may be going to hit the fan, you need to find out why and then take action.

Everyday CEO stuff

This is not management, but the sort of everyday tasks and functions the CEO should be doing.

First you should establish what your lead key performance indicator (KPI) is. At Restore, in the early days, I was expecting us to go under at any moment if a supplier demanded payment or the bank decided they'd had enough – and all I worried about was the cash. This meant for a few months that (despite having no interest in the equity at the time) I had to postpone being paid myself. So all I really wanted to know every morning was what the company's bank balance was.

This became a good habit. Later on, when the business was obviously solvent and trading well, the first figure I wanted to see every morning was still the bank balance. This involved a bit of extra work when we had many entities with their own bank accounts but it was still what I wanted to know. I got used to the big cash movements – like the wages going out, rents being paid and the VAT payment dates. This became my lead KPI and would generally determine my mood at the start of the day.

Secondly, unless you're in an immature business where it's all about the top line, or have built a spectacular moat (a defence which keeps others off your turf), you should always keep costs down. The saying 'Look after the pennies and the pounds will look after themselves' is not usually true for individuals where a move in, say, house prices may dwarf what can be achieved by cutting costs in weekly shopping. But it is absolutely true in a business employing thousands of people. Here, £10 a week each saved by 5,000 people works out at an £2.5m of profit, which may be the difference between a year showing solid profit growth and a year when margins go backwards.

So, the CEO should keep a lid on costs everywhere, particularly as people are usually much more careless about the company's money than their own. There are quite a few simple tips here. One is to minimize the number of company credit cards floating around the business. Having to claim expenses that need to be signed off significantly reduces the plastic flash which drains the company's coffers.

A smart CEO also understands that costs usually float up when revenues increase. A request for an extra HR or marketing employee or another vehicle is far harder to turn down when business is good. So expenses tend to power up when revenues are buoyant. This means operating margins often go up in a recovery phase but then drop as cost control slacks and revenues don't move up at a similar rate. And then you get the switchback effect when revenues start to slow while the cost caravan carries on. Think of costs as daisies – they will grow if unattended and need to be mown regularly. Everybody will thank you for keeping it tight so there's limited need for cost-cutting when times get tough or business turns down.

You should always be alert to the presence of unnecessary, ineffectual or lazy staff, whose departure is usually welcomed by their colleagues. Here, it's useful to find ways of comparing individual units or teams with each other. I like businesses with many similar sites doing the same thing where I can benchmark branches against their peers to see who's carrying more cost than they need to.

For all this, however, you need to be careful with the Darwinian approach to performance. You don't need or want to be as insensitive as General Electric's Jack Welch was about it. Most people's takeaway from his somewhat self-congratulatory book *Jack: Straight from the Gut* was that he demanded that the weakest 10 per cent of the workforce should be culled every year. This is wrong.

It was also a system open to being gamed. Welch's managers put retiring, ill and even dead colleagues on the hit list to satisfy their boss's ridiculous edict.

BEING THE CEO

Incidentally, one of the worst-managed operations I ever saw was GE's site at Yeovil. Their lunch was being eaten by a small, local competitor which was clearly twice as nimble and far more productive, quite probably because it wasn't in thrall to a macho egomaniac. It is true that the fittest companies are the ones that survive, but a well-managed business where almost everyone is doing their best is more likely to achieve this than a hostile environment where everyone is covering their own backs.

Another area where the CEO can have a real influence on day-to-day operations is on where to focus energy. Most managers will be familiar with meetings where 90 per cent of the time is devoted to the problems, 7 per cent to business which is doing OK, and 3 per cent to the business that's performing well: 'Good results again from Wales – let's move on.'

Most CEOs like to solve problems – and laggards need to be adjusted or improved. But the easiest way to get a business to fly is (to use a rather ugly phrase) to 'sweat your sweet spots'. Spend a lot of your time focusing on what you already do well – and do more of it.

In a related vein, it's crucial to keep an eye out for individual star performers. As CEO of Brandon, I would notice whenever a particular manager had transformed the branch they were running. Although they were not my direct report, I would make a point of visiting them along with their line manager and ensuring that they were recognized and that the next time an opportunity came up, that person would get a good shot at the promotion.

One such manager went on to become a star director. Several years later, after I'd left Brandon myself, he became disaffected with the new management, and I was lucky enough to be able to back him by investing in his new business, which has boomed.

Interestingly, when I spotted another star and suggested he might move up a level in due course, I was turned down. 'I really enjoy my job and love my monthly bonus, why would I want to move into a role where I have to manage other branch managers?' Fair enough – not everyone who is great at their job is ambitious and you should respect that.

Of course, it's worth pointing out here that some star performers are very high maintenance, particularly on the sales side. Sometimes it's worth pandering to them but it's also good to point out to them that they're a bit of a pain in the arse and they've really got to perform to be worth the effort. And of course, you occasionally get toxic stars who demotivate everyone around them and think their performance means they're untouchable like the star striker in *Ted Lasso*. You need to get rid of them.

CEOs should understand tempo too. When is the business ready to move forward and when should you be polishing the fire engine to get everything right before moving to the next stage? Growth is never tidy but the CEO needs to recognize when untidiness starts to become flying by the seat of your pants.

I had a newish division where we'd hit a sales sweet spot and invested in a lot of kit rapidly to process the flood of orders. When I visited the site, it was clear that some of the equipment was not working as intended and people on the shop-floor were under intense pressure and unhappy. I had visited to see why customers were ringing to complain about schedules not being met as well as to gee up the people and hopefully to improve performance (although, in truth, I didn't really have a clue about how this might, practically, be achieved).

The previously excellent site-manager grabbed me and dragged me off the floor. In an emotional, expletive-filled rant, he told me in no uncertain terms that I'd under-resourced the operation in terms of training and infrastructure and didn't understand how much I was asking him and his team to achieve. Suitably chastened, I left the facility and went back to mollify customers and manage their expectations. This meant telling them we'd oversold and asking them nicely to cut us a bit of slack. It's not a great position to be in, but if you have screwed up, owning it is better than passing the buck or sticking your head in the sand.

Finally, 'Never waste a crisis'. You should be very wary of creating uncertainty and chaos in pursuit of a business goal, but if you're in uncertain times anyway, use them as a chance to do the things you've been hesitating about. We saw a lot of this during COVID. Companies used it as an opportunity to ram through changes, especially in areas like IT. One IT director told me that in the first three months of the pandemic, his business accomplished five years' worth of change in terms of its systems. Similarly, during the pandemic, many restaurants quickly pivoted to delivery models with high levels of digital customer interaction and many medical practices upscaled their on-line capability rapidly.

Manage your advisers

Another key area for a CEO is managing advisers. This can be a slightly dysfunctional relationship, particularly in the circus that is the big public company world. You may want something from them too – don't expect that you will get that plum non-executive directorship if you endlessly question fees on equity placements or the hourly rate of your lawyers. Worse still, advisors are the ultimate fair-weather friends. When times are good, they'll happily blow smoke up your arse, but when the tide turns, they won't have your back.

When Johnson was going down the tubes, the professional feeding frenzy was something I was aware of even in my debilitated, reduced state. I estimated, at one point, that the cost of a phone call to piece together a survival plan was £25,000 an hour before the banks applied their reconstruction fees. On the call were law partners and assistants for every one of the nine banks in the syndicate as well as PR advisers, auditors, brokers (and their lawyers). All of them had their meters running and it's unlikely anyone queried their rates.

Often they didn't even bother to hide their self-interest. A 'Big Four' accountancy partner made it very clear to me that if I didn't appoint his firm, not only would I be off their Christmas card list, they were unlikely to recommend me as a sensible manager once the smoke had cleared. Even in good times, the CEO should view the financial services industry as a tax on their business – and one which often goes to pay for second homes. This is not to say these people are worthless, and you do need them. So it's a balancing act – you should acknowledge their value but recognize that their fees are exorbitant – and not hand out the company's money unnecessarily or in a way that is to your own advantage.

I find the easiest way to deal with professional fees is to think in terms of your average employee's annual salary. It's a different world but while your managers agonize about whether a branch could do with a couple fewer staff, agreeing to a 3 per cent placing fee rather than a 2 per cent fund-raising fee, rather than 2 per cent, could equate to the annual cost of 15 colleagues.

Not using these people, alas, is not an option. If you don't play the game, the money doesn't get raised. The best a CEO can do is minimize the business's exposure to the pocket pickers and do what they can themselves. As an experienced M&A operator, I hardly ever use advisers when we are buying a business – and usually save my salary several times over each year this way.

Remember too that you are the person who signs off the advisers' invoices – and remember this when they acknowledge your business acumen. They are acutely aware that their revenue stream sits with you. They know how much they depend on you as CEO. You will no doubt have told them you want them to be straight with you. And yet, they are in it for the fees you pay them and so have an incentive to tell you what you want to hear. This is true whether they're Goldman Sachs or a tiny local design agency.

When new management comes into a company it is a very nervous time for professional advisors. All of them know that they are reliant on senior management's patronage, and they will have worked hard at building and maintaining the relationship. When I left one role, the recently appointed chairman and incoming CEO changed virtually all the advisors within two years. On one level I felt that this was a form of ugly patronage, and dangerous given the previous advisers' depth of knowledge of the business. Particularly unnecessary was the way in which the long-term property adviser's services were dispensed with in a one-line email. He was a one man band, not a big firm. On another level I accept that people like advisers to be those they know and trust.

Big decisions

In 2000, the catering group Compass merged with the TV company Granada. It was a controversial merger which left a nasty taste in the mouths of many in the media and arts, not least that of John Cleese who famously faxed Gerry Robinson, the man behind it all saying, 'F***off out of it, you upstart caterer.' Robinson's later response to this was rather good – he said that a CEO only needed to make two or three decisions a year.

I don't wholly agree with this. Being CEO is about the big decisions, but you can only make them by having a great feel as to what is going on, which is not easy if you spend your time in an ivory tower. However, the point that as CEO you shouldn't sweat the small stuff is sound. You should employ people you trust and that let them get on with it. The big stuff is you – and it's the big decisions that really change companies.

Often these are pivots (to use a currently fashionable word). When I was working at 3i, an example of a great pivot was Bond Helicopters. Previously a crop-spraying business serving Scottish farmers, Steven Bond recognized that the skill set of his business was experienced pilots who understood the Scottish weather and flying regulations. He realized that this was what the nascent North Sea oil industry needed and this was the foundation of the world's largest helicopter fleet for the oil industry.

This illustrates the need for big decisions but also that businesses often turn into things you do not expect. Part of the fun of being a CEO, particularly if you're an entrepreneur, is how the market sometimes morphs your business into something very different.

One of the UK's most successful businesses, RELX plc had its roots in printing as Reed Group. My distant cousin, Sir Keith Skinner, sold the Skinner printing business to Reed and eventually became its CEO. Spotting how commoditized printing was becoming, with a correspondingly poor return on capital employed, Keith morphed Reed into a publishing company, which included merging Reed with the Dutch scientific publisher Elsevier. A generation later, the renamed RELX is a global leader in information and analytics.

On a different level, a friend set up as a tutor on financial matters for unsophisticated but affluent families. His product was excellent but the business only really took off when he switched his target market to graduate trainees in professional firms who needed a better understanding of financial markets. All these examples demonstrate that a CEO needs to perfect both what they are currently doing while being alert to the possibility of 'the Big Switch'.

In a business that I was involved in setting up, the pivot was realizing that, while our customers needed a man-in-a-van service to ensure that they were operating in accordance with legislation, what they really wanted (and needed) was to outsource all their compliance requirements. The CEO recognized this and it became a software-driven business whose goal was to help our customers sleep well at night knowing their compliance is covered.

Sometimes the pivot is a transformational deal which takes your company into new markets that are a logical extension of what you do. You need to think about this in terms of where you are in the industry cycle and where the opportunities lie. Is there a price-insensitive franchise that can be grabbed? Is there a disorganized market which as a well-run company with related skills you can grab hold of? This is one of the really fun parts of being a CEO.

Being a leader

There are many leadership styles, some more consensual than others. My primary advice on this is that you can't sustain behaving unnaturally for long so you're best sticking to how you really are; in today's parlance, you need to be your 'authentic self'. I know that my style is not as consensual as it might be: I'm fairly combative, I like taking contrarian views to establish the best option and then moving on with a plan of action.

I've arrived in companies as the CEO with limited knowledge of both the company and its specific market. This means that getting the initial tone right can be difficult. You may have the title that you are chief executive but, as they say, the sheriff's badge does not make you the sheriff. You are an outsider – and it's not the same as an internal promotion where people know you and know that you've 'made your bones'. Here, you need to show people you can lead.

With my style, the key elements are humility and humour. On joining Restore (then Mavinwood), my introductory remark was always, 'I'm from head office to help', which is generally recognized as one of the world's biggest lies. Most of the relevant people realized that I was being tongue-in-cheek, self-deprecating and willing to learn from them. But they also recognized that on another level it was actually true. I was joking-not-joking.

As a new CEO you also need to realize that recognition is not going to happen overnight. Respect needs to be earned – and trust built. Having just talked about humour, it may seem odd to say that you must have no interest in being liked; rather you should aim to be respected. If you're lucky, people will like you but this will be because they have come to respect you. If you aspire only to people liking you, it's likely they will struggle to respect you and then you'll struggle as a CEO – and in the end they won't like you, either.

One of my favourite aphorisms on CEO style comes from the great Felix Dennis. Dennis was one of the best business brains of his era and was jailed for less time than his fellow 'criminals' in the notorious 1960s *Oz* magazine obscenity trial because the patrician judge felt that his upbringing in poverty meant that he must have been led astray by his brighter and better-educated contemporaries. In his brilliant book, *How to Get Rich*, he notes that a business leader should 'Think big, act small'. Sensible people admire the brilliant business person who doesn't make a show of themselves and lets their business savvy and achievements do their talking.

In this vein, when things go right, you should always acknowledge the contribution of luck which will have played a major part. Be generous in giving the credit to those around you. If your organization performs well, people will know you're doing a good job – and they'll respect you for being magnanimous. Finally, enjoy the good times as CEO – fortune's wheel can always turn quickly and the tough times may be no fault of your own but that doesn't make them any easier.

6
THE BOARD

'Democracy is not about making speeches. It is about making committees work.'

LORD BULLOCK, BRITISH HISTORIAN

What the chair and CEO relationship should entail, what it looks like when it works – and what happens when it goes horribly wrong. How to run a board meeting, how to prepare for it and why you should keep it short. What to look for in non-executive directors and how to reward them properly.

The chairman and the CEO

One of the things I like about UK plc boards is the clarity. You have a chair and a chief executive. The CEO runs the company and the chair runs the board. This was one of the many recommendations of the UK's 1992 *Cadbury Report* and was intended to avoid the obvious conflict of interest where you effectively have someone overseeing their own behaviour.

Elsewhere it can get very confusing. In private companies you can combine the role. In, the US over 40 per cent of S&P 500 companies still combine the role, although this figure is falling. Just to further confuse things, American companies sometimes have CEOs and presidents who are second in command.

In the UK, there are a few exceptions to this. Occasionally an executive chair (usually doing a few days a week) can work where the CEO has to be in the trenches for day-to-day operations. Executive chairs will usually take on parts of the CEO's role – for example dealing with stakeholders such as investors and bankers, undertaking mergers and acquisitions and crafting the corporate narrative.

But generally the roles are separate and this is a good thing. However, along with running the board, the chair also has to be the confidante, motivator and champion of the CEO. They should be there to provide energy, enthusiasm and support at all times. All relevant information should be shared between the two and frank and open communication is critical. They are the closest thing the CEO has to a manager.

This makes for an odd dynamic not dissimilar to a parent-child relationship (with some companies, I'd take this further and cast the other non-executive directors as sometimes wise, sometimes doddery, aunts and uncles). The difference here, of course, is that the parent can ultimately kick the child out in this relationship.

All this is why the relationship between the CEO and the chairman is the single most important in the company. It can be very good and very bad.

Good chair

I've had successful and unsuccessful relationships with my chairs. Some have become great friends – I respect them immensely and they been a huge positive influence on my life and work. Others less so, and there is one I would still cross the street to avoid.

But let's start with the best. This chairman had been recently appointed because the previous board had fallen apart as the company collapsed. He was used to tricky situations but here, he wasn't confident that much could be saved from the wreckage. However, he was happy to have a crack at it if a sensible CEO could be found. That was me.

My appointment was rushed through. There was little time for a formal process and it helped that the majority shareholder was not that fussed. I was asked very directly about my own previous failings. I think it was partly to understand what I'd got wrong, partly to see if I'd learned anything and also, most importantly, to check I wasn't damaged goods.

The first year was tough. The spectre of insolvency was ever-present, especially in the early months. But my chairman was a rock. Particularly at the beginning he made a point of popping into my office at least twice a week just to say hello and get an update. Once he found me lying under the desk (it was not an open-plan office!) reflecting on the latest bad news. I crawled out and told him that a chunk of our profit had turned out to be an illusion and that we were now not only unable to meet the banking covenants but were also making a loss.

'Not great but could be worse,' he replied, smiling. 'We only owe £40m and have a pretty good chance of reducing that over time. I've just come from a meeting where the company owes £500m – and has no chance of getting back to profitability for at least two years.' He then added, 'And our richest shareholder is politically connected and won't let us go bust before a General Election!' Exactly what you need when you're lying on the carpet contemplating life in a monastery.

As well as being a source of wise counsel, this chairman was also a staunch ally. On another occasion our other big investor had been venting his frustrations at me. Basically, he was blaming me for the performance of his investment under the previous board and he'd been selling his shares at risible prices. When my chairman heard of this he said we needed to go and see the man. In the meeting, the chairman took the lead. He pointed out that I was a new CEO who was trying to sort out the chaos and that pinning my predecessor's mistakes on me was both unfair and counterproductive. Alas, he failed to mollify the man and the meeting ended acrimoniously (rather nastily and oddly, the investment manager left saying he'd rather attend bathtime at home than talk to us any more), but, even so, having the chairman stand up for me with an irrational investor felt like a great vote of confidence.

Throughout our working relationship, he was a sounding board and a source of excellent, occasionally surprising, advice. When an acquisition target consistently failed to respond to my approaches, his solution was punchy. 'We've got to buy this business to get where we want to go. So think of the biggest number that still works for us and send it as a serious offer direct to their board.' Very simple, but it worked.

I've also worked with an entrepreneurial chairman – and this was a good relationship. He held my hand as I learned the ropes as CEO. His style was unconventional and he focused on motivating people, understanding customers, and was always looking to turn a buck. By working closely with him, I was able to bounce ideas off an experienced operator who taught me a lot about running a business, while letting me make my own mistakes.

Although I am currently a CEO, I am at the stage in my career where I where my next position is likely to be a chairmanship. And by reflecting on the chairs I have worked well with, I can now see the sort of CEOs I'd be able to help – and those whom I should avoid.

Bad chair

While many chairs have been good some were notably less pleasant to work with. One seemed entirely oblivious to the problems I was facing. This company was also a disaster which I had joined to turn around – and the board with the exception of me had overseen the debacle (the chairman himself had been in place for five years). As I uncovered a series of ever more horrendous problems, and shared them with him, he would barely engage. Rather he breezily wished me good luck and would offer comments like, 'Well that's why you're here!'

This was a business that had its priorities very wrong. At a subsequent board meeting, the first item on the agenda was the dates for next year's board meetings. Over the next 20 minutes (the meeting was scheduled for two hours) the non-executive directors compared notes on when and where they were going skiing and what summer holidays they were planning.

Soon, I couldn't restrain my frustration. 'I assume you've read my board report,' I said loudly enough to shut down the discussion of the merits of Verbier and Zermatt. 'This company is in really, really deep trouble. There are unlikely to be any board meetings next year unless this board addresses these issues now – because there won't be a company!'

The chair looked up from his diary with an irritating kindliness. 'That may be the case, Charles, but I think it's easiest to sort out these dates when we are all together.' They returned to the pressing problem of finding a suitable date in July, over a year away, that wouldn't clash with a non-executive director's fortnight in Tuscany.

Not much later (and entirely predictably) things had gone from bad to worse. It had become clear that the leader of the banking syndicate that held our loans was aiming to take control of the business. Just to make things really terrible, the syndicate leader was the bad debt recovery team from a major bank, renowned at the time for recovering their loans in a highly aggressive style. So I set up a conference call for the board to run through all the options I could think of.

There weren't many of these and none were very appealing. I was also hoping for other ideas from the board or, at the very least, a steer on which of my options they preferred and some thoughts on how to play it. After I'd finished, there was a lengthy silence, broken eventually by the chair: 'I think you've just got to do your best with them, Charles.'

It went on. I suggested the board might use their contacts and connections to point out how aggressively the syndicate was behaving and suggest more constructive ways forward. This was a pretty reasonable idea. Not only did our board include a former banker, a corporate financier, a peer with a business background and a chair of a company that had a significant financing arm, but the problematic loans had been arranged under the current board. 'I think that's unlikely to achieve anything, Charles, and this quite a big ask of a non-exec,' came the chairman's reply.

I tried again. 'It would be useful if you and other members of the board could attend the meeting with the banks, particularly as the board has more knowledge of the history of the loan and the relationships.'

'I don't think any of us were really involved at that level,' the chairman said. 'We'll let you know if anyone can make it but otherwise, I think you've just got to

THE BOARD

tough it out.' In the end, of course, nobody was available. There were 16 brutal debt-recovery bankers – the skinheads of the finance industry – licking their lips on one side of the table and me on the other.

The chair's lack of support for his CEO was not the only problem. His general ineptitude contributed hugely to the dysfunctionality of the board and this, in turn, resulted in a business which destroyed value rather than creating it.

Here it's worth giving a short rundown of some of the horrors I uncovered:

- *Massive fees being run up with external advisers on deals that never happened.
- Capital projects being embarked upon where a simple sense-check showed a pathetic return on investment.
- *No simple and obvious internal controls from the chair like signing off the previous CEO's expenses.
- Huge investment in irrelevant and expensive IT projects (the largest cost £25m and delivered nothing but chaos – and I had to write it off).
- 'Ugly' transactions such as giving away a business to keep its terrible financial results out of the full year results.
- A smell of unhealthy collusion between the former CEO and one of the divisional MDs which was noticed but not acted upon.

All of the above are exactly the sort of things that a sensible chair and their board would be alert to and would be probing the executives about, rather than breezily dismissing them before returning to the best slopes in Courchevel. Clearly, this board was a nightmare, but you can also have problems where both the CEO and the chair are good at their jobs – but the chemistry is wrong.

I'm a reasonably emotional CEO who wears his heart on his sleeve. I like delivering on a vision and believe that, while structure and controls are important, business is about the outcomes not the processes. So, you could argue it would be a good idea to put a person like me with a process-driven chair. In fact, when this happened it didn't work out.

I don't like the idea of board meetings focusing on governance and processes to the exclusion of narrative, motivation and where we need to go next. I am also uncomfortable with an increasing reliance on advisers – I feel they run up costs and also reduce the sense of responsibility. My relationship with this chair was tense as we were approaching the world of business from very different angles. But I can't hold this against the man in question – and I can also see that it was difficult for an incoming chair to work with a well-established CEO who was used to his way of doing things.

A dysfunctional relationship with a chair can have very real human consequences. The worst day of my working life was when the only fatal accident occurred under my leadership. Because the site was relatively close, I could get there within two hours.

The grief and trauma of those at the site was intense and we all felt some degree of responsibility for the event and the horror for the victim and his family. The trauma was not diminished over the following weeks and months as we undertook an internal enquiry. It's a very selfish thing, but having a weak relationship with my chair at the time didn't help me to manage the situation, particularly as the board offered me no support with running the internal and external inquiries.

What makes a good board?

Bad boards can destroy businesses and good boards can help build them. But what actually makes a good board?

I once ran a smallish company which was growing quite fast. We'd outgrown our serviced offices and were looking for premises of our own. The best site was central and cheap but our search team (of one person) said there was a significant problem. The board room (aka the meeting room – most head office-lite businesses don't need more than one meeting room) couldn't accommodate more than six people. What if the board grew as we did?

In fact, I saw this as a plus. British naval historian Cyril Northcote Parkinson wrote over 60 books, the most famous of which was *Parkinson's Law*. The law itself states: 'Work expands so as to fill the time available for its completion.' Another of his witty but actually quite profound aphorisms was: 'Deliberative bodies become decreasingly effective after they pass five to eight members.'

I'm with Professor Parkinson here. Once a board gets much beyond five, there tends to be an inner circle and an outer circle. The former communicates informally before meetings to work out the direction of the meeting, and after the meetings to decide which actions to take. So, if you want a board where everyone is expected to contribute, it should be no more than six people.

Perhaps surprisingly, the current fashion is for taking this even further – the idea is you have only the CEO and group CFO as board executives with other executives attending as required. This works well: it keeps the board small and establishes that the CEO is responsible to the board for the entire business, with back-up from the CFO on the details of the financials. By contrast, with boards where the CEO's other direct reports attend all meetings, responsibilities tend to get sprayed around and diluted.

So the number of executives on the board should be as few as possible. But what about non-executive directors (NEDs)? I believe that broadly the same rules apply. They should be few in number, be there for a reason and bring useful perspectives.

Here, diversity is important – because you want the board to be looking at the company from different angles. At its simplest, for NEDs, this means having people with different skill sets and backgrounds. A very effective board I sat on as CEO had a tough industrialist, a financier who understood investors and a CSR (corporate and social responsibility) specialist. It was chaired robustly by a generalist who ensured everyone contributed and we all listened to each other. The board was scrupulous, challenging and helpful.

All non-executives should carry their weight. The days of having 'good eggs' on boards are thankfully largely behind us. But even so I can recall several NEDs who have been put in place for the wrong reasons. One was a man who had suffered a setback in his career and been imposed on our board by a powerful shareholder who felt he owed the NED a favour.

To their credit other board members worked hard to oppose this appointment, up to and including threatening to resign. The chairman even sent the man a three-volume 'synopsis' of the Companies Act to check that he really wanted to be a NED. Nonetheless, he joined the board... and despite his best efforts he couldn't really contribute anything. He 'left' very soon after the shareholder sold out, having done little except cause disruption.

It's always a mistake to have ineffective people on boards, not least because you want them small. But one very good reason that the quality of the board is critical is that boards regularly choose the CEO and their other members. In one business I worked in, the wrong choice of replacement chair led to a knock-on series of further weak board appointments, including the executive members. The end result of this is that a once-dynamic growth business became a compliance-obsessed nonentity. One rotten apple eventually spoiled the whole barrel.

For this reason, I'm also a great believer in starting boards right. A start-up which I chaired is majority-owned and managed by a seasoned and highly successful entrepreneur. At a very early stage, he established a formal board including a couple of impressive NEDs. Even though revenues were still below £1m a year he put in place a board structure and practices, which can, and hopefully will, support a multi-million-pound business. Part of how the company will get there is recognizing the importance of a good board at a very early stage.

This brings us to what it's like being a NED more generally. On one highly effective board where I was a non-executive, the chair had good attention to detail and drove through good process but also expected the board to get stuck into the big narrative questions and dig into the company performance. Here, I enjoyed asking simple, challenging questions, while trying to avoid the sort of hobby-horsing I have seen other NEDs getting hung up on. I am ruthless about poking into opaque areas, particularly those where I have slipped on banana skins myself as a CEO.

I also try to give advice on areas I know well such as dealing with shareholders and bankers. Offering this sort of helpful counsel to the CEO is a big part of a NED's role. Other contributions a NED should expect to make include providing good contacts, whether they're prospective customers, bankers, shareholders or advisers, and spreading best practice and sharing knowledge from other boards they have been or are on.

The role of the non-exec director can be very rewarding. But you need to fully understand what you are getting into before you say yes. Too often NEDs are overpaid and underworked. But when things go wrong, the reverse is true. The NEDs in a company that has got itself into trouble, especially one that is public, will find themselves in the firing line, with a full-time job on their hands.

The basics for an effective board meeting

Other than the right number of good people and a decent chair, the key to an effective meeting is a well-thought-through board pack. And the first rule for this, like all internal communications, is keep it short.

I arrived at one business two weeks before the next board meeting. Most of the sizeable finance team were busily preparing the board pack, having already spent much of the previous week on it. The final version, when it eventually appeared, was a brick over 300 pages long. Nobody was going to read all of it. Nor should they. The content had barely changed for five years. The few recent alterations had been made at the request of a director who probably hadn't thought them through but they too had now become part of the edifice.

On another committee I belong to, the monthly board pack can run to well over 150 pages, with 120 of them comprising a couple of adviser's reports such as a detailed building survey or a legal interpretation. Even if these appendices are read (and it's apparent that they're usually not), the significant points are lost in the mass of extraneous information.

All this is sadly the norm – and it's a waste of everyone's time. Board papers need to be short, snappy and written from scratch.

The exception to this are the financials (as distinct from the CFO's written report). These should be in an identical format to the previous month's to allow easy comparison. They should be kept as simple as possible, with a P&L for performance against budget and prior year for the group and individual divisions, with forecast performance to the year end, together with a group balance sheet and a cash flow that includes the most recent cash balances.

I also like to have a one-page debtor analysis with a 'rogues' gallery' of the top ten late payers. Group debtor days (how long on average it takes to collect the group's debts) are an indicator of how well the debt collection is going and also flag up operational issues such as when customers aren't paying because they're not happy with what they've received.

The other reason for a rogues' gallery is that a large and unexpected bad debt can be hugely destructive – and the gallery acts as an early-warning system. This is a lesson I learned the hard way. In one business, we had done a lot work over a long time for a bank. This client insisted the work was billed through a third party which was coordinating their facilities management procurement (a surprising decision until we twigged that the client's procurement manager had a family interest in the third party). This appeared to lead to some confusion in the billing process between the bank, the third party and us, which resulted in us not receiving payment for several months.

We failed to pick up on this quickly enough and the amount owed shot up to over £1m. Next, we discovered that the third party had financial difficulties and was using the money they were receiving from the bank to fund their problems rather than paying us. We were in trouble. Various payment plans were put together but the third party eventually went under, the bank felt it was our problem and we had a hole in our P&L of nearly £1m. This was a sizeable chunk of our annual profits. A rogues' gallery would have alerted us to a problem when it was big, rather than enormous.

Tracking debtors may be critical for some businesses but is a minor matter for others such as those selling to big companies (still watch out though), government or consumers. In some businesses the sales pipeline is of critical importance and tracking prospective major contracts is what you want to know about. In one fast-growing B2C business I'm involved with, the cost of acquiring new customers and tracking the most effective methods to deliver them is critical to the business model and the company's long-term success.

Some companies like to have a traffic light system in the financials, highlighting the good (green), the worrying (amber) and the bad (red) numbers in the pack. Personally, I prefer a written report from the CFO highlighting their areas of joy and concern. Although the traffic light system may seem intuitive, these gradings are often generated automatically without anyone really considering or interpreting them. A sensible executive must be able to pick out the numbers they are pleased or unhappy with and highlight them in the narrative.

The board pack may also contain relevant attachments needed such as analysis of particular acquisitions under consideration, new banking terms or pension fund reports. These will be helpful but need to be summarized in the CEO's or CFO's reports so that readers understand why they've been supplied and what they're looking for.

So, how short should these reports be? Very short – the CEO and CFO reports should rarely be longer than two pages. They should set out what these individuals think are the key issues in the business and should always start with a summary Health & Safety report. I have also asked divisional MDs in certain roles to prepare one or two paragraphs on the key issues in their businesses and to incorporate these into the pack.

The great thing about my six-page board pack is that nobody has an excuse for not having read and understood it. Those who have to write it may be less thrilled (we're back to 'If I had more time, I would have written a shorter letter'). But actually it's good for them too – it means that everyone contributing to the pack has to sit down once a month to think about what really matters to them in their area of the business.

Board meetings should be short, too – the chair should aim for no more than three hours, although enough time should be allowed in case a subject requires further examination and interrogation. Care should be taken with any new members too – they should be helped up to speed and encouraged to ask questions. And the chair should be sensible in ordering the agenda rather than slavishly following a template. I'm sure all readers have sat in meetings where minor issues have been discussed at length and there isn't enough time for weightier matters to be addressed fully.

That said, several chairs I've worked with are process-driven, seeking to get through the meeting as if its point is to get to the end of the agenda rather than challenging and seeking actions. This can work if the other non-execs take on the role of challenging and exploring, but too often key issues are funked and required actions postponed.

Sometimes big decisions and urgent issues do not arise on a timescale which dovetails neatly with the board's schedule meetings. In a world of ubiquitous video-conferencing, and if the board is small enough, impromptu board calls can ensure that all directors can be involved in the decision-making process.

If you can get it all right, there is nothing nicer than a slick board meeting where everyone is fully informed, performance can be assessed and decisions made with full intelligence.

What the board should do

It is important that the board doesn't let itself become a process-driven box-ticker. Many do – and they become a dead hand on the tiller of the business. They fail in their duty to guide, challenge and support the executive. The companies run by these boards tend, in the long term, to underperform at best and collapse at worst. But this is not to say that that governance is unimportant. It is – and

THE BOARD

it starts with duties of the nomination, audit and remuneration committees and extends far beyond.

Of these three committees, the most important is the nomination committee, which is why it is usually headed by the chair. The most vital job of the board is to ensure it has the right CEO. And, as noted earlier, if you start appointing duffers to other roles on the board, the effect is often steadily corrosive.

This is worth a short digression. In the UK, good governance guidelines suggest that non-executive directors should serve two three-year terms. In my view this limit is not always a great idea. Knowledgeable NEDs with long experience of the company can be very valuable resources – and many highly successful private companies not required to satisfy governance guidelines have extremely long-standing NEDs.

The audit committee is what it is – and generally needs an accountant as the chair who will understand the audit process and the issues the auditors raise. I've found that many auditors bog the company down in comparatively irrelevant discussions about the carrying value of individual businesses and allocating values to notional concepts like the customer base.

With the audit committee, the fun really only starts when there are arguments around the treatment of certain costs, especially when a public company which is desperate to hit its market forecasts starts jiggering around with capitalizing costs. Surely the costs of the sales team who have just delivered that huge contract should be allocated over the length of the contract rather than thump this year's P&L? And that's one of the less controversial treatments I've come across.

The remuneration committee sets the directors' pay. It sounds like the most interesting committee, particularly where there are no controlling shareholders. But in reality, for public companies, it has become a complex minefield where ever more Byzantine schemes are devised to incentivise directors and where an endless stream of consultants are brought in to benchmark against corporate peers and promote best practice.

Benchmarking pay in particular is a problem. Once you start, no remuneration committee wants to tell the CEO that they should be below the second quartile for pay in their peer group. So there is an inevitable spiral of pay inflation. Runaway executive pay has long been an issue – and publically disclosing directors' pay (which started in 2008) has had no effect. In fact, I suspect it may have made things worse. As I write, my current pay package seems absurdly high and out of touch with what the rest of the people in the business earn, but it is line with 'the market'. I think I am paid too much for doing my job. Remarkable rewards should be available, but only for creating a great business and generating remarkable returns for shareholders and, to a lesser extent, other stakeholders. But 'the market' in the UK doesn't approve of remarkable rewards for outperforming

CEOs so underperformers and overperformers are generally on a similar gravy-train.

Beyond these three committees, every board should have Health & Safety as a priority, the chief executive's report should start with this – and at least one meeting a year should focus on H&S, whatever the sector and chance of accidents. There are other areas which should be addressed on an annual cycle, such as insurance, properties, sales and marketing.

Similarly, the annual budget process which typically takes two board meetings (very few budgets should be accepted first time round) needs to be scheduled into the board-meeting calendar. And it's helpful to have the remuneration committee meeting around the same time so that correct numbers for pay and bonus schemes can go into the budgets.

In a group structure, it is also useful for the board to be given individual presentations by divisional MDs, ideally on their turf and once or twice a year.

One ineffective board I sat on required the divisional MDs to attend several board meetings a year with their cohorts, but only to give a presentation on their individual business. This was hopeless. The MDs, irritated at having to spend most of the day getting to and from the meeting for a 20-minute presentation, were summoned in one-at-a-time much like prisoners going before a jury. They didn't even get to hear what was going on in the other divisions.

For this reason, in multi-site, multi-divisional companies, I'm a fan of holding some board meetings at operating sites as well as at head office. This works well with the relevant divisional boss or manager arranging a tour around the site. There is nothing quite like seeing a business in the flesh. To be fair, this is easier to propose than it is to execute – but you are much likelier to pull it off successfully if you have a small board.

What does 'non-executive' mean?

Although you want to avoid people who treat NED roles as sinecures, the right level of engagement of the non-executive directors is hard to gauge.

I had one NED who was determined to meet all the key operations people, particularly women as we had few women in senior management positions (not atypical in a blue collar company where the majority of the workforce were male). I thought this was a good idea but it created significant friction with the divisional MDs who felt the NED was a loose cannon in their operations by taking particular interest in certain individuals.

The appropriate line, perhaps, is for NEDs to feel they have access to all operations but understand that it is on the basis of 'hands off, eyes on'.

Occasionally chairs in public companies handle some of the investor relations and join in with investor presentations. This can be a good idea when a CEO is new and less experienced in this area but, in general, the investors want to see the person responsible for the performance of the business, and that is the CEO. However, shareholders will want to have a line of communication with the chair. This is particularly useful when they are unhappy with the company or there are issues about executive directors' pay – and the CEO should start worrying if investors ask for meetings with the chair without him or her being there.

An area of confusion, particularly in quoted companies, is whether the non-executives should hold shares in the company, and if they should be involved in performance-related incentive schemes. In some companies any non-executive's shareholding is frowned upon. In others, non-execs are expected to have a token shareholding. In still others, NEDs may have substantial shareholdings relating to a family interest or being a retired founder.

In my experience of companies where there is a powerful shareholder on the board, their preferred title is often deputy chair, suggesting that there is something slightly different about them. If a company has a deputy chair, you may find that they have a particularly strong interest. You often see this in organizations like league football clubs where the moneyman wants power without responsibility.

As an investor, I very much like seeing non-executives with significant shareholdings in companies. It aligns their interest with me as a shareholder and ensures they are part of the roller-coaster ride of shares going up and down. My favourite buying signal is when a NED of a company I have invested in starts buying the shares in volume after they come out of a close period. They know that it will be difficult to sell shares in a quoted company where they sit on the board, so will be doubly cautious before piling into the company's stock.

There are also situations where it is appropriate for non-execs to have incentive schemes related to the share price, particularly when the company is in its early stages. As a NED, I joined the long-term incentive plan of a listed shell company as it started its journey. If I may dispense with false modesty, I was a very important adviser to this company over the years. Even so, I felt slightly over-rewarded here as the company's share-price increased 1200 per cent and delivered a huge capital sum for comparatively few hours worked.

Incentivizing NEDs can be tougher in family-owned private companies – which want good NEDs but may not want to issue shares. These are slightly different beasts and the answer is for the non-execs to be decently paid.

One poor compromise I've seen here is where the chairman was close to the family and was not paid in line with market rates but instead was given shares – and not a particularly generous allocation. I picked up on his slightly baffled irritation when he retired and sold his stake back to the company at a discounted rate (reflecting his minority status). Understandably, he felt rather hard done by – it didn't add up to much after 20 years' service, during which the company had flourished to the benefit of the family owners. He should have been paid properly.

7
THE BUSINESS OF MANAGEMENT

'Such a complete retirement served to imply a satisfactory amount of trust in their offices and to be trusted displeases no seaman worthy of the name.'
JOSEPH CONRAD, *THE MIRROR OF THE SEA*

The genius of Peter Drucker, good and bad styles of management and locking together power and responsibility, then letting people get on with it. Plus how to keep people busy and happy, how to manage the whole person and recognize what motivates different people and why; ultimately, a company is only as good as its people.

Drucker said it best

There is no shortage of management books in this world – and if you count titles such as Sun Tzu's *The Art of War,* Machiavelli's *The Prince* and (yes) the *Bible*, they have been with us for thousands of years. But if you want to read only one management author, I'd choose Peter Drucker every time. Read him and you don't need much else.

I'm rather ambivalent about most management and business gurus. By and large they only have one decent idea (which is probably somewhere in Drucker's work already). This becomes a 5,000-word feature in a business magazine such as the *Harvard Business Review*. If they play their cards right and are lucky enough to catch the zeitgeist, they can spin it out into a bestselling book and a lucrative slot on the business speakers' circuit.

Nonetheless, this my contribution to the genre. I can't make any great claim to originality. But what I have to say is based on experience. Unlike, I suspect, the majority of management writers, I've been there and done that. I have run and managed half a dozen companies.

There are numerous styles of management. At one extreme, you have total micro-management where nothing happens without the boss being involved. And at the other you have completely hands-off management. Here, I always think of Lord Arnold Weinstock, who was CEO of GEC, which one of the UK's largest multinationals, sitting in Mayfair endlessly analyzing the numbers coming in from his business divisions (until, eventually, the great GEC was rendered worthless by a banker with a vision).

It's tempting to say that all management styles have a place. But they don't. Bullying dog-eat-dog, where you pit colleagues against each other, and crude financial incentivization are proven not to work over time. Even now, it baffles me that, in the 1990s, so many us of fell for the aforementioned 'Neutron' Jack Welch's gung-ho rubbish (where he sacked the bottom 10 per cent of his workforce every year). He wasn't a great CEO – he was a macho bully.

Other styles are less obviously awful but still to be avoided. I dislike the wheedling style where emotional pressure is applied to get people to do what you want. I also struggle with the currently prevalent passive-aggressive style where the managed have to second guess what the manager wants and get blamed if they guess wrong. Often with this style, bosses will claim they are empowering staff, but really this a political dodge whereby the manager retains power but passes over responsibility. I'm not hugely keen on the over-friendly style either. It's usually OK when times are good. But when tough choices have to be made and you discover yourself giving your 'pal a written warning or making them redundant, it's a whole lot less effective.

So what are some styles that do work? One is acting as a coach. You offer those you manage advice and guidance. Another is by setting an example – 'This is what I do, now copy it.' Both have to be done judiciously – so you're not hanging over people's shoulders and micro-managing them (in the first instance) or hectoring them (in the second). A more hands off-approach is to agree and set out detailed instructions and then monitor performance against how closely these instructions have been followed.

Style can be dependent on sector too. In creative companies, and charities, the style is often co-operative and collegiate, with the manager acting as a coordinator rather than a leader. This can work very well where people are highly motivated by a very tangible, often quite personal, end product – for example in advertising and TV. But you have to be careful here: creatives are the most controlling and mercenary people I've come across. They are high maintenance, aware of their value and continually evaluating their options.

One style I really like but have never been in a position to deploy as a manager is 'Management by Older Sibling' (this assumes the younger sibling is being managed by the older). In MBOS, the manager lets their people get on with things but keeps a close eye on what's happening and steps in with very direct advice and / or instruction when things are going off-track. They also act as a mentor. But here, they are unafraid to be blunt because the relationship is strong and the younger sibling understands that the older sibling wants them to get it right for their own sake.

One of the best managers I've ever worked with used this style to great effect. A tough man from the wonderful but sometimes rough naval city of Plymouth, he'd worked his way up from the shop floor and was respected by his team for being forthright but also caring passionately about the business and those who worked in it. When I first saw him in action, I was amazed at his bluntness, which disguised a brilliant mind. He understood exactly when people didn't get it – and could explain to them what they were doing wrong in words of one syllable. But he also cared deeply about them and wanted them to get it right.

On one occasion, a lad who was rising up the ladder quickly was offered a job by a competitor with a significant pay hike. That evening, the Older Brother visited him at home, sat down with the young man and his partner and told them why this would be a bad decision, tempting though it was. He explained that the competitor was well-known for sharp practice. They wanted the man for his customer contacts and, once they had them, they'd sack him for not being up to scratch in his new role. He also courageously noted that the YB should think hard and recognize that he wasn't worth the salary offered at this stage of his life. The OB added that numerous opportunities would come his way at his present employer if he stayed. The OB was persuasive. The YB stayed and moved into the OB's job when he himself was promoted.

Power and responsibility

I wholly understand that one should adjust one's management style according to where a person is on their career journey. But my preferred management style is simple. It's based on locking Power and Responsibility together and driving this as far down the organization as possible. It is largely about empowerment. If you tell people what you want, give them the power to do it and leave them to get on with it, they will. In fact, they usually amaze me with their enthusiasm to do so.

Power without responsibility is a lot of fun – as any newspaper columnist can tell you. The early twentieth century Conservative Prime Minister Stanley Baldwin memorably castigated the press barons of his day for this and described their lust for power without responsibility as the 'prerogative of the harlot throughout the ages'. However, while fun, it is no way to run an organization – and it is telling that our most chaotic recent Prime Minister, Boris Johnson, was a former newspaper columnist.

If power without responsibility is fun, responsibility without power is awful – and is one of the worst things you can inflict on anyone in management. It must be avoided whenever possible as it means you're asking someone to do something without giving them the tools do so. In my experience this typically arises in situations where key functions such as HR or purchasing are centralized. Those at the centre without day-to-day responsibility make key decisions and those trying to run the actual businesses have to accept these. How can I be expected to take responsibility for my division or branch if someone else is choosing who I recruit or whom I buy from? I have responsibility without power and will usually feel that I can't be held accountable for my operation's performance. This is not a place you want anybody to be in.

The Power and Responsibility model works best in operations where there is a clear hierarchy and for this reason it may not work well in sectors like the creative industries where the focus is on collaboration and inspiration. However, few companies (and no armies) work this way. There is no need to produce complex organograms but reporting lines prevail from the factory foreman to the financial controller to the sales manager. Most entities of scale have a well-defined management structure and trying to pretend otherwise leads to opacity, politicking and misunderstandings.

If you manage using the Power and Responsibility Model, there are some basics you need.

- Clear objectives have to be set and monitored. These should be based around the KISS (keep it simple, stupid) principle which means the manager has to have clearly thought through what they want and have got buy-in from the person they are asking to deliver.
- People must agree that they understand what is being asked of them, that they have the tools to deliver, that it can be delivered and they're happy to be measured against the goals.
- Eyes On, Hands Off – you want visibility of everything that goes on. But you don't want to be standing over people while they work.
- Appropriate reporting in place so monitoring and discussion of performance is clear, agreed and can be done quickly.

The biggest challenge with this model is that individuals and individual operations may have conflicting personal goals within the business: Salesman A and Salesman B may be charged with achieving sales targets and be competing for many of the same customers. Branch A might view a customer on Branch

B's patch as fair game. Division A may not want to share its customer list with Division B in case Division B cocks up and impacts Division A's relationship with its best customers.

This needn't be a serious problem – in fact the odd conflict over 'poaching' often reflects a business with well-motivated people. However it is where management skills come in. When conflicts arise, a respected manager will listen to all parties and look to rule with clarity and fairness, and to be respected for their judgement.

Sometimes this means allocating the rewards (not just financial bonuses, but also acknowledgement and career prospects) appropriately. For example, divisional managers may be partially rewarded according to group performance or branch managers may have part of their rewards based on the performance of the overall geographic area where they are based. It's also about creating transparency and the right culture. As CEO you set the tone and, if you set this right, you create an environment where people want to work together and benefit from being part of something bigger.

I am not in favour of centralization – as it usually means centralization of power, not responsibility. I view it as dehumanizing and ineffective – it takes agency away from individuals and leaves a mush behind. Even Margaret Thatcher's greatest admirers understand the extent of the damage she created with her instinct for centralizing control – and this is something the UK, the most centralized country in Europe, still struggles with.

As a CEO, I would always avoid centralizing anything until pressurized from below. In one company the divisional MDs were irritated that I continued to obstruct a centralized marketing and branding initiative for the group. When I was finally forced to address the question at a management meeting, some wag had put 'PMUATW' in small letters on the flip chart. When I was forced into a corner by convincing arguments that the time had come for such a centralized action, I reverted to my long-held view that it was unnecessary, contrary to our management philosophy, and was 'Pissing Money Up Against the Wall'. A huge cheer went up as I'd come up with the phrase everyone had long been expecting, and the 'PMUATW' was pointed out. I conceded that I'd reverted to a hackneyed prejudice and the centralized re-brand proceeded – and was a great success.

Finally, as a manager centralization leads to all sorts of problems. Everything becomes matrix management. You find yourself endlessly asking who you should thank and who you should kick because you can't work out who has responsibility. So, lock together power and responsibility, and give people as much of both as you possibly can. Then let them get on with it and amaze you!

Business clichés are often true

Many well-worn workplace homilies are no less valuable for being homilies. 'If you want something done, give it to a busy person' is one of my favourites. People get on with things efficiently when they are busy. In the right cultural environment, staff will expect an almost immediate response from their managers (and their managers from them). This rarely results in poor decision-making; it just makes things happen quickly and effectively.

This has been underscored by my experience of many part-time workers. With constrained time to do things, they just get them done. It's particularly true of parents with childcare responsibilities. People who have to leave at 3pm on the dot, get the job done – and done well – by 2.45pm. One of the most efficient colleagues I ever had worked a four-day week, one of which was from home. I often felt slightly shamed by her productivity compared to mine.

'Busy people are happy people' is another maxim I love, although I prefer the highbrow version from Lawrence of Arabia's *The Seven Pillars of Wisdom* which states" 'Happiness is a by-product of absorption'. The purest expression of this I've found is not in work but in sailing. I'm a very, very amateur sailor and helming a dinghy places enormous demands on my concentration. Thanks to Lawrence, I fully understand why sailing makes me so happy.

'It's about outcome not process' also rings very true for me – and, again, this is fundamentally about empowerment. How people choose to do things is largely their own affair, as long as they stick to key codes of behaviour and uphold the company's culture (which, as a good CEO or manager, you will ensure they know). It's great watching people take the initiative to achieve agreed goals – and nothing pleases me more than staff discovering they've found a better way than the one I suggested.

Interestingly, in this sense, I feel work is rather the opposite of life. With the former, it's about the destination, not the journey. With the latter, it's about the journey, because we all know what the final destination is.

Taking over as a new boss

Even if you've run companies before, taking over as CEO is always daunting. In fact, I'd extend this to taking on many management roles, sometimes even those where you are just managing a team you were formerly part of. You need to work hard to establish your credentials, often with people who may be suspicious and even hostile. And you need to work out what your key tools are – usually these will be your direct reports.

The first step is to understand who these people are and what they're doing. Sometimes this is less obvious than it sounds and occasionally what you'll discover is downright counter-intuitive.

A friend of mine was appointed to run one of the UK's major cultural institutions. On appointment he asked his PA-to-be to set up meetings with his direct reports so he could meet them individually before he took up his post the following month. She was slightly taken aback: 'I'm not sure you're going to get round to meeting all 28 of them before you start.'

At this point, he realized his suspicions that the organization had become unwieldy were well founded. In case you're wondering, in normal circumstances, it's reckoned that a manager can operate effectively with no more than eight direct reports – and even that's probably too many.

When you come into a business, it's an interesting exercise to assess the people around you and then what they think they are being asked to do. As noted earlier, it's imperative that those you manage understand in depth what they are being asked to do and why. The 'how' can, and should, generally be left to them. But this is also something you ought to check regularly when you're in a management role. Often structures and roles get bent out of shape, sometimes imperceptibly over time.

When you arrive in a new role, you often have to look quite hard for the facts and even the truth. Everyone has their own nuanced and, unsurprisingly, self-interested view of what they're doing and what others are doing. 'Success has many fathers, while failure is an orphan' is another great truism because it's true. None of this means that your reports are lying, just that, like all of us, they see their truth through their eyes, talk up their successes and glide over their failures.

A skilled and experienced manager has to work through these mists most of the time, even when she's familiar with the people and the situations. In my short time at Johnson, almost all of which was spent fire-fighting, I never really got to the bottom of what was going on in the present, let alone what had happened in the past. It was almost impossible – I was hearing dozens of wildly different narratives about the same events – and this, in itself, was a sign of how much trouble the company was in.

Even so, you don't have to be Poirot or Freud to work out some things – there are obvious tells. For example, if someone says it's not about them, it generally is, and if someone says it's not about the money, it always is. This is why it's so important to understand those you manage and get to know about their personal lives. Most people, but not all, enjoy talking to their boss about their life outside work, and you need to learn as much as you can.

It's pretty common for people who do their job well to go off the boil. Sometimes, it's because they're jaded, sometimes because they're encountering something they're not good at dealing with (some people thrive in difficult market conditions, while others struggle, and vice versa) but very often it's because life outside work is troubling them.

If you don't know what their home life is like or you can't talk to them about it, you won't be the best manager for them – and you might have a view of their performance which is incomplete. If someone has serious problems in their home life, their work may well suffer – but the reason is nothing to do with the job. You don't want to lose a good employee because you don't fully understand the context of their performance.

This goes further – sympathetic management treatment of someone with non-work problems is always a morale booster for colleagues. In one company I ran, an excellent branch manager had his life upended by the illness of his newborn daughter. When she tragically died six months later, he was the only working parent with a child on the paediatric ward who had been given fully paid leave for the duration of her life. His colleagues who had done their own bit by putting in extra hours to cover for him were immensely proud that the company they worked for had stood by him in this way. That the decision to keep him on full pay had been made by his line manager (although sanctioned by me) was also greatly appreciated.

In another instance, having suffered from mental illness myself, it was obvious that one of my direct reports was being knocked sideways by a nasty divorce. We agreed that he should step down for a year but I would find him a role if he felt fit to work again. Fortunately he recovered and returned to become a brilliant leader of a new division we had started in his absence. Again, his peer group felt that they were working in a great company.

This is so important. You should do these things because they're the right thing to do. But they will also improve morale, boost productivity and make your business a more attractive place to work. They are the very definition of enlightened self-interest.

Age and motivation

In a world where age discrimination is rightly outlawed, age is a sensitive topic. But that doesn't mean you can be blind to age. To manage people properly, you need to understand what their aspirations and life goals are. Age has a huge has impact on these and, therefore, what people are looking for out of their job. A smart manager should understand this.

I sat on the board of a company where the dynamic, very young CEO had boundless energy; he was wholly focused on the success of the business over the next five years. Another business I chaired had a similarly dynamic but older CEO who was highly ambitious for the business but knew that this was his last throw of the dice – and he wanted to get it right. Another company I chaired had a brilliant CEO. He was in his mid-50s and wanted to work reasonably hard but getting secure decent cash for the next 10 years was his priority.

Of course, I haven't treated these three CEOs any differently. But pragmatically, I recognize they all wanted different things. And that has applied to so many people I have managed over the years. Ignore what individuals want out of life at your peril.

A recent example of where I failed to judge this properly was a situation similar to the third CEO. An impressive MD of a company where I am a major shareholder seemed reluctant to expand his business, despite being well-placed to do so. The business was running smoothly, there were interesting growth opportunities and I felt he was capable of running a bigger business. Yet he kept, rather awkwardly, turning down growth opportunities that came our way and I thought we should pursue.

Eventually, the other big shareholder pointed out to me that I was discomfiting the MD with my continuing focus on growing the business. The MD liked and respected me – and so he felt obliged to think about growing the business because I wanted him to. But he didn't want this. Rather he was content to continue to polish the fire engine and run an excellent company.

The other shareholder knew this because he was of a similar age. Like the MD, he wanted a strong, reliable dividend stream and had no interest in taking any risks with it. I backed down, recognized I had failed to understand the needs and aspirations of those around me and became very comfortable with the steady dividend flow. As for the MD, he's hugely relieved that I am no longer endlessly pestering him to expand the business.

There's a broader point here that goes beyond age – and this is simply that not everyone is like you. I am ambitious, like growth and, until recently, felt that maximizing monetary returns for myself and others was imperative. But others often don't think like this. A lot of people are not trying to climb the greasy pole or increase their influence / power / wealth. Understanding people's different aspirations is critical to being a successful manager.

Have your people's backs

As well as understanding your people, you should always have their backs, within reason. I think about this most often when I come across the saying, 'The customer is always right'. This phrase and its variants was popularized by early modern retailers such as Harry Gordon Selfridge, John Wanamaker and Marshall Field.

It's true that customers pay the bills, that you need them, and that getting more of them, whether you work in hotels or tool hire, is the key to success. But, as I touched on earlier, this does not make them unerringly right. Indeed, it is not uncommon for them to be dishonest, stupid, over-demanding and bloody-minded. In a proper management structure, customer complaints should be taken extremely seriously. But when it is obvious that your employees have done their best and behaved appropriately, you should back them to the hilt.

As noted elsewhere, a perk of being the top person in an organization is that you can tell the customer to get lost. You should do so without hesitation when this becomes necessary, and you should let your people know that you are doing it. The pleasure and morale boost you give your people when you support them in a run-in with a customer is palpable, whether it is the credit controller dealing with a tricky payer or an operations person who has gone beyond the call of duty for a customer who will never be satisfied.

'A company is only as good as its people' is a far better maxim than 'The customer is always right'.

Why mean is good

In his 2015 book *Other People's Money* (OPM, which is also a pun on opium) John Kay looks at how spending other people's money (in this case a financial sector gambling with wealth it did not create) is one of the biggest threats to the capitalist system and was basically the cause of the 2008 financial crisis. This is also a common criticism of governments – indeed with government it goes one further. They are spending other people's money (taxpayers') on other people (not themselves). The end result is that they don't really care about the money.

Regardless, the overall point is the same. It's a lot easier to spend the company's money than your own – and this is very dangerous. This is something you need to understand as a manager. There are many beneficiaries of this, such as managers of restaurants in financial districts who know that people who don't look hard at prices because they're on expenses are exactly the customers they want.

I've seen this in several troubled businesses I've worked for. Those at the top spend OPM freely – and so does everyone else. In one company I joined, the former CEO was well known for his legendary expense account and general abuse of company assets – and this was not helped by him signing off his own expenses. Not everyone followed his example but enough did at all levels and, over time, the impact was pretty much terminal for a company that should have been watching every penny.

At another troubled business I arrived at, the previous leaders of the group were still in place for a rather pointless 'handover period'. I was accompanied by them to one of the failing division's board meetings, and a typically ineffectual meeting it was too. Afterwards, we repaired for lunch to the poshest local hotel.

Here, we were warmly welcomed by the maître d' and led unctuously to the best table, where a three-hour lunch began with endless bottles from the higher end of the wine list. It was clear that this was standard practice. Extraordinarily, when I slyly noted my discomfort at this decadence, the response suggested that I was rather unworldly and pious.

I'm a bit of a stickler for this though. I once upset non-exec director of a board where I was CEO. He'd arranged a lunch with a mutual acquaintance and it didn't feel like company business to me, so I contributed my share of the bill and felt they should do the same. He clearly thought I should put it on the company. A bit awkward and uptight? Maybe. But it sends out a message to everyone. I don't abuse expenses and you shouldn't either.

Sometimes profligacy reaches extraordinary levels. Early on in my career, when I was in finance, I worked on a potential investment in the US. As a junior, I was thrilled to be flown out twice to Texas, once business class and, when travelling with my boss, first class. Later, when it looked like the investment was going to proceed, the entire non-executive team of six were flown round-trip first class. It all seemed great, although I was left scratching my head as I worked out that the travel costs alone added up to 10 per cent of the investment made. Surely this couldn't be how companies were meant to work?

Perhaps at this point you're thinking that I have a bee in my bonnet about this – but time and again, I have seen profligacy with company money and business failure go hand in hand. Your job is to look after other people's money (usually shareholders') not spend it like it's nobody's money.

So what should be done? Every manager must impress on those they manage that the company's money should, as far as possible, be treated like their own. This should start at the CEO and end on the shop floor.

The key to this is giving people power and responsibility so that they can and do take ownership of their part of the company. It's also why strong financial reporting is needed. This means that managers can clearly see their operations' financial performance and see where they can economize or need to invest. Ideally it should also show them how they are performing against their peer group.

As part of this, I always try to ensure that managers are charged for everything they have control over and nothing they don't. Having an overrun in head office costs and allocating them to cost centres further down the chain is unfair and annoying, particularly when they impact adversely on performance. It does not incentivize the right behaviours.

If head office costs run at 10 per cent of group revenues and you're targeting a 10 per cent operating margin for the group, it is far better to ask the divisions to deliver 20 per cent operating margins than sticking them with their share of group overhead. You should try to achieve this at all levels of the business where people have their own profit and loss responsibility. Being responsible for your own P&L at any level is stimulating and generally fun. It involves you in a key way in what you are doing.

Besides (and as noted elsewhere) costs have a tendency to grow, particularly in good times and, like daisies, they need to be mown regularly. It is easiest to do this where the money is being spent by the people who can see what is and isn't necessary. It amazes me how tough people can be once they start thinking of the company's money as their own. I mean this in an entirely positive way – they starting abhorring waste, taking personal responsibility and urging the same responsibility on those they manage.

Those unfamiliar with this type of management style tend to confuse it with the effectiveness of financial incentives. They think the manager is being tough and monitoring every penny because some of that money saved will end up in their pocket. But this not my experience. I believe it's because you're empowering people. While everyone likes to enjoy the fruits of their labour and extra money is always welcome, it's usually about pride and job satisfaction.

Perhaps the most rewarding element of setting up this model is creating businesspeople out of people who have never thought of themselves as such. Seeing tool hire branch managers, many of who left school at 16 with few qualifications, learn how to read P&Ls and understand more complicated concepts such as cost of capital and effectively running their own businesses was one of the most rewarding parts of my own management career.

Higher up the pyramid, there are basic housekeeping rules that need to be in place such as managers in the chain openly scrutinizing their direct reports' expenses (my favourite chairman always went through my expenses in detail in front of me before signing them off, a practice I adopted on signing off others' expenses) and reducing the temptations of company credit cards and cash availability.

But much of cost-monitoring is based on sensible financial reporting. Why have costs escalated this year compared to last? Why does that branch or operation need more people or vehicles to generate the same revenues as this one? Is that manager hampered by having to operate out of a property which is too expensive for the business's needs?

What is to be avoided is the high-handed nonsense about cost-cutting coming down from head office with no understanding of conditions on the ground. You often see this in companies where, for whatever reason, profits are falling. The panicking CEO will issue a ridiculous 'one size fits all' edict like 'Everyone must

THE BUSINESS OF MANAGEMENT

cut costs by 5 per cent', which achieves little and probably points to why the business has got itself into trouble.

This is not to say that people at the top cannot have significant impact on costs. Deciding the general quantum of annual pay rises is an obvious area. Understanding what properties are needed and are affordable (taking on the right or wrong leases has huge impact on the profitability of a business over time) is a key activity for senior management. But the most important way of controlling cost is setting the tone on OPM.

Where senior management often has to spend a lot of money is on professional fees. As noted elsewhere, these are a necessary evil, and there is no point in trying to buck the crazy costs of professionals like lawyers, tax advisers and, most painfully, the City operators. However, it helps to understand that, as the CEO, these are your costs and you should work as hard at keeping them down as you expect your frontline troops to do with their costs.

The key to an easy life as a manager is having a successful business which people will generally enjoy working in. One of the biggest contributors to this is doing better than your competitors – and one of the biggest contributors to that is keeping your costs down. Never ignore this or be ashamed of it. Besides, if you do convince your people to keep a lid on costs, you can pay them more. By treating the company's money as their own, they get more money which really is their own.

8
PEOPLE AND PAY

'When you hire good people, and you provide good jobs and good wages and a career, good things are going to happen.'
JAMES SINEGAL (US BUSINESSMAN)

Why the role of HR should be administration and support, not executive and managerial, why appraisals matter and why recruitment, talent and succession are too important to be left to chance. Plus the often counterintuitive world of pay and bonuses. How incentivizing people is a bit of an art and why many companies get it completely wrong – with schemes that are either too complicated or simple, but which encourage the wrong behaviours.

The role of HR

This has always felt pretty simple to me. Managers are responsible for managing their people and the role of HR is to support and advise them in doing this. A company I was close to appointed a chief people officer and my heart sank. Either this will be a non-role which offers responsibility without power or it will be the next stage in centralization and the destruction of the power / responsibility model.

None of this is to say HR is unimportant. But its role must be advisory and administrative, not executive. There will be many occasions when advice is needed, particularly on legal and technical issues, and there also needs to be support in terms of maintaining appropriate records. In small companies I tend to use one of the HR outsourcers – technical HR advice at the end of a phone line for a few thousand pounds a year.

I can think of numerous situations where HR's input (whether external or in-house) is needed. In one business I ran, a fitter returned from lunch blind drunk – and the branch manager had to be advised on how to deal with it. In another, a warehouse manager had to deal with a Romanian warehouseman storming up to him to complain that a Polish colleague had called him a gypsy. In an office-based world, life may be less aggressively rough and tumble, but there will still be interpersonal disputes, accusations of bias, bullying claims and so on. HR is there for all of these.

HR can also help with the technical points of management. Where someone is underperforming, they can advise on the steps to be taken over a period of time to move them out of the business with the necessary warnings being issued in the right sequence. Where training programmes are needed, HR can research and coordinate their delivery. Some of the outsourcers also supply excellent and regular e-learning for areas like Health & Safety. And HR can look at pay scales and conditions, and work with senior management to ensure the business is kept up to date with best practice.

However, a manager must make the big decisions about their people and their development. A manager who can't manage their reports and constantly leans on or hides behind HR may be better off sticking to their area of expertise rather than management. Here, it's worth remembering that management is a skill in its own right and not everyone can do it. Just because you are a great salesman, it doesn't mean you are suited to sales management. An excellent programmer's career path does not have to involve becoming head of IT. This is an issue you see everywhere. Technical competence is no predictor of management ability.

Recruitment and talent

Recognizing and developing talent is critical to a company. You need stars to emerge in your business, not least because it is far cheaper to grow your own talent than to buy it in (there is no better example of this than professional football). External recruitment has other problems too. When you recruit someone you are effectively making a bet about their future performance based on dozens of unknowns. You will often recruit the wrong person even after the most rigorous processes. Doing so is very expensive in terms of company performance, and cleaning up the mess is time consuming and unpleasant. It's disappointing that the latest UK government doesn't understand that employers are never going to get recruitment right first time all the time and need some sort of probationary period for new recruits.

When it comes to internal appointments and promotion, much of the art of talent-spotting is understanding people's ambitions. Where someone is doing well and has real ambition, it needs to be recognized and opportunities for development and advancement ought to be provided.

Those with talent should bubble up through the business, but management plays a huge role in creating an environment where this happens. Senior managers need to keep an eye not only on their direct reports but on those below them. Talent spotting should be seen as part of the culture – and managers should not view promising junior staff as threats to their own position. There will perhaps, always be a slightly random element to talent spotting – but even small companies should make it more systematic and also have formal processes in place to deal with promising talent.

This is another reason I believe that senior management should get out of head office. As a CEO, I relish visiting operations. I'm not sure my instincts about people are particularly good, but it is frequently obvious to me that somebody has potential that isn't being fully used and that those in the management chain above them need to look at this.

For similar reasons, it's also good for senior managers to get involved with the people in an acquired business. I remember once meeting the man who had been number two to a domineering owner-manager. The owner-manager was about to leave and the deputy in question had always been blindly loyal to his boss, was underpaid and didn't understand quite how good he was at his job. Two years later he was thriving as the manager of a business 10 times the size, being paid twice as much and had been identified as a potential divisional MD.

There's a lot to be said for simply showing talented people recognition, too. When visiting a branch whose performance had been magnificent following the arrival of a new manager, I asked the man how he had achieved the turnaround and where his aspirations lay. He explained simply what he had done differently and added that he'd probably move on now. I asked him to stay where he was and give me six months to find something appropriate to his talent. A year later he was managing 30 branches brilliantly.

Succession management

Talent-spotting and succession management go hand in hand. It can be easy to overlook succession management, so a basic grid, setting out senior positions and who might take on key roles in the future, is helpful. However, it shouldn't be set in stone or function as a series of promises. Rather it should serve as a reminder of who is around and a guide.

In one acquisition I made, the lumpen, stodgy plc from which the business had been bought had stipulated that all divisional MDs must have ready-to-go succession plans with candidates in place. The result was a lot of people in jobs which were beneath their abilities (some had been recruited as successors-in-waiting). They were being paid high salaries and often had little to do. I have never found making cost savings so easy. It was like being given a list of overpaid people we didn't need.

I too have failed in succession-planning, however. I once had a brilliant divisional MD from a humble educational background. He was an extraordinarily effective manager – hard-working, well-respected, worldly and smart, but he'd started from the shop floor. I recognized that my time left as CEO was fairly short and that a successor would be needed. So the divisional MD was sent on senior management courses and I involved him slightly in some of the areas where he had no experience, particularly on the quoted company side. I thought I'd done enough, but I hadn't.

When the time came to find my successor, the nominations committee (in which I was not allowed to play a role) interviewed my preferred candidate but only really out of politeness to me. He didn't get to the final interview stage – and this was wholly down to my inadequate succession planning. I hadn't spent time explaining to him what I was doing on the plc side, I hadn't exposed him to bankers and investors, and hadn't familiarized him with the board membership and its workings. With more thought from me, better development planning, more stress on building his relationship with our CFO who could handle all the stuff he didn't know about, and slightly better politics, I could have produced a stronger candidate who would have done a brilliant job.

Succession planning is particularly key for top jobs and, as someone who has changed careers frequently, I have to recognize a pattern – that successful businesses tend to promote internally while struggling ones tend to look outside. This, incidentally, is why I rather unintentionally became a turnaround person. If you're running your business well, you know who the next CEO is. You probably don't need or want someone like me coming in from the outside

Probably my worst performance at succession management was in a business I had built but which I had run out of ideas for. I'd worked in tandem with a brilliant chair but we were both running out of steam. So the plan was for me to move on, for him to find a replacement for me and then move on himself. The fly in the ointment was that he had a degenerative disease which was accelerating. I and others felt that he could no longer fulfil his role. He was slightly reluctant (and I now realize this was out of the best interests of the business rather than himself) but accepted the situation. So the first step was to replace him rather than me.

It was inappropriate for a CEO, particularly one planning to leave, to be active in the appointment of a new chair. And the former chair was not felt to be in a condition to organize his replacement. So a newish non-executive director ran the chair recruitment process with no effective input from me. The new chair was a reasonable appointment but not the right type for what was a pretty entrepreneurial business. His first responsibility was to replace me. Again, a decent but culturally unsuitable replacement for me was recruited, correctly with little input from me. Shortly afterwards the established non-executives moved on, and the leadership of the business had completely changed to one with no affinity for the culture of the company.

Lesson? Don't leave succession management to chance.

Family businesses and succession

Family businesses have their own succession dynamic, and there's a good reason that one of the best TV shows in recent years is called *Succession* – and it's set in a family business. If you are going to keep it in the family – which is to say, have it run by bloodline relatives – you need to think very hard and plan. And be very aware of the 'rags-to-rags in three generations' cycle which frequently flows from handing on blindly to the next generation.

However, many UK family businesses do this very well and draw strength from the numerous benefits of such companies. These tend to be things like staff loyalty, long-term thinking and genuine paternalism. I am particularly concerned that the current UK government's drive to sort out the national debt is being placed largely on the shoulders of businesses of this type. Depressingly, many owner-managers now believe that passing on such businesses to the next generation is likelier to be a burden than a gift.

However, there is still enthusiasm for passing on businesses of a significant size. The key here is not to have too small a number of candidates (in *Succession*, there are four siblings). Successful multigenerational business usually have a wide gene-pool of cousins to choose from. And the trick is to pick which one or two of these will lead the business, based on capability and willingness to take the management role on rather than going to the first person in line. The families who pull this off successfully are amongst the wealthiest in the UK and run companies such as Jardine Matheson, AB Foods, and Warburtons.

All of these businesses choose from the family gene pool but cast their net widely within it, rather than following the primogeniture principle. The next leader or leaders of the family business can be expected to be steeped in the business and also very aware of their responsibility to hand on a healthy company to the next generation. This promotes long-term vision as well as giving the management a sense of custodianship rather than self-interested ownership.

Another succession option is picking people out a long time ahead of their time to succeed. The brilliant (but unpopular with Republican classicists) Augustus failed to organize his succession, leaving behind him a chaos of nutters. His extraordinary legacy survived despite this. However, it took almost a century before Rome get its act together on succession: 98-180 AD was the rule of the Five Good Emperors. All four of Nerva's (the first Good Emperor) successors were 'adopted' by the existing Emperor early on, some with no blood connection at all. This was the height of Rome's power. Marcus Aurelius, the last of the Good Five, handed on to his son Commodus (correctly cast as the villain in the film *Gladiator*) and it was a downhill ride thereafter.

How to pay people properly

This brings us to pay, another issue that vexes bosses. It takes up a huge amount of mental energy and causes real angst. It shouldn't. In fact, it should be one of the easiest ways to keep your staff happy. Unlike getting rid of bastards or managing underperformers out of the business, which is unpleasant, pay can be a genuinely positive thing – if you approach it right and do it right. Bonuses and long-term incentive plans (LTIPS) are a little trickier, so let's start with basic pay.

When it comes to pay, what most people care about is their peer group. They want to be paid in line with others who do the same job and in line with the market. Essentially they want to be paid fairly. As a boss, you should pay them a little bit more than the market rate if you can. The message this sends out is that you care, you value them and you recognize they're great people. Do this and they'll be happy.

Pay differentials between peers and near-peers are the most emotive and problematic area and can be highly destructive if not resolved or clarified. I once had a senior divisional MD who made over five times his annual salary under a share option scheme. By any yardstick he was doing incredibly well. And yet, when he discovered that the more recently appointed CFO (who he considered his peer) was earning considerably more he was furious. It took all my persuasive powers to convince him not to resign. You see this a lot in the City and Wall Street. The banker who gets a £1m bonus is delighted until he discovers the guy next to him got £1.2m.

Sticking to this basic rule where you pay people in line with their peers and a bit better than the market will not only deliver happy staff, it will also make your own life as a manager much easier. If you have an employee who rates themselves very highly, is greedy or is an aggressive negotiator, the temptation is to give in (and a certain type of smart employee will always look a bit disappointed when you give them a pay rise, even if they're cheering inside). Over the years, this problem can compound and in extreme circumstances an employee like this can easily wind up earning 30 per cent more than their peers.

But if you pay everyone as equally as you can for a similar job, you can always fall back on this. You say, 'I can't pay you more than Clare who does the same job – you both perform well and you're both earning 10 per cent more than the market rate.' It also helps you with gender issues – women are much less likely to ask for pay rises than men (although this may be partly as women seem to

PEOPLE AND PAY

better understand that the more highly-paid you are, the more exposed you are if your performance or the company's performance falters).

Pay should be what is known as a 'hygiene factor.' This concept comes from the American business psychologist Frederick Herzberg's Two Factor Theory which stipulates that there are two kinds of factors in job satisfaction: growth factors and hygiene factors.

Growth factors motivate. Hygiene factors like pay and comfortable chairs do not motivate in their own right, but if absent they may lower motivation. Thus, if you do not pay people a fair salary they will be dissatisfied and unhappy. But once you are paying them a fair salary any extra will not motivate them much. They will not work ten per cent harder or be ten per cent happier if you are overpaying them by ten per cent.

In my experience, paying more does not get you better people when recruiting (although a sensibly crafted bonus scheme can help here), as most people judge their value on what they have been paid in the past or what they aspire to. This is backed up by research. A famous study looked at earnings achieved by Harvard Business School alumni in the years after graduation. What they found was that those who were paid more were those who expected to earn more, rather than those whose performance at Harvard had been better.

This plays out across entire sectors. People who work in finance or marketing are generally far better paid than those in production because that's how the market is structured. This may also reflect the class system in the UK. The people who go into these functions are more likely to have come from middle-class backgrounds and have gone to private schools, and they are likelier to have expectations of a certain lifestyle which possibly includes being able to pay school fees.

Here it's worth briefly mentioning the two things that do motivate people – the growth factors. One is responsibility and power. As mentioned earlier in this book, this is the doctrine of empowerment and I am a huge fan of it. Don't micromanage your people. Leave them to get on with their work and they'll be happy. All you have to do is recognize good work (a call out of the blue from the CEO congratulating a branch manager on a good month is massively valued), make decisions at your level and be on hand if they need you. The second big factor in workplace satisfaction is you want your organization to be respected. Your staff should feel as if they are part of a bigger entity and that the bigger entity is something to be proud of.

Bonuses and incentives

If you can provide these three things – responsibility, recognition and an organization staff respect – you're 80 per cent of the way there. However, the remaining 20 per cent is considerably more difficult. This is related to several of the other points (and pay) and the question here is how do you get your staff to buy into the company's long-term success? Most companies do this via bonuses and incentives and they often get these wrong. I know this, not least because I have got them wrong.

Awarding share options is a case in point. Many young company managers think that holding out potential equity gains to staff is the key motivator. This is not right – both in terms of motivating staff and generating returns for yourself. I've come across innumerable start-ups where staff are expected to work for below-market rates of pay in the hope that the founder's vision will deliver. Very often the share options used to do this end up being worthless.

Similarly, on acquiring a business, the incoming management shouldn't think anyone is buying into their grand vision. Rather, staff want the normal stuff: slightly above market level wages, responsibility and being part of a success. They are, very sensibly, there to do a job and get paid, not to share in your dreams.

At a later stage, many companies cite the ability to award options as an advantage of being public. This means they can reward employees at all levels with the right to buy shares at a fixed price. If the shares go up, the options can be exercised after three or more years and a profit taken by the employee. If the shares go down and never get above the exercise price, nothing is lost by the employee. So the employees' goals are aligned with the shareholders. Options incentivise people to stay at the company and to care about how the whole company does rather than just the parts of it over which they have influence.

Options have worked very well for me and other movers and shakers I know. The people who can really make a difference at the top like backing themselves and are generally prepared to accept less than market rate rewards in exchange for making big gains on equity. Many entrepreneurs through acquisition hold this as their key driver. Similarly when owners are absentee landlords, relying on the hands-on management to create value, encouraging these managers to create value for themselves alongside value for the landlord makes sense. I have often done this in start-ups where the financial backers have a majority stake but are reliant on the management to create value, as in private equity transactions. It can also be appropriate where a retiring owner steps back from day-to-day management.

But it is often a mistake to assume that everyone in a senior position is desperate for equity. Yes, it's nice to have but may not be as big a motivator as job security and a decent package. Where this is the case, the motivational element is much smaller than the dilution in ownership and ultimate value. Even in public companies, the value of share options as a motivator is less than might be expected when spread widely. Many recipients don't read the business pages. They don't look up the company's share price every morning and they

PEOPLE AND PAY

have no interest in the stock market. And so, below senior management level, share options don't work very well.

They're just too abstract and remote for most employees. Furthermore, few staff below senior management can have a real impact on the share price as individuals, so the idea that their performance and the value of the business are linked is alien and doesn't make much sense. It is often actually dysfunctional; a company should always understand that equity is the most valuable element in business (as entrepreneurs and savvy business people know), therefore to hand it out when it is valued so lowly by the recipients is madness. You're delivering little motivation to people who can't affect the outcome at a massive cost.

I have first-hand experience of how this doesn't work in practice. When share options were awarded thoughtlessly (and at my recommendation) to the 100-plus branch managers in the public tool hire business I ran, the outcome was: no additional motivation, an element of confusion, and a potentially significant dilution in the ownership of the company. Best of all, when the shares went down below the exercise price, there was some sense that something ethereal had been lost which was a source of minor grievance. There literally was no upside for anyone involved.

In one private company I control, the key people were suspicious of being directors and the nebulous concept of long-term capital growth. A simple cash bonus related to their performance, coupled with a generous salary, was what they wanted. They did want the business to be a success but they didn't feel remotely concerned about how their efforts were creating value for me. They did their jobs happily and really wanted me to do well – but this was because I'd put up the money that allowed them to do what they wanted to do, not because they were growing the value of the company.

So, how should you motivate and incentivize people via financial reward? A far more effective way of doing this is one of the very few successful bits of UK tax-based motivation – the SAYE (Save As You Earn) scheme. Under this, all employees are allowed to pay into a savings scheme. At the end of three years, the money saved can be used in two ways. One is to buy shares at a discount of 20 per cent below the share price on the date the person first started saving. The other is to take the money back with interest. If the share price has done well, they buy can the shares and sell them at the higher current price.

Perhaps you've spotted that the SAYE scheme works in a very similar way to share options; in fact the chief difference is that people really like it. Why? Well, this is really one for the behavioural economists but my personal view is that people feel more involved in the process; it is their own action in participating in the scheme and paying into it. This makes it more real to them, less abstract, and so far more rewarding.

Keep it simple, stupid (KISS)

At the operating level, the best financial motivator is simple cash. Now, I know we've said that pay is a hygiene factor – and it is in terms of salary. However, you can use bonuses as a form of recognition and people do seem to like this. Here you want to be as straightforward as possible.

In the tool hire business, after the share option scheme had achieved little in the form of motivation, we moved to paying the branch managers a share of the profit their branch made (over budget). This went straight into their (and their staff's) monthly pay packets. It was a figure they could see, grasp (and spend) immediately, and it aligned them completely and demonstrably with the performance of what they were managing.

Moreover, it included something for everyone, right down to the guy who swept the yard. He might not have realized what it was all about but he liked the extra £100 a month in his pay packet when the branch had a good month – and the branch manager liked the feeling that she had made it happen for him. It was incredibly simple and it worked for everyone.

However, even though it was very simple, it allowed us to incentivise quite sophisticated behaviours too. As mentioned previously, in a hire company you don't want branch managers to have large quantities of kit lying idle. Rather, you want it all hired out producing a return. But if you measure idle kit on a national level, there is no incentive for individual managers to minimize the amount of stock they have lying around idle. You do not differentiate between the branch that has 5 per cent sitting around and the one that has 50 per cent.

So you charge the managers for the kit they have on site. The company is expected to make up to 20 per cent a year on the capital it deploys, so that's what you charge the branch managers. If a lot of kit is lying idle it will hit the branch's performance and the pride and bonus of the manager. This strongly disincentivizes having large quantities kit lying idle (and stockpiling kit for one-off events) and encourages managers to seek a return on your capital investment in line with what your investors will seek from you.

You should also try to smooth bonuses out. We based monthly bonuses on average profits over the three previous months. This negated behaviours such as finagling bumper months and weak months, meant that a bad month had an impact for three months and smoothed the bonus payments. It also involved setting budgets every month for three months forward so that the targets were always realistic.

Once concepts such as a charge on capital employed and three-month rolling averages were explained, both the concepts and the rationale were immediately understood and the scheme worked brilliantly as being clear and fair. The managers could see exactly how their performance translated into pay. They felt fully in control of their businesses and would focus on every line which they could control of their P&L, from the number of vans they chose to operate through to keeping the electricity bill down. The charge levied on how much equipment they held wholly reflected what I had been tasked to achieve by my shareholders who wanted to see a maximum return on the money they had invested in a capital-intensive business.

I try to introduce this wherever possible. In the document shredding division of my current business, those in the warehouse are paid extra if the quality of the bales they produce is higher than average. So rather than chucking all the files in with the associated paper they look to separate it out to achieve high-quality bales.

What doesn't work

Possibly the worst bonus schemes I have seen revolve around paying a percentage of salary. These have become popular for all the wrong reasons and I've often seen them both in businesses that I've acquired from large corporations and in businesses which I've come in to run.

I once bought a records management business from a large company which wanted to get rid of it because its core activity was not RM (several businesses such as transport groups had acquired or developed RM businesses as part of their other activities). The management team of four were on salaries between £100 and £150k. They had a bonus scheme where they were paid an extra 25 per cent of their base salary when they hit their budgetary targets, 50 per cent when budget was exceeded by 10 per cent, and 75 per cent for 15 per cent.

With the business budgeted to make £2m, the scheme paid out £125k at £2m, £250k at £2.2m and £375k at £2.3m. Can you spot the first problem? In this narrow range virtually all the extra made (and sometimes more) went to the management team. Moreover, there was no incentive to do any better. Why bother stretching yourself to make £2.5m or £3m when your own bonuses max out at £2.3m? In fact, the only people this scheme really worked for were managers themselves, the accountant who devised it and perhaps some people at head office who were more concerned about reporting that the division was on budget than the business actually performing well.

The perverse incentives didn't stop here. During a good year, the management team might start massaging the figures down to £2.3m. This would mean that their bonus paid out in full, their targets for the following year would be lower (than if they made, say, £2.7m) and that these lower targets would be easier to hit, because they'd pushed money over on to the following year. In a weak year, the self-interested strategy would be to let the business slide. Why bother making any effort if you're going to miss your targets anyway – and besides, lower results, again, mean lower targets the following year.

For me, all this illustrates the problems you get with a lazy, box-ticking approach to financial incentives. Too often there is central management function, made up of people who just want a budget number for the group results that is likely to be hit. They are too unengaged to think beyond that. This leads to the kind of manipulation I saw and this, in turn, destroys honesty and transparency across organizations, right up to the person who's taking responsibility for the whole shebang. This poor culture is a pretty quick route to underperformance against what can be achieved.

Understanding this kind of thing can be a real source of advantage for you. When we bought the specific business referred to above, it was (unsurprisingly) making £2.3m a year. However, it was also carrying so much fat that we could take out over £1.5m of costs before any of the synergy benefits (cutting duplicated functions, sharing expertise, tax advantages etc.) With these, the business was soon making us £5m a year. What had appeared to the selling company's board to be a high price turned out to be a spectacularly good deal for us.

Back to pay. The solution for divisional management bonuses is straightforward, although like any bonus scheme you need to keep refining. Something like: of any profit above 90 per cent of budget, 20 per cent goes to the team. And there should be no limit on the size of the bonus: an extraordinary year will deliver big bonuses, but that's not a problem as you'll be thrilled to pay it out.

It also makes the group take a better approach to pay full stop. A lower bonus means you have to pay people properly to do their jobs. This means bonuses are there as an addition to salary, not as part-substitute for it. Bonuses return to their proper role, which is allowing staff to share in the business's profits when it is doing OK or well. This contributes to individual staff taking responsibility for their area of responsibility as it has a direct impact on their pocket. Steering clear of percentage-of-salary bonuses also means your key people are not grossly overpaid in a good year and scrabbling around for the mortgage in a bad year.

On top of this, you should add in some share options for the most senior divisional management who can have an impact on the overall business. At this level, they need to be motivated by the performance of the group as a whole and encouraged to look out for other divisions. The need to stay with the business during the option period can tie people into the business too when things are going well. All this holds pretty much true for most senior management.

Before we leave pay behind, it's worth looking at a final example of what doesn't work. In some circumstances, usually start-ups, the company cannot afford to pay employees properly. Instead it pays them a reduced rate and gives them share options which, in theory, could be worth vastly more than the foregone salary if things work out. This model tends to appeal to young, clever people who have often seen it work spectacularly well for others and trade stories of the secretary who never had to work again.

Perhaps the most extreme example of this is the artist David Choe. He was persuaded to take stock instead of cash for painting the walls of Facebook's first office and is now worth around $300m. But it probably won't be you and I'd be very wary of taking stock instead of a decent salary as an employee or offering it as an employer.

If you're an employee, if you're that good, you should be founding a company yourself or getting paid properly. Moreover, many really driven entrepreneurs will be doing everything to make the business work and won't be as attentive to the impact on your potential goldmine when fund-raisings are needed as you might like or might have expected when you first signed up. If the business fails or is picked up at a disappointing valuation, the entrepreneur will usually be in a far better position than you to extract value from the wreckage.

There's also often a slightly messianic, culty air around start-ups which require the employees to believe in the project despite having far less equity participation than the founders. I remember working briefly for a 1980s forerunner of Rightmove, the UK online real estate platform. The entrepreneur was genuinely shocked when I asked to be paid as agreed for my efforts. Could I not see that asking for my salary could have a negative impact on his great vision?

From the employer's angle, there are downsides too. If the business is any good, you'll be giving away equity too cheap. If things don't go as planned, you risk having very upset people when your dreams and promises to staff don't pan out. So if the business is that good, work harder yourself or raise enough money to pay people properly, rather than borrow their time and industry, with no certainty that you will be able to pay them back.

Again, we're back to the basics. Pay them slightly above the market rate with a bonus scheme that's transparent and easy to understand. They'll be happy and they'll deliver for you.

9
THE TOUGH SIDE OF PEOPLE MANAGEMENT

'Firing people, that's unfortunately part of doing business.'
　　　　　　　　　PAUL WOLFOWITZ, PRESIDENT OF THE WORLD BANK

The nasty stuff at work. Sacking people and redundancies, identifying useless people – and how to let people go as decently and humanely as possible. Using crises, the Ancient Greek view on redundancies and what happens in those strange organizations where nobody is ever sacked. Finally, managing bastards and why, very occasionally, useless people have value.

When people have got to go

Sacking nasty, destructive employees can sometimes be cathartic and even enjoyable. But removing underperformers who might be quite pleasant people is much less so and making redundancies is one of the worst tasks you can face as a manager. However, these things often need to be done – and done as humanely, decently and expediently as possible.

　　I'll start with redundancies. When these are not removals in disguise, they have the downside of being deeply unfair – the individuals involved are often victims of circumstances which are far beyond their control such as downturns in the global economy. There is literally nothing these people could have done to save their jobs and this can make them feel like helpless pawns.

　　That said, mass redundancies are not all bad. When you shed large numbers of people, individual self-esteem need not be battered (because it isn't any one person's fault). And when, say, a local facility in a multinational is closed or production is moved off-shore, there is minor comfort in your peer group being in the same position, irrespective of ability. The community knows that it is nothing to do with your performance and capability.

I once came into a company where the head office function had become absurdly bloated. Those at head office were getting in the way of the operating businesses, creating grief all round at extraordinary cost. I quickly reduced the head office count from 54 to nine. This not only saved a lot of money, it reduced the operating businesses' costs (no need for several people generating information for head office), simplified and speeded up decision-making, and created more dynamism in the operating companies. While unfortunate and unpleasant for those made redundant, none of them could take this as personal or reflecting poorly on their performance. It was simply a change in management style of which they were a victim. And easy to explain this to future employers.

For all this, there isn't much to be said about how to manage a mass redundancy, beyond the technical, statutory stuff. You need to get this right and you should behave as decently as possible and choose your words very carefully when you speak.

However, there are plenty of situations where matters are far less cut and dried than this. I have been involved in buying numerous businesses where an acquisition results in what are often called 'synergies'. What this means in practice is that, often in the acquired company's head office, there will be a number of duplicated functions such as finance and HR, marketing. Cost savings can be generated by eliminating this duplication.

When such an acquisition takes place, it's usually pretty easy for everyone to see what is coming, the logic to it and who will be exposed. Redundancies rarely come as a surprise and, what's more, the integration of functions and systems takes time. Those who will be leaving the business have plenty of time to look for alternative positions and the process is generally pretty humane. The new management may also have opportunities to redeploy people elsewhere in the organization.

Here, as with mass redundancies, it helps if those who are going to lose their jobs understand that it is not a reflection on their performance and there are others in the same position. This allows those affected to see that it's not personal and can help their pride and self-confidence. As an employer you should be publicly clear about all this so that the next potential employer knows that these people are leaving for reasons unrelated to their own abilities. When Elon Musk sacked half the staff at Twitter immediately after taking ownership, those losing their jobs (and their potential future employers) at least knew that it was nothing to do with their own capability.

I've recruited many great people who had been made redundant elsewhere, usually for no fault of their own. There is no stigma, particularly if a redundant candidate is accepting and carries no animus towards their previous employer and their misfortune. The ideal approach is to view the situation as an opportunity to try something else.

Worth mentioning here is that all this points to being cautious about recruitment when the going is good. You do not want to bring on hundreds of new staff only to have to make them redundant when times get tough again. Better to hold back on additional recruitment until it is clear that a long-term shift has occurred in the business. Think Mark Zuckerberg at Meta (formerly Facebook) hiring 12,000 people in early 2022 and then making a similar number of redundancies later in the year. This is also an argument for using consultants (generally not something I'm keen on), freelancers and contract staff until you know the additional workload will be sustained in the long run.

Getting it right and wrong

My own experience of redundancies has been mostly on this sort of smaller scale, rather than total restructuring or shutting down large operations. I have arrived at businesses and quickly realized that costs and revenues in some operations are massively out of line or that there are people, particularly managers, who are doing non-jobs. One of the worst days of my working life was having to sack a number of supposedly underperforming senior managers at a business which I had recently joined as CEO. I offer this as an object lesson in how not to do it.

It was obvious from day one that there were too many managers relative to the overall size of the company. My predecessor, who was still involved in the business having stepped up to be the chair, had told me about this, even going as far as identifying which people he felt should be removed. He had not acted on any of his findings but the reasons he gave seemed plausible.

He said that I was the new broom who needed to arrive and make an impact; he had historic personal relationships with several of the people who might have to leave and it was important that this exercise was undertaken by someone who didn't have these relationships; I would also be able to set up the structure I wanted. I bought into this rationale, although I could also see that he wanted someone else to wield the axe.

Fine. I understood the need for action and I had some ill-formed, theoretical concepts of what to do. In order of descending usefulness these were from: my stint as the editor of a management magazine, books with titles like *The First 100 Days*, and a malevolent idea I'd picked up from a film producer that a sacking or two in the early days of shooting sharpens everyone up a bit and keeps them on their toes. Within two months of my arrival, I had my hit list of superfluous managers, which had mainly been compiled by my predecessor.

On the fateful day itself, I drove, with the group HR manager to do the technical side, to the workplaces of the five people with the black crosses on their back. I was dreading these meetings and, as it turned out, rightly so.

Two of the five had an inkling that something might be up and probably knew they'd been phoning it in. Explaining to them that the company's costs were sky high and that I had to put this right wasn't too bad. But the other three were a different story. They were confused and distressed and, in retrospect, rightly so as they weren't swinging the lead and had not been told that they were failing. Moreover, as word of my Grim Reaper-like tour got out (and bad news travels at the speed of light in business) other managers started asking what car I was driving so that they could be prepared for the arrival of the executioner at their office. Arriving at one branch where the area manager had his office, he met me in the doorway, asked if I was really there for what he feared, noted that his job was his life, and asked whether I knew that his wife had recently left him. The following five minutes were awful – I never want to put someone in that position again nor to be responsible for that happening.

At the end of a long and harrowing day, I returned home and got blind drunk. I felt a mixture of remorse, regret for the pain I had inflicted, and that this couldn't be the right way to do things irrespective of the company's circumstances. Nonetheless, it taught me a lot.

Many of us have stories about monsters who have lost touch with humanity and relish their power over people's livelihoods. Joseph Conrad's Kurtz in *Heart of Darkness* was not unique. Some of these stories have a humorous edge, such as Robert Maxwell bumping into someone working in his office building, firing him on the spot for being scruffy, and handing out the estimated redundancy payment from the cash wodge in his pocket at the time. The 'employee', who had never been in the building before but had been sent by his company to fix the photocopier was, naturally, thrilled.

But sadly these stories are not just folklore. I had, at an early stage, a small degree of sympathy for a CEO who had left behind a mess which I was trying to sort as his replacement. This sympathy was based on his personal circumstances and the fact that he had clearly been over-promoted to a role where he was clueless.

I visited a particularly distressed operation and was surprised to hear that my predecessor had been there before his departure. I was impressed by that as he wasn't known for getting stuck into problem areas, until the local manager noted it was on the day the CEO's football team was playing in the area. The next anecdote from the local manager was truly shocking. The receptionist at the site had failed to recognize the CEO and not unreasonably asked him to move his car which was parked in an awkward place. When he left the site the CEO noted to the manager that he didn't want the receptionist to be working there when he next visited. From then on, I was happy to trash his reputation whenever his name came up.

So, how do you get it right?

- You must always make it absolutely clear to those you are managing what you are asking them to do, agree it with them and then monitor their performance against it.
- If someone is not delivering what they have committed to do, discuss with them. Try and understand why it is not happening and how matters can be improved.
- If the situation persists and it is down to their inability or reluctance to do what is reasonably asked of them, you take action at this point.
- While it is important to take soundings from other people in the business, you must make your own decisions, rather than acting on another's recommendation. The latter is only acceptable if you are instructed to do something – in which case the person instructing you has made the decision and it needs to be clear that they, not you, are responsible for the action.
- This is particularly true when coming into a business. Here you need to assess the quality and effectiveness of your direct reports, along with the reporting structure. Once you've done this, you need to work out what you want people to do, make it clear to them and then carefully monitor and assess how they are doing.
- My experience is that most people are pretty good at their jobs as long as they care, are prepared to take responsibility and are clearly told what is expected of them. Those who don't fit these requirements can be sweated out of the business – good management will often mean they choose to leave rather than have their shortcomings exposed.

Performance management in three meetings

We all have friends who are occasionally (or regularly) incompetent in elements of life. That's fine. You don't necessarily look for technical competence here – and if their incompetence becomes too difficult or offensive for you to cope with, you can drift away from the relationship. However, incompetence cannot and must not be tolerated in the people you manage. It has to be dealt with – and often the only way of doing so is to sack the person.

There is (rightly) a lot of regulation around sacking someone or making them redundant, particularly in Europe, but I have never found it unduly restrictive where someone is doing a bad job and the right procedures are in place. Most managers I know understand the critical importance of people being capable of what they are needed to do. They know that having people around who cannot do their job properly is a killer for any organization in terms of its survival, success and for the well-being of all who work there. They can see that one person's incompetence affects everyone around them

However, most will also admit they have often been too slow to deal with people who are not up to scratch. This is usually because the managers are decent people: nobody should relish telling their reports that they're not up to the job. But you must grasp the nettle. I have never come across a situation where the removal of an incompetent employee, particularly in management, has been the wrong thing to do, whatever the short-term cost.

You will dread it the first time you do it, but once done you will wish you had acted earlier – and it does get easier. I have got to the stage where I no longer dread it or delay. It needs to be done and as quickly as possible. Everyone else will thank you. The release of energy and enthusiasm inside an organization where a failing manager is removed is stunning, particularly as most of the unfortunate person's colleagues and reports are normally well aware of their failings and ahead of the senior management on the need for removal.

So, how do you identify incompetence? Many managers will say follow your instincts. I agree with this to an extent. Managers' guts tell them if something isn't right. My particular 'tell' is looking at an upcoming internal meeting and not feeling good about someone who will be attending. I know at this point that my instincts are telling me there is something wrong which I need to assess and probably address. However, you should also be cautious about instinct as you are making decisions that will negatively affect someone's life. So trust your instinct, but verify with facts.

Even so, I have still funked it on occasion. One example that always comes to mind is a divisional MD. I had taken him on to impose order on a chaotic and floundering business division. Even at the time, my instincts screamed that this was an MD who would be able to impose order, but not move the division forwards after doing so. Other colleagues made the same observation. Nonetheless, I made the decision that having order now was the most important thing.

My fears proved very well founded. He imposed order. But soon afterwards, sales started to fall, despite him bringing in a new and very well-paid sales director who he had previously worked with. Because I had recruited the MD and he had delivered half of what we'd agreed (the order) I didn't act as I should have done, although his performance was far from satisfactory. Eventually he retired early, reflecting the pressure he was under. But, even so, a year in the development of the business was lost because he was the wrong person to run it – and I was reluctant to remove him.

It is similarly difficult in situations where you or the company bear some responsibility because you have been involved in the person's career development. Here, the person who was a promising employee often winds up promoted to a position that is beyond their abilities. This, of course, is the Peter Principle in action. The principle, which is named after the Canadian educator and 'hierarchiologist' Laurence J. Peter, states that there is a 'tendency for every employee to rise in the hierarchy through promotion until they reach a level of respective incompetence'. This, a bit like the best-known of Parkinson's laws ('work expands so as to fill the time available for its completion'), sounds like a sly joke about organizational inefficiency, but is actually wry observation about the nature of the world of work. You see both everywhere.

It might seem obvious here to demote the person. But in practice, usually for reasons of pride and the stigma attached to a demotion, moving people down happens very rarely, so, again, the solution is usually to have the person removed. I have often seen people who are sacked for incompetence join a competitor company in a role one rung below that from which they previously held. A sales manager who was sacked from company A goes back on the road as a salesman at company B. This may be a slightly messy process, but it's a good outcome

Whatever the reasons, the approach to performance management and removal should be the same.

The three meetings

- First meeting: you appear not to be delivering what was expected of you. Why? And what do you need to achieve it?
- Second meeting: we're still not achieving what we had agreed and expected. Why not and how can this be changed?
- Third meeting. I think we can both agree that this isn't working and that it is best to part company.

In my experience, if you need to arrange a third meeting, the person knows what's coming. Indeed, there is often an element of relief on both sides and the meeting is more about the terms of the departure than actually having to sack the individual.

Telling people they have to leave

Sometimes termination meetings can be very cordial. A few years ago, I came into a company as CEO where the CFO was a pretty decent and competent man but the business was in a big mess. The business had been floundering before his arrival and his role had, from an early stage, been to act as a lightning rod to protect the CEO rather than get stuck into the finances. As a result, with the CEO gone, he barely had a role as the finances were really being run by the group financial controller.

I told him this when we were on a train together, and he thought for a moment before asking me whether I thought he should go.

When I said that he probably should, he replied, 'Don't blame you. Good call. What's my deal?' I've stayed in touch with him and there is no bad blood at all about it.

Other meetings are much more difficult – to the point where people refuse to acknowledge what you're saying. I once dealt with a lovely man who had been the first ever employee of a company which had 100 staff when I joined but now had 500. He was a strong example of the Peter Principle and was in a job about three rungs above his capability.

Despite sitting down with him regularly to set out what was expected of him and how far short of it he was falling, he just couldn't see where this was going, possibly insulated by his history with the company. I offered him several lesser roles which he turned down flat. At the fateful final meeting, he literally couldn't understand that I was asking him to move on. I did the best I could: I was offering him a consultancy role that, initially, would provide 75 per cent of his salary and which he could build into a decent business. I had rightly dreaded that meeting as however blunt I had been in my warnings he seemed incapable of taking on board that he was massively underperforming and his ongoing employment was under threat. His response to the short, formal letter I gave him at the meeting was to stare at the page, re-reading it for 10 minutes without speaking and then leave the room, again without speaking.

After he left the company, and to nobody's surprise, the outcome was a massive unblocking of people and corporate potential. It worked out for the man himself too: he built a nice advisory business providing sensible and well-informed Health & Safety consultancy to a sector he understood well but was a commercial disaster in. Despite this positive outcome, I now know that, with the greater experience, I could have handled the relationship better. I could have been much clearer about what I wanted, what wasn't being delivered and where all this led.

Your final act should be to create the right narrative around the person's departure. You want them to retain their self-esteem and confidence, even if you cannot wait to see the back of them. Narratives that work well often include elements such as the person wanting to get back to what drew them to the industry in the first place, a tough market and character clashes. This is also why they need to go elsewhere – such narratives work less well where colleagues know that the real reason for departure was underperformance.

There's an element of self-interest here, too. There is no point in creating enemies unnecessarily and many industries are small worlds. Even if someone is deeply unhappy at the time, they may come to see that you had no choice and behaved as well as you could in the circumstances. If they subsequently find a job to which they are better suited, they may even thank you in the long run.

The saying 'never waste a crisis' is also relevant here. When your market is declining or the economy is struggling, letting people go is far easier for them to understand as well as easier to justify internally. COVID enabled many managers to address people issues in their business, sometimes out of necessity but also because the opportunity was there.

A good friend of mine who runs a family hospitality business saw his revenues collapse during the early months of COVID. He'd built up an adequate 'rainy day' fund (and boy was it pouring) and made use of government support schemes, so the business was not in danger of going under. However, the crisis did allow him to huck out some long-serving deadwood in an organization whose culture had been to leave underperformers in place, hoping, in vain, that they'd improve.

Those he let go could tell themselves it wasn't them, it was COVID, and he could tell stakeholders and senior management that he needed to make the business leaner because who knew what the future held? There was enough truth in both of these assertions that the narrative worked. And, in retrospect, my friend reckoned it was one of the best things he had ever done, with morale and effectiveness across the organization immediately picking up.

I have seen numerous businesses using the opportunity presented by the COVID crisis to do similar things. Yes, it's a bit cynical. But it's nowhere near as cynical as many people think – and using a crisis in this way can actually deliver a good outcome (or the least-worst outcome) for everyone involved.

Performance management outside business

Performance management of the sort I've described may be harder to implement in the public and third sectors. A culture of 'jobs for life', a natural acceptance of underperformance or a focus on esoteric success indicators can create a difficult environment for a manager who wants to be effective. This is one of many reasons (full disclosure: another is the money) that I have limited experience of these sectors.

That said, I find organizations with cultural or other barriers to sacking people fascinating. What do they do with their underperformers? The answer is they often find creative ways of sidelining them or giving them impressive-sounding but fairly powerless jobs (politics is a case in point here).

Another method that works for individual managers in large organizations is simply to send useless people far, far away. Here I'm always reminded of Lawrence Durrell's marvellous short stories about diplomatic missions in the *Antrobus* collection. Durrell's narrator maintained that the only way to get rid of an incompetent underling in the Foreign Office was to promote them so that they reached a level where they would be posted elsewhere. Once you start looking you realize this sort of perverse incentive is surprisingly widespread in large organizations.

I have also come across situations where the absence of a hierarchical structure or Byzantine arrangements mean that there is no means of assessing and reflecting performance, particularly where boards of trustees are too distant or dysfunctional to undertake these actions. Here, you can often see and feel that something is wrong, but to actually prove it you need to build a case and this takes real detective work.

I once worked with a charitable organization where the organizational structure meant that the de facto CEO had very little accountability. He was the only person who understood what was going on and a series of random committees held notional control over individual areas. The CEO was the only common member of all these committees and this gave him extraordinary power, combined with the ability to avoid responsibility. Personally, he was a decent and pleasant man, but wholly inefficient and ineffectual, because he had been allowed to do only what he was interested in, with no one in a position to point out his failings or rein in his dodgy and off-piste enthusiasms such as building development. He was a poor delegator (no surprise as his power was based on not delegating), was never prepared for any meetings of the many committees he sat on and all his many direct reports spent most of their time trying to second-guess him.

I took this as a challenge as there was a clear impact on the charity's core activities not least in terms of its financial viability. My approach was to play to one of my strengths and not to challenge him directly. I decided that the best way to find out what was going on was to follow the money and get to the bottom of the financials. Then I consistently and doggedly challenged all the financial information being provided to the trustees (who had very little commercial nous themselves) particularly wherever I was on a committee. I also sought appointment to as many related committees as possible so that I could get a grip on the broader picture rather than the tiny slice which my committee was exposed to.

A key element was to understand the accounts which no one apart from the CEO and his competent but browbeaten and second-guessing financial controller could follow at all, with costs and income streams appearing to pop up in unintelligible lines of the contorted accounts. Drilling into the numbers is something I enjoy. There is a narrative there which can generally be uncovered eventually and explained to others. Having got a handle on what was going on (although to this day there is quite a lot I never bottomed out), one could then start to see where the strategies were wrong and / or not known apart from to the man himself as well as identifying the inefficiencies. I could then ask the right questions at the committee meetings and point out to everyone around what was happening and let them pick up on what shouldn't be happening.

As others became aware of how dysfunctional the management structure and information flow was and understood more about what was happening, the CEO's position weakened. As a result he felt undermined and under pressure. Eventually and reluctantly he acknowledged that it was best for all if he retired. His departure immediately lightened the mood for everyone and his replacement's openness has meant a properly functioning organization with well-informed decision-making which is far better placed to deliver on its purpose. The turnaround here has transformed a loss-making but important entity into a national champion.

Who wields the axe?

A key question when removing people is who should do the actual deed. To me, this comes back to the importance of locking together power and responsibility in the organization. This means that the person who makes the decision should take responsibility for it and for managing the meetings leading up to and including the delivery of the bad news. In large companies, some prefer to let HR take the lead and I have some sympathy here. Getting rid of people is a technical process with numerous legal and related issues. Moreover, HR have the experience here and so know their way around presenting it in as unpleasant a way as possible. In smaller businesses, this isn't an option.

Personally, whether it is a big or small organization, I feel this is part of leadership. Doing it yourself shows respect for the person involved. By all means, take along an HR person or notes from your outsourced supplier as support, especially if you're inexperienced in this area. But the bad news must come from you. As for the approach shown in *Up in the Air*, the film where George Clooney is a disconnected, dispassionate consultant who flies around the US telling people they've been fired on behalf of his clients, it is shocking and depressing that such roles actually exist. Shame on those who outsource the unpleasant parts of management like this.

The good news, perhaps, is that these final meetings rarely turn really nasty. If the communication leading up to the final meeting has been clear and the outcome is obvious, there is usually less horror than expected. Indeed, on multiple occasions, I have received extraordinary calls from managers who have just sacked someone. They have reported that the experience has been better than expected, sometimes even good.

Why is this? To invoke the Classics here, Xenocrates the Greek philosopher said you can only have a finite amount of pleasure or pain from one experience. This explains, for instance, why you rarely enjoy that party you were massively looking forward to as much as you thought you would. You have used up so much of the pleasure in anticipation. Pain works in the same way. When you have spent weeks dreading the moment of telling someone they are losing their job, you have used up all the pain. Thus, particularly when the news is not taken too badly, you often leave the meeting that's been looming over you feeling strangely elated.

There is no need in a properly managed business for senior management to do more than highlight that the cost base has got out of shape in individual areas of operation. Generally, where the axe should fall is best left to the local managers who should already know that their cost base is unsustainable. It is they who should look out for opportunities to trim, ideally based on natural wastage but not funking where something more brutal is required.

Managing bastards

So far, we've looked at sacking people who are merely incompetent. But what about people who are actually nasty? People who play politics, shaft colleagues, treat others badly and make trouble – or worse? What about them – and what if they're good at their jobs?

Genuine bastards (and I'm using this in a gender-neutral way) are actually pretty rare in business. A lot of people who you think are real bastards are just situational bastards. They're in a bad situation and this makes them behave badly. Improve their lot, *et voilà*, no more bastard. There are also large numbers of people who have some negative character traits but who are valuable and, with careful management, can work out. For example, if someone really delivers the goods but is very high maintenance, you might find a way of giving them the attention they need because they're worth it.

But every now and then you encounter an immutable bastard – someone who is toxic because they're toxic. In a work context, this is usually a person who will damage the business or other people in order to better their own position. They will lie and deceive and manipulate and screw you over. In my experience, they are also very canny. There is only one solution here. They are not going to change – so you have to sack them.

This is true even if they are good at their job, because the toxic effects they have on the rest of the company will always outweigh any good they do. The classic example of this is the superstar salesman whose behaviour is tolerated because their figures are so good. Once you factor in how miserable they make everyone else, you soon realize they're still a net negative.

My own biggest bastard was the manager of one of the business units at a company where I had recently been appointed CEO. The warning signs were there for all to see. At our first meeting, he roared up in an Aston Martin. One of the first things he told me smilingly was that the best thing for me to do was to sell him the business as soon as possible. He didn't even bother to frame it as a joke; rather it was said with considerable malice and in a way that that made it very clear that the subtext was 'F*** you.' Of course, I understand that not everyone in a troubled company is going to welcome a new CEO with open arms. But a direct 'I don't give a s***' challenge to your authority is a huge red flag.

The red flags kept coming. This particular division had offshored the manufacture of its products to a series of ever-cheaper developing countries – which ran the gamut from Morocco and Ukraine to Vietnam and eventually Bangladesh. In fact, this was the key to its continued success. It meant we could hold prices for customers while maintaining profit margins. When I (very courteously) asked to see the contracts – not an unreasonable request from a CEO to a divisional head – I was told that they were all in the bloke's head and too complicated for me to understand.

Again, this should have sent alarm bells ringing. What he was saying was, 'No. I am not giving you this information.' Again, effectively, 'F***you.' At this point I should have said to him, 'Yes you are because I am the CEO, I answer to the shareholders and business is not a democracy. If you have a problem with this then I have a problem with your continued employment.' Shortly after my first meeting with the bastard, I asked to come to one of the bastard's division's board meetings. He said, 'If you insist you can, but we'll have the real meeting before or after you come.' Again, f*** you. I was reminded that the outgoing CFO had warned me that this man was a problem and one who needed to be dealt with.

So why didn't I? All the usual reasons. Nobody enjoys direct confrontation and we all like to think that, with a mixture of charm and persuasion, we can convert even the most difficult employees to our cause. When a problem is not truly pressing, it is always tempting to give it time and see if it resolves itself.

The biggest factor here though was that the bastard had leverage. At various points in the past, this division had been an independent business. This meant he was viewed by his staff as still being the CEO. They were fiercely loyal to him, not me. They were not bastards though. In fact, they were mostly great, hard-working people who were passionate about their jobs. But they had been corrupted and lied to. The manager had told them that I was screwing his division over by favouring another division over his. It was entirely untrue, but they believed it. They saw me as the enemy.

I voiced my concerns but the company board's response was that with so many problems across the group we had to tolerate his behaviour until we were out of the woods. Unsurprisingly, with similar funks having become part of the company's culture we simply headed further into the woods.

He knew I couldn't tolerate him but his stance with me was, 'If you sack me, I will take my senior management with me. Then you will be left with a near worthless division. You will have nobody who understands the contracts and you have nobody who knows how to run the business.'

It was blackmail and it worked. But I should have called his bluff and that I didn't would cause me huge headaches further down the line. Later, I discovered that he was also playing politics with his division's results and forecasts. This would be one of (admittedly several) reasons we breached our banking covenants (agreements). The disaster breaching the covenants set off would eventually slash the company's value by over 90 per cent. On top of all this, he was leaking negative stories to the press. He was sabotaging the business from within.

I now realize that I was overestimating his leverage and his people's loyalty. Most people are loyal to bosses but only up to a point. Their greater loyalty is to their income and family. Had I sacked the bastard, his management team would have grumbled and hated me for a few weeks. But they'd have adapted the new reality pretty quickly. I now believe most, if not all, of them would have stayed. The lesson here then is that once you know you have an immutable bastard, you have to sack them immediately. Fail to address the problem, whatever the short-term cost, and you are storing up far greater trouble for the future.

This story has a happy ending of sorts though. The man in question outlasted me and went on to buy the business just as he had told me he would. However, having very belatedly realized just how toxic he was, one of my last acts as a CEO was to line up an alternative management team to step into his shoes and replace anyone who left with him. This meant he no longer had the leverage he once did. Having been so sure of himself and believing that the company now had an alternative to falling in with his plan, he and his backers paid a high price for the business, taking on significant debt. This was despite there being no further supply-chain savings to be made and a likelihood that his profit margins would come under pressure. It went bust within a year.

I didn't entirely funk sacking every bastard though. On another occasion, I found myself dealing with a manager who was physically intimidating his staff. He was good at his job but bullied those under him and customers were complaining. It was clear he had to go. Even so, I tolerated his behaviour for far longer than I should have, not least because I thought he might knock me flat (for which he reportedly had history in his local community) if I told him he was fired. I also excused my cowardice by noting to myself that his area of business was not underperforming.

Eventually I screwed up my courage to do the sacking in person and also asked my secretary to ensure that two of our toughest engineers (who had reputations as Friday-night brawlers) were near my office, should things go wrong. In fact, the bastard in question was expecting it. He appeared to look shocked, his shoulders slumped and then he overturned my desk and stormed out. The results were gratifying – the cloud over his business and his people lifted almost immediately. I should have sacked him sooner but at least I sacked him.

In another group CEO role, I inherited a divisional MD who was running the business that he had sold to the group. He was a 'Hail fellow, well met' chap, whose chumminess disguised his laziness and focus on his own interests. His business was going through an understandably rough patch, but I received continual assurances that it was soon to come good. I was fighting fires across the group and a friendly face asking me to trust him to sort things out was a relief, so I let him get on with it and didn't probe to deeply.

It took well over a year of continuing losses before I cottoned on that he was doing nothing apart from hoping that the market would improve. As the fires went out across the group, I finally focused on exactly what he was doing and only then realized that he had been feathering his own nest with chunky 'entertainment' expenses, retaining his old pals and removing those who might blow the whistle on him. When my insistent probing got too much for him, he resigned and set up his own business based on trying to pinch his few profitable accounts. I virtually never resort to legal sanction but, in this case, I turned up at his house with lawyers in tow to tell him that I would pursue him viciously if he persisted in his new venture at the group's expense. As a lazy and fundamentally weak man, this did the trick and I could start to sift through the wreckage of his division.

In all three cases, it took me far longer than it should have to lance an obvious and nasty boil. It's the same as it always is with people who are an insoluble problem. You get rid of them. Here again, I failed to grasp the nettle promptly because grasping nettles is not pleasant. But not grasping them is much worse. The problem eats away at you and saps your mental energy; it's always there in the background. And the second you deal with it, you wish you'd done it months ago.

On the other hand

Very occasionally, the human element is more important than the efficiency of the organization. I was appointed chair of a small members' club. It wasn't a role I relished but the club is a curious one where a member wanting to be the chair is immediately discounted on that basis alone.

My predecessor pointed out that, as all the members knew, the club secretary was superannuated and a priority of my chairmanship was obviously to find a replacement for him. The secretary was a delightful man who had taken the role 20 years previously after a distinguished and long career in the armed forces. He was incredibly loyal and hard-working, but was believed to be approaching 80 years old (nobody knew his actual age) and the quill-pen based systems which he had inherited were still in place. Despite his enthusiasm for the club, there were increasingly frequent muddles attributable to virtually non-existent IT and his occasional senior moments.

In my first few months, I suggested that we might consider putting in place some sort of succession plan on a timescale to suit him. He was nonplussed. The following day, I received a formal and polite letter, noting that if I wished to be rid of him, he would tender his resignation immediately. I called him straight away to recant my suggestion, noting that it was up to him to choose when he wished to resign. The subject was never mentioned again and he was still in post when I enthusiastically handed on the chairmanship five years later.

Feebleness on my part? I certainly paid for it by having to double-check quite a lot of what the secretary did, and field a few members' complaints about the club's inefficiencies. But the club could afford to be run inefficiently, it still provided its core service to the members, and the secretary was a very decent man who loved his role. I don't think I funked a decision there.

10
BIG MONEY

'But a certain limitation of mind seems to be an indispensable asset, if not to all public personages, at least to all serious financiers.'
FYODOR DOSTOEVSKY, *THE IDIOT*

How start-ups are funded, the relationship between CEOs and their banks and what happens when you and the bank fall out (it really ain't pretty). A little history of the financial sector, the ins and outs of private equity and quoted companies, how to deal with investors and, finally, using the Indian Rope Trick to grow a plc.

Banks in principle, and a little history

If you've got your business flying, at some point you're going to have to deal with the financial markets. You may not need them in certain sectors but generally there comes a point where every ambitious company needs to engage with Big Money.

Bankers have taken a reputational battering in recent years and rightly so. In fact their decline in public respect pre-dates the 2008 financial crisis – and this is down to how banking has changed.

Banking used to be a well-rewarded function with some social responsibility for processing non-cash transactions (which is why the main banks are called 'clearing banks') and managing a flow of funds from those with money (depositors) to those who needed money (borrowers). It has now morphed into a honeypot for those working in the industry whose irresponsible behaviour has negative impacts on wider society.

To be fair, this isn't exactly new. In 1940, Fred Schwed wrote a book called *Where Are the Customers' Yachts?* The title came from a story about a visitor to New York around the turn of the twentieth century who was admiring the yachts of the bankers and brokers. Naively, he asked where all the customers' yachts were. Of course, none of the customers could afford yachts, even though they dutifully followed the advice of their bankers and brokers.

In the twenty-first century, not much has changed. The primary cause of the financial crisis was over-lending to uncreditworthy customers and selling these loans on to unsuspecting third parties. This allowed the intermediaries, particularly the bankers, to make a lot of money as they took a percentage of every sale.

It's important to make the distinction between banks and investment banks here. The former's main role is taking deposits and lending while investment banks are a misnomer as their function is primarily advisory and financial trading activities.

The confusion between banking and investment banking has arisen before. The US Glass-Steagall Act which was introduced in 1933 was designed to prevent depositors' money being used in the casino of financial trading. By the 1960s it had become less robust and it became weaker still in the 1980s. It was repealed in 1999 and the repeal was perceived as acknowledging that it was no longer functioning as intended.

The response to the financial crisis in many countries (including the UK following *The Vickers Report*)) was to the ringfence the retail operations of the banks from their wholesale and investment banking activities. But, whatever one's thoughts on the morality and pay packets of the bankers (and the total absence of confirmed culpability for any individual as governments poured billions into the banking system to save the banks from what they'd created), it's a rare CEO of a company of a certain scale who hasn't had to deal with them. They are a necessary evil.

What a CEO wants from banks

Ideally, a CEO wants their bank to be like any other supplier, providing goods to which value can be added by their company's processes. The cost should be keen and the service efficient. And, like any other customer, the terms of payment should be met.

The difference is that the bank ultimately wants its goods back, or at least it wants to know that it can get the goods back. This is not so different from other suppliers. However, other suppliers have few tools to ensure they get paid beyond cutting off supplies and taking the company to court for non-payment. Once delivered and invoiced, the goods cannot be recovered, particularly in the case of services. Banks are different. They know that it's easier to put money in than to get it out – and so they have developed many tools to get their money back out, should they wish to do so.

These include sitting at the front of any queue for repayment. This means that, in most tricky situations, they are the stakeholder most keen to pull the plug. They can then recover money from those who owe money to the company ahead of other suppliers. They usually have access to management accounts so they can keep an eagle eye on when they can get all or most of their money back from a struggling enterprise.

Many entrepreneurs will find a bank willing to lend money, with a small clause that a personal guarantee is required. Be very careful! Signing a PG means the bank can take all your assets if your company cannot repay the bank. They'll probably stop short of kicking you out of your house but they will definitely expect you to pay rent once they own it. Until I had reached the fortunate position where I knew I could comfortably cover any debts of a business I was a significant shareholder in, I never signed a PG. I don't recommend anyone does, however high their confidence is in their business.

Banking covenants are another area to watch. These are small, individual agreements signed between the bank and the company. They mean the bank can call the shots as soon as there is a covenant breach (which, with a struggling company, there usually will be) and can often effectively end the life of the business.

The banks are ruthless. Arguments that putting companies into receivership is bad PR and so on will have almost no effect. The jolly bank marketeer who was your best friend when you took out the loan swiftly disappears behind the credit analysts who crunch the numbers on whether the bank is going to get its money back.

So a CEO, as well as their CFO, needs to understand the *modus operandi* of the banks and work out the scenarios where the bank might start muscling in. They should negotiate hard on the bank covenants when the sun is shining and the bank wants to lend. The banks know the value of the covenants and too many optimistic entrepreneurs unthinkingly sign off covenants making them a hostage to the banks when the business wobbles.

Creative debt

The famous UK industrialist Lord Hanson always said that a key element of the success of Hanson Trust, the doyenne of conglomerates in the late twentieth century, was down to his business partner, Sir Gordon White. 'Gordy,' he explained, 'introduced me to gearing.'

It's not complicated. Gearing refers to a company's debt-to-equity ratio, which means the extent to which a firm's operations are funded by lenders versus shareholders. Debt in a successful company with decent cash flow is far cheaper than equity (partly because interest paid on debt is tax deductible, which is a long-running bone of contention). So, if you want to grow and you do so by borrowing money cheaply, you'll end up with far higher returns for your investors, including hopefully yourself.

This can be taken to extremes by private equity companies who will tolerate far higher debt levels than quoted companies. At the other end of the borrowing spectrum are family-owned companies who don't want to bet the ranch just to make more money.

Sometimes, the debt is overcooked and, particularly in an economic downturn, the company can't foot the interest bill, let alone repay the capital. But for many private equity operators, this is part of the maths. The odd company goes down but that doesn't invalidate the overall model. And the private equity firm usually holds much of its investment in the riskier part of the debt which, like the banks, ranks ahead of the company's suppliers in the repayment queue. So, even if things go wrong, hey-ho, they often get back much of what they put in.

This occasionally results in scenarios so awful they're almost funny. I know of a private equity company which put a delivery company that it owned into receivership on Christmas Eve after all the parcels had been delivered. This meant the amount of money owed by its customers was huge and therefore recoverable by the lender-owners. Its suppliers who had actually delivered the Christmas presents never got paid and many followed the company into receivership, losing their businesses and their investments.

So, if you're going to play the 'creative debt' game, understand the rules – and examine your conscience. There will be a lot of temptation to make a fortune by doing the wrong thing.

How to keep the banks off your back

The key here is to understand the cash movement through your business. The only daily KPI I insisted on for many years as the CEO of a successful business was knowing the level of cash and debt in the business.

I needed to do this in the early days of that business as we were constantly about to exceed our borrowing limits. But once we were out of the woods, I continued doing it for the next decade. I knew the days on which the payroll and VAT payments went out, even when the banks were very comfortable with their debt position and regularly offering us more money.

Many dramatic collapses – such as Carillion in 2018 – occur when management has lost touch with its cashflows. In Carillion's case, huge revenues at low margins meant that cash generation was impossible to trace. This was combined with a massive numbers of debtors and creditors who were owed or owed many multiples of profit, not that there was any of that when the final scores on the doors were calculated. Naturally the banks could get their hands on the mountains of money owed to them when the emperor was revealed to have no clothes – unlike Carillion's suppliers and even the government.

For most businesses, working capital turns into cash when the business shrinks as debtors exceed creditors so more money is collected than paid out. But in areas such as retail, the money arrives in the till before suppliers have to be paid. A downturn in sales usually means that as the money shrinks in the till, suppliers have to be paid and the cash is rapidly sucked out of the business. Without a decent cash buffer at all times, a retailer that is playing fast and loose will often be revealed when a recession hits.

Decades ago, there was something to be said for the relationship you had with your local bank manager. But there is no point cultivating modern 'relationship managers' at banks now. Gone are the days of 'Captain Mainwaring' – the 1930s bank-manager co-opted into the Home Guard in the TV comedy series *Dad's Army* – types topping up the local garage owner's borrowings on the back of a chat at the golf club.

Certain banks looking to gain a foothold have been successful in allowing their local bank managers to be a more sophisticated version of Captain Mainwaring though. These banks are bringing back the long-forgotten model where the local bank manager had a reasonable amount of responsibility for both making loans (typically under £500k in today's market) and monitoring the loans themselves. This has worked, primarily because smart local companies like to know that the person lending the money has a feel for the business. But with many large banks, trying to find the faceless credit analyst who can give you a feel for where their algorithms are going to place you is pointless. So, keep an eagle eye on your cash position at all times.

What happens when you fall out with the banks

I'd like to tell you it's not as bad as you think. But actually it's worse.

I was once appointed to run a business that was 'in workout'. This is a euphemism for when the banks want to guarantee the recovery of their money and so want to influence how the company is run. Once was enough. I never want to be in that position again, except where I'm brought in on the understanding that they are the boss. And I don't really fancy that either. But it's worth a brief look at where I went wrong and why it was so bad.

I made the truly cataclysmic error of assuming that because the business was fundamentally OK, the banks would cut me some slack. They wouldn't. I also imagined my role was to protect the shareholders' interests. This meant I failed to understand that the banks held all the cards (as mentioned earlier, they just wanted their money) and it was in their gift to determine if anything was to be left over to the shareholders.

The situation was not helped by the lead bank 'selling' my company's debt to another of its divisions whose terms of engagement were similar to those of a bailiff: they would be paid a percentage of whatever was recovered. This division was headed by one of the nastiest financiers I have ever worked with. His team was incentivised by their bonuses being determined by how much debt they recovered compared to the amount they had paid for debt internally.

If the company went into receivership, the likely outcome for the specialist banking division was a full recovery as the business was owed a lot of money. So the harder they pushed the business in this direction, the bigger their individual bonuses were likely to be. Even the anodyne report by the UK's Financial Services Authority into this particular banking division in later years notes this 'could have led to poor behaviours if staff believed (for example) that they would get better pay and rewards by focusing on the division's commercial objective, which risked the consequential poor treatment of customers.' Pity the poor bloody company who falls foul of such divisions (and have some small sympathy for its idealistic dreamy CEO who was still fighting the good fight).

It wasn't just the bankers either. As part of the 'recovery process', accountants were instructed (at huge cost) to review forecasts. A shrewd and unpleasant divisional MD, who was hoping to acquire his division from the wreckage, promptly slashed his internal forecasts in his presentation to the accountants. This left the company with forecasts in breach of its banking covenants – something which, as a plc, had to be announced publicly. I suspect this man also had a nice sideline of leaking bad news to a hungry press.

Following the announcement, a visit from the credit insurers followed. These poorly understood operators guarantee payments to suppliers. Having credit insurance removed is tantamount to the suppliers being told that they are unlikely to be paid for their goods and services. So the company loses most of its suppliers, unless the banks undertake that the bills will be paid.

Probably the most directly unpleasant experience is the one mentioned earlier where eventually, I found myself alone in a room with the bankers, the rest of the board having discovered they were 'unavailable' that day. I was surrounded. There were 16 of them and I was beaten. It was the financial equivalent of being beaten up by a gang of skinheads.

One of my oppressors moved in again and raised his boot. This was the Americanised German who'd flown in from Frankfurt for the sport. 'Mr Skinner,' he barked, 'did you not say three months ago that this particular division was worth over £100m?' He looked around the board table at his fellow gang-members who nodded appreciatively at the elegance of this latest assault.

I struggled weakly to my feet. 'No,' I said. 'In time, given proper investment, it could be worth that much.'

This was the cue for the next punk to step in, eyeing his notepad like a skinhead springing his flick knife as he approached a quivering opponent, possibly looking to slice an ear off as a trophy. 'Did you not say one of the struggling businesses' business was to be sold for at least £12m? Could you now explain why the best offer you have is less than £10m?'

Rather feebly, I offered, 'Given the market's awareness of our current weak banking position, it is unsurprising that potential purchasers are taking advantage of our need to raise money rapidly and thus reduce their indicative offers.'

'Are you not aware that the deterioration in profits that you have revealed today puts the company in severe danger of breaching its banking covenants at either or both of the tests at the end of this year and at next half-year?'

By now, after the measured thrashing of the last two hours, it seemed that recklessness was in order. I gave it my best and final shot, 'Yes, but given your group's requirement that any covenant renegotiation would be on the assumed basis that the covenants were breached anyway, it seemed in the best interest of shareholders to attempt to pass the covenant test…'

Before I could dig myself into a deeper hole, the man from the building society which was new to banking leapt in for the coup de grace. 'Are you not aware that your fiduciary duty as a director of the company is to act in the interests of those with the primary financial interest in the company and' – he glared triumphantly around the room – 'that now appears to be this group.'

The room sighed in admiration at this beautifully executed manoeuvre – even the men from the Far-Eastern bank who had been impassive in the face of the earlier savagery nodded sagely and appreciatively. I was now Alex after his treatment in *A Clockwork Orange* or Winston Smith slumping out of Room 101.

'What is it you want?' I croaked. A sigh of satisfaction echoed around the room.

I was taken out by the banking advisers who, by this stage, had assumed the role of paramedics. They patched me up – so I could return to hear the terms. There were no real surprises here. Of course, they had no wish run the company (why would they when beating up well-meaning CEOs paid just as well and was far more fun?). So they'd leave me to it, subject to the usual tributes and with advisers swarming over the company to maximize the spoils for the conquerors.

The lesson is clear. Make sure you understand the terms of engagement with the banks. Woe betide the CEO who believes the banks want to support a business when it's in trouble. Their only driver is recovering their money – and, to be fair, that's what their job is.

The ABCs of PE

Private equity has come a long way over the last 30 years and is now a popular asset class for many institutional investors like pension funds.

The fundamental idea is that large companies can be owned privately, with the majority of shares held by one or more PE funds whose goal is to increase the value of the company over the period of its ownership. This will typically be three to six years as the fund will normally return money to its investors within 10 years – and take a chunky cut of the profit generated in addition to management fees.

Like any mature market, private equity is now heavily segmented. Huge PE firms with billions under management compete with global trade buyers and one another for multi-billion dollar companies. Mid-market PE firms woo large private companies and stalk smaller public companies looking for opportunities where the public market may not have spotted value. And smaller firms look for retirement sales, businesses with dynamic management whose growth plans they can fund, and potentially valuable mismanaged companies.

Angel investors like backing entrepreneurs who want to move things forward but may need money and advice to do so. A friend and I recently acquired 20 per cent of an IT consultancy where the owners wanted to take some money out of the business but also wanted help in professionalising the business for a sale ahead of their retirement. The key element in our decision to invest was respecting and liking the owner-managers.

Finally, there are small and large venture capitalists who are genuinely deserving of the old-fashioned name. They don't shuffle the financial pack but take genuine risks by backing early-stage investments. Their skill is finding the next Google and avoiding the next 'fake it til you make it' business like Theranos.

Venture capital (VC)-backed start-ups and early-stage investments have been the top-performing area for private equity in recent years. Many companies, especially tech companies, have been valued at huge multiples of sales (they are almost never making profits at this stage) and the big winners have more than made up for the much more numerous losers. But the market has become crowded and the glory days of pre-revenue next big things may be drawing to a close.

A little more history (this time on private equity)

Today's enormous, high-profile venture capital and private equity industry is a far cry from the first major UK VC firm, Investors in Industry (now 3i), where I toiled for seven years.

3i was set up after the war to address the 'Macmillan Gap'. This was named after the Macmillan Committee (nothing to do with the Prime Minister, Harold Macmillan), which had identified a need to provide capital to private companies that wanted to expand but couldn't find sources of funding. It was owned and funded by the nation's clearing banks (whose arms were twisted to achieve this goal).

For many years, 3i had the market pretty much to itself and developed an independent and buccaneering spirit, despite its quasi-state ownership. It almost always took minority shareholdings and let the management get on with it. It never sold its holding unless the whole company was sold and much of its returns came via dividends.

A major boost to its holdings came when a junior lawyer noted that private companies could avoid death duties by having a minority shareholder. EDITH (Estates Duties Inheritance Trust Holdings) duly ended up with 20 per cent plus holdings in many of the UK's bigger private companies.

3i was probably at the height of its powers in the early 1990s when it had a network of regional offices which invested in businesses of all sizes. A young 'controller' like me would often find themselves investing £50k of 3i's money in a local, expansion-minded engineering company and such small investments were considered part of the training for larger investments.

3i made many good investments, but, as the years passed, it also wound up with a long tail of 'the living dead'. These were investments which had often been made years or even decades earlier. Typically they were companies which were stumbling along, paying no dividends and often supplying no or limited management accounts.

This led to many situations which now seem like something from a sepia-tinted past. On one occasion, a highly driven clothing entrepreneur who would go on to be a great success rang me out of the blue. His trouser delivery from a Scottish company was chaotically late. It was a 3i investment and could I apply pressure? I managed to get hold of the 3i controller in Aberdeen who was notionally responsible for the investment. After a bit of digging around, the controller responded that we were indeed an investor but he'd never heard of the company and there had been no communication for over five years: he couldn't help.

In the early 90s, this gentlemanly way of doing things was changing fast. 3i had become increasingly independent of its generally uninterested bank shareholders and was considering a public flotation. It had opened international offices across Europe and in the US. The sale of its stake in the airline British Caledonian had netted it £100m. What was the financial sense in backing an ambitious corner shop to the tune of £50k which could only ever be a trivial distraction in terms of meaningful returns?

Moreover, the financial landscape was changing. Large management buyouts (helping management buy out the existing owners, usually by borrowing) were increasingly where the big returns were being made. New concepts were being introduced. These included management buy-ins (new management being backed to buy and manage private companies) and BIMBOs (buy-in-management buyouts – an acronym unlikely to be coined today). The latter usually meant a couple of dynamic managers joining the existing management team.

However, the biggest reason the market was changing was 'carried interest'. This is a form of compensation paid to investment executives in areas like private equity, hedge funds and venture capital managers – it means they get paid a percentage of the fund's profits. Somewhat confusingly for laypeople, it has nothing to do with interest rates. The term actually dates from the sixteenth century. Captains of European ships sailing to Asia and the Americas would take a 20 per cent share of the profit (their 'interest') from the 'carried' goods to pay for the cost transport and to compensate them for the risk of sailing across oceans.

3i staffers had been reasonably well paid, but, increasingly, new competitors were being run along the lines of US private equity firms. Leveraged buyouts (which were basically MBOs but with much more debt chopped into different slices of precedence) were becoming all the rage across the Atlantic. KKR's acquisition of RJR Nabisco was probably the most famous of these and gave us one of the greatest business books ever written – *Barbarians at the Gate* (written by Bryan Burrough and John Helyar; 1989).

The managers of private equity firms would raise capital and acquire majority stakes in companies, charging management fees and taking a chunk of the proceeds, through carried interest. Ultimately this has meant that one of the quickest and easiest ways to generate huge riches for senior management teams was to manage a private equity fund rather than manage a business.

Many 3i employees could see which way the wind was blowing and left to set up their own private equity firms. 3i was floated in due course and the regional offices closed down. It is now a successful, but unremarkable, private equity firm (its fortunes boosted by one spectacular investment in the European supermarket chain, Ahold).

The closest thing the UK now has to the original 3i is the British Business Bank, a government-backed bank making soft-ish loans. Unsurprisingly, several old friends of mine from 3i work there.

The private equity cycle

PE funding raises an interesting question about authority – specifically when is a CEO not a CEO? An owner-manager has the power and authority to call all the shots (subject to occasional constraints from their banks). The non-owner CEO will often be hamstrung by controlling shareholders particularly when it comes to major strategic decisions. The CEO of a plc has to be mindful of the interests of their shareholders, but, in conjunction with her board, is generally in charge. And a private equity CEO?

Fundamentally, the CEO of a private equity-controlled business answers to their investors – and with PE, this usually means they're at the mercy of the investors' timeline. As a number of PE CEOs have told me, PE firms are focused on their exit right from the outset. Even when they're only considering an investment, they're thinking about how quickly they'll get out and how much they can make.

Some elements of this are absurd: the quicker the turn can be made, the higher the rate of return. A 50 per cent return over two years represents almost 25 per cent per anum, while 100 per cent over five years is just under 15 per cent per year. (You might reasonably think, 'Yes, but the security of nearly 20 per cent over five years has its attractions.')

But you're forgetting carried interest. PE has something called a 'hurdle rate' – this is the point at which carried interest kicks in. Normally this is about 8 per cent and the managers and fund share in anything above this.

So with a hurdle rate of, say, 8 per cent the 'quick flip' looks much more attractive – it's 14.25 per cent vs just under 7 per cent – over twice as much. If you want to be a member of the yacht-owning classes it's a no-brainer: you go for the high-earning quick flip, not the steady, long-term performer. The CEO won't be going to be allowed to get in the way of that.

However, with so much money sloshing around the PE firms, the traditional quick flip, which tends to rely on a dim-witted seller and no competition, has become rare. A great – which is to say terrible – example of how asymmetric-information quick flips used to work was British Rail's (pre-privatization) sale of Porterbrook to PE. Porterbrook was the division which owned BR's rolling stock. It was sold to PE in 1986 and flipped a few months later at a £300m profit for the PE backers and management.

The normal model now for PE is to access as many opportunities as possible and comb through them in the hope they can find an angle. The lengths they'll go to are impressive. Once, when I was looking for a chair or CEO role, I thought it might be worth contacting a few PE firms to see whether they had anything of interest. I was flattered how many responded but quickly realized the point of their call was invariably to see whether I had anything to bring to them where they might find an angle.

The sort of angles they're looking for include soft-soaping the owners and / or management to buy the business cheaply, identifying an exit to a buyer who is going to miss the opportunity this time but will pay more at a later date, seeing a structural change which can be made to improve margins, or a belief that, with better management or more investment, the business can deliver better returns.

Once acquired, PE-owned companies are pretty focused. The good ones and their CEOs will have a plan and get on with it. Usually it depends on the timescale. If the flip is a few years away, they will be prepared to take a lot of pain early on, with restructuring costs and other write-offs taken through the balance sheet early.

Then, get a bit of growth into the business with limited concerns about sales costs on the P&L. Next it's time to dress it up, to show topline growth (courtesy of the recent spend on sales) and improving margins (now is the time to slash costs). *Et voilà*! Improving revenues, profits up and ready for beauty parades in front of brokers desperate for a flotation mandate. Or a trade buyer who wants to enhance earnings. And failing that – flog it off to another PE fund who needs its next investment and can see their own angle.

PE operators are aware of the cynicism of stakeholders and the general public regarding their mission. The person in the street may not know what carried interest means, but they know that PE operators want to pay themselves huge bonuses, generate decent returns for the money invested in their funds and be able to roll the dice again.

As a result they often try to put a positive spin on these things. But it's unconvincing. My children's private school was acquired by a PE fund and much was made to concerned parents of the fund's educational links. Foremost amongst these was that CalPERS, the giant Californian teachers' pensions fund, was an investor in the PE fund. You can be pretty damn sure that CalPERS had no specific interest in investing in British private schools (just as the BR pension fund might have been invested in the fund that milked Porterbrook). However, any figleaf, no matter how flimsy, is handy when you're in private equity and don't want the stakeholders to get concerned. The stake was duly flipped in a few years.

So – private equity or quoted company?

First, a word about private companies – where the business is owned by an individual or a group such as a family.

Private companies have their own issues for an external CEO. Owners can be weird, irrational or downright difficult and many owners never fully let go of the reins. Long-established private companies (particularly those a couple of generations away from the founder) often have numerous descendant shareholders many of whom want to meddle or want rentiers' dividends based on what they believe they're entitled to.

Although this sounds (and can be) funny, it can also destroy companies. A once-great private cleaning company has numerous shareholders and has been brought to its knees by family members demanding dividends and arguing amongst themselves, like the sisters in Gormenghast over whom the cursed crown should rest with and why they've been let down.

However, external CEOs are not that common in large private companies. So, if you are a CEO of a sizeable business, the choice is usually between PE-owned and quoted companies.

The advantages of PE are many. The ability and willingness to take on a lot of debt tends to bring long-term advantages, particularly when you can post back the keys when it all goes wrong and move on to the next company where the benefits of high gearing are delivering above-market returns. But this is me being a bit glib and so below I've listed the main advantages of running a PE-backed business.

- You can get on with running and even restructuring the company without having to report what you're doing in the public arena. Many businesses need a good clear-out and it's pretty ugly to do this in public. Far better to wield axes and change structures when the only formally published material is the accounts which are lodged at Companies House nine months after the year end. These will, naturally, show huge losses due to complex financing structures resulting in zero corporation tax being paid, even by strongly performing companies.
- Most PE operators are very bright, as the rewards involved attract the smartest and best. They have probably researched the market deeply and thoroughly partly to justify their role.
- As active board members and with their teams of analysts behind the scenes, PE owners cut through the crap to get the most out of a company. They are intolerant of stupidity, vested interests (beyond their own) and ignorance about the macro trends.
- They can be helpful (although the question remains about why they stand at one remove from the trenches if they really like business).
- They generally have money to hand. When you're trying to buy a business for your company, a key point is being able to tell the vendor or his adviser that you have the money to do so. Often trade buyers (who are trying to run their own businesses and manage their balance sheets) are at a disadvantage against a PE fund which can write cheques at short notice because that's what they do.
- Many PE operators are sensible, particularly once they've done a decent number of deals. A friend who has chaired the British Venture Capital Association and witnessed the changes in PE over the last 35 years told me that he's reached the point where he only gets involved in

deals where he likes the people and the product (unsurprisingly leisure companies feature strongly in his group's portfolio). Possibly this wouldn't pass muster under some regimes but he's experienced, brilliant at picking winners and worth giving money to as an investor despite setting himself a limited range of investable companies.

- You're going to get paid much better if you get it right in a PE-controlled business than in a quoted company. Executive pay is rightly under scrutiny in the publicly quoted world, where mediocre performance in a midcap company seems to deliver £1m plus pa. But if you get it right as a PE CEO, you're going to see rewards that dwarf this.

- As a PE-backed CEO, you may also have the opportunity to 'go again'. A friend in technical film production went through four PE funds, taking money off the table every time his company was flipped between funds. Ultimately a French trade buyer was the patsy. They paid too much and lost my friend as CEO through their Gallic idiosyncrasies (although he'd got bored and made too much money by then anyway).

- Therein lies the slightly guilty secret of the PE industry. Values should ultimately be decided by long-term cash flows, and valuations should be benchmarked against public company valuations. However, there are always PE funds with money that needs to be invested and funds which need to sell businesses to return money to investors. Secondary and tertiary (and beyond) deals between PE funds keep the money churning through their system. You don't want to be in the PE fund which ends up with the overvalued company when the music finally stops.

I once advised a very successful young man who was running a public company. The company (but mainly him) was approached by a PE firm. They suggested the company should be taken private. The CEO would make much more money, could undertake further growth with plentiful access to capital, and wouldn't have to stand in the limelight revealing the company's ups and downs to the markets, the media and competitors. Should he do it?

It was up to him but my advice was 'No'. There were two reasons behind this. Firstly, he would remain his own boss if he delivered for his broad range of shareholders. Secondly, he could build a great company, which was responsible to all its stakeholders, rather than simply be part of a financial process enriching those he was answerable to.

I'm not sure he was that interested in my advice but the company remained public. However, the self-determination of running a public company is not all a bed of roses.

Why be a public company?

The difference between running a public company (which is listed on an exchange) and a private company should not affect day-to-day management. A company is not generally going to be any more or less successful because it is listed. But the public markets require specific skill sets and, like the banks, you need to understand the rules of engagement.

Businesses float for many reasons but often without the directors and major shareholders really understanding what being listed is all about. Public markets are strewn with unhappy managements and shareholders, who often feel a bit like fish flapping on the beach after the tide has gone out.

They're everywhere including the UK: the HUT Group traded at a 90 per cent discount to its much-vaunted offering price within a year, the HSS Group staggers on at a 95 per cent discount to its initial price, and has become one of the many corporate living dead – companies with tiny valuations whom everyone has given up on. But let's start with the good reasons to list on a market because there are plenty of them. These include:

- Owner managers feel this is a way to get some money out without losing control.
- Private equity firms may want to find an exit for their investment at a better price than a trade buyer or another PE firm will pay. Listing may also represent a technical exit for calculating the managers' carried interest plan.
- Growth businesses want to have access to future capital without having to find one-off investors.
- The profile of being a public CEO appeals to the CEO's vanity.
- Fragmented shareholder bases will like the liquidity. That is, investors can sell shares (not necessarily in huge quantities) easily at a price which is set by the markets.
- Current and future share option schemes for staff can be cleanly structured with a genuine exit available on maturity.
- A listed company can acquire other companies for shares either through placing shares or the vendors taking shares in payment.
- The publicity produced by going public may attract customers and the status of being listed may encourage suppliers and customers to gain confidence that they are dealing with a serious business.
- Finally, most of the world's great businesses of scale are public. All of them will have had to have 'gone public' at some point.

There are also plenty of downsides to being a public company, many of which are mirror images of the upsides.

- The shareholder director who imagines they have money on tap which can be accessed by selling shares will discover pretty quickly that the market considers directors' share sales, even on a tiny scale, as displaying a lack of confidence. It will punish the share price when directors sell. 'Liquidity events' (polite phrasing for receiving a chunk of cash) are always rare and holding shares in a smaller listed company is far from the 'money on tap' opportunity some might think. Over 25 years I've been involved in public companies, I've been fortunate to have a few, but careful planning, an acknowledged valid reason and market timing all need to be impeccable to turn shares you're connected with into spendable cash.

- The golden rule that it's always way easier to put money in than get it out works equally well when you're involved in a public company. Accountants understand this better than anyone, which is why a cautious CFO buying some stock in his own company is almost always a good 'buy' signal.

- The media much prefers to pillory a failing CEO than to praise a successful one. If you do well, you'll probably be ignored.

- Raise money for a deal or a significant investment that doesn't work out and you'll pretty soon find you and your company are *persona non grata* and have no access to future capital for at least a couple of years.

- If times are tough, staff find watching their shareholdings tumble and share options falling 'out of the money' demotivating.

- When something doesn't go right, your suppliers and customers will know very quickly – and your competitors, already pleased to have real-time, detailed information on your business, will be out there telling them.

- An unhappy shareholder may decide that they want out at virtually any price and will sell out every time there is a buyer, destroying both your share price and liquidity in the stock.

- As a director of a public company, you've got to get used to the rules. You need to start to think pretty hard about what to say when your mother asks you how work is going. Any stray comment may end up in the wrong hands and if you disclose any sensitive information, even accidentally, you'll be looking at a run-in with the regulators.

- You need to get used to paying lawyers, brokers, accountants at every turn with many straightforward actions requiring compliance with listed company rules and public disclosure. The sums involved are pretty hefty (think enormous documents and £250k), although less if you're quoted on a junior market such as AIM in the UK
- Large transactions (such as acquiring a sizeable business) may be subject to shareholder approval and require public fundraising. These can be time-consuming and put public companies at a relative disadvantage, compared to, say, a PE buyer who can write a cheque on the spot.
- You need to learn how to manage mechanisms such as the Regulatory News Services. Sometimes disclosing information 'because you have to' can be played to your advantage: announcing add-on acquisitions regularly; highlighting good contract wins; well-regarded shareholders buying into your stock; the likely impact of a competitor going under. But this is not necessarily part of the typical CEO skill set.

Understanding public company investors

My first real job was in investment management and I wasn't well suited to it. This was partly down to my stunning ignorance of the field on arrival – for the first few months, I thought that you bought shares from the company in question. With the rashness of youth, I also tended to take views on companies very quickly and not very objectively. This was memorably demonstrated by my first internal note being about Racal, the electronics business which was the parent company of the nascent Vodafone. In the note, I said that mobile phones were unlikely to catch on.

I was only there for a year, but that year gave me a half-decent understanding of professional investors that came in very handy later on.

Today's transparency, wide access to information and the speed at which that information is available means that even the most diligent fund managers struggle to have an edge. This wasn't necessarily the case 40 years ago when public information was harder to come by and insider trading laws were less established.

I remember once a very small stockbroker came to give a presentation to our investment team about a mid-sized plc. It appeared he knew very little about the business but he kept repeating with a broad grin that the company was going to 'do the numbers'. After the meeting, everyone went back to their desks, and placed orders with the stockbroker for the stock for their funds (and a few for themselves, fairly typical in those days) and the stockbroker received a big commission cheque for his efforts. The company's exceptionally strong results came out a couple of weeks later, the shares surged and the investment team congratulated themselves on their stock-picking abilities.

Those days are long gone. I believe that few fund management firms now deliver the required value to beat the market – and that investment trackers are the best exposure to equity markets for most stocks. There are a handful of investment areas such as genuine venture capital and small companies where fund managers can probably beat the market.

As a public company CEO, you need to understand what's driving the people who are the conduit for the money you want to get your hands on. The first thing to appreciate is that good professional investors make dispassionate decisions. As Dostoyevsky noted in *The Idiot*, 'But a certain limitation of mind seems to be an indispensable asset, if not to all public personages, at least to all serious financiers.'

Having a few successful financiers as good friends, I'd agree that many of the very best investors have a degree of the emotional dysfunctionality that comes with being dispassionate (it's alright, reader – they know who they are). But, although the bar is set very low, I'd say that investment professionals are probably amongst the nicest and smartest of the various tribes roaming around the bloated and extraordinarily greedy financial services industry.

Over the years, many fund managers have been very supportive of businesses I have run, providing money for expansion and often offering sensible advice. But never forget that their role is to make money for their investors. Their job is not to help the CEO out unless they feel it's in their fund's interests. They monitor their performance against other funds, know that a bad run will culminate in the removal of investors' funds and ultimately the risk of them of losing their job.

Fund managers have many different styles, including owning long-term, high-quality stocks, trading frequently to take advantage of what they perceive as market pricing anomalies, high-growth, momentum, specialising in sectors or types of company and so on. Long-term holders will probably hold few stocks but know absolutely everything about the companies, including studying anything that might be relevant to their investment.

A hard-working friend whose performance has made him an investment legend confirmed to me recently that he hadn't bought or sold a share for three years, apart from investing more in some existing holdings. People like this tend to be helpful investors who ask the right questions and often note things about your business and / or market which you weren't aware of.

Some investors want to get to know the management well over a period of time before investing. One highly successful fund manager saw me and my CFO every time we were making presentations but never invested. The fifth occasion we met him, it was the end of a long day, we were running late and our CFO was going to miss his train unless the meeting was very short. Believing the meeting would be the usual waste of time, we said that we only had 10 minutes, quickly ran through an abbreviation of our presentation and explained that we had no time for questions. The next day, the investor started buying our shares and built up a significant shareholding over the following year.

Generally successful investors in smaller quoted companies 'follow their winners' – they keep investing in companies as they grow if the business is going well. Occasionally they will take an initial position in a company almost as an option to be able to put more money into it as it grows. This means that when business is going well and the company needs more cash, you can tap up the market almost at will like a cash machine.

Just don't ever feel your investors are looking out for you and be aware that some of those kindly faces at meetings may be thinking very differently to you. Often I have presented to investors who are really only interested in finding out more information on the market and its implications for other shares they own. Some years ago, one of our suppliers, a quoted company, had developed a new product that was supposedly going to be a game-changer. In several meetings I found myself being quizzed in forensic detail about one of our smaller divisions to which the company in question was a supplier. The investors had little interest in us – they were trying to work out whether they should believe what the other company's management was telling them.

Finally, there is often a slightly sinister edge. When I was managing a company which was in trouble, a US hedge-fund manager contacted me frequently. He appeared very interested in picking up our shares at their new all-time low, asked extensive detailed questions and was clearly interested in my state of mind. Only when I discovered someone was shorting our shares on a huge scale did I put two and two together.

The rules for a public CEO

There's really only one rule for a CEO and their company if they want be highly regarded by the markets. HIT YOUR NUMBERS – and ideally exceed them by a little. Your numbers are your forecasts for the financial performance of the company, typically for the next two years. These forecasts are normally fed through to the wider world through the house broker's analyst who will be guided by the company as to what they think the future holds.

The moment all fund managers dread is an unexpected announcement (usually issued at 7am, which is why fund managers are up then) from a company they are invested in, reporting that profits are likely to be lower than previously indicated. These profit warnings can be dressed up in various ways and often will only appear in the third or fourth paragraph of the announcement, after some slightly upbeat points being made earlier on. But everyone knows that it's about the profit warning.

Investors hate these because not only do they reflect the fact that the company is going to make less money than expected, but it also suggests the management doesn't know what it's doing and something more fundamental is wrong. This is because everyone knows you must hit your numbers, so most senior management teams will try everything to avoid not hitting them.

The thinking is that if they've tried everything and still haven't got there, the problem runs pretty deep. This is why share prices get hammered on a profits warning and this is compounded by many shareholders wanting to sell their shares before worse news come out. The adage that 'profit warnings come in threes' is worth bearing in mind.

Profit warnings have their own language. I have put out an announcement that profits are 'broadly in line with market expectations'. This means, when translated, that profits are going to be 3–5 per cent below forecast; the company shares opened up 30 per cent down.

Obviously the simplest way to avoid this is to take under-promising and over-delivering to an extreme, where the market forecasts are always conservative and always hit. However, there are problems with this:

- The market will get used to the company beating its forecast and start to build in expectations that it will do this.
- Forecast numbers which show little improvement against previous results will suggest lower rates of growth and the share price will reflect this.
- The share price will reflect the caution and could be lower than it should be, meaning that raising new money will be more dilutive for existing shareholders
- Successful businesses generally take risks. If you're ambitious for your company, you've got to put your neck on the line sometimes.
- The CEOs who will do anything to avoid missing forecasts are numerous and in my view aren't going to make investors much money. Too many CEOs prefer to oversee a cautious, meandering business and receive too much pay for acting as custodians rather than getting on with the hard business of maximizing returns.
- My experience is that such over-cautious listed companies often get into ruts and deliver increasingly poor returns. This is fine for an owner-managed business but not when you're being paid to deliver the best for your investors.

Only very foolish investors would expect a company to show consistent profit growth, but this is what most forecasts look like. Anyone who has run a business knows that, with the exception of companies like utilities, revenues and profits rarely square off against budget.

Particularly in smaller companies where performance is more volatile, most sophisticated investors know that some level of legal sand-bagging of profits in good years is undertaken to cover up for shortfalls in bad years. The CEO and his CFO are expected to manage this smoothing within limits. Examples of this include timing invoicing at year-end, delaying slightly in good years; taking provisions against bad debts and releasing them when needed; managing year-end cash balances by paying or not paying invoices or upping and downing credit control, and other legal shuffling.

When a CFO leaves a listed company, the first thing the new CFO will want to know is how much there is 'in the larder' and where it is. Incoming CEOs, as well as exiting CEOs, should know this too. But don't get on the wrong side of this, by emptying the larder and then thinking a few strokes of the CFO's pencil can fill a hole.

This is so often where big collapses happen: the construction firms overestimating work in progress, the contracting companies taking up-front payments and taking them into this year's revenues rather than spreading them out over the length of the contract, the roll-up businesses buying poor-quality but earnings-enhancing businesses to get them through a tricky year and storing up problems for the future, and so many more.

I've seen some shockingly uncommercial activity undertaken in a desperate fight to hit the numbers. A struggling company I'd joined had in the previous year effectively given away a business having a bad year so those activities could be recorded as 'discontinued', meaning the loss in that operation would not be part of the parent companies' full-year results. This was in spite of any actual value the business unit may have had.

When a profit warning comes without a truly exceptional reason like COVID ('poor weather' is rarely if ever accepted), savvy investors know that the elastic in financial reporting has been stretched too far and may well have snapped completely and a slew of further bad news is on its way.

Of course as a public company CEO you will have to formally announce what's gone wrong. Advisers will be insistent that news about any further problems is disclosed promptly. It's not just the stock market that will be following this either. Customers expecting to pay their annual gym membership may think twice if there's a chance the gym may go under. And suppliers will start getting concerned about their credit terms while the credit insurers will greedily lap up any bad news to see if they should remove their exposure. These disclosures thus often accelerate problems and a dreaded downward spiral ensues – which, again, you have to report publicly…

It doesn't stop there either. Next up, if you disappoint, you will be meeting the institutional shareholders. The best hope here is that the markets have been going well, their mood will be up and there's a chance of some thoughtfulness. Go to see a fund manager under pressure in tough markets with disappointing results and you're going to find out pretty quickly that they don't think much of you and your management skills.

So, how do you tread the difficult path between being ambitious for your business and not disappointing your shareholders?

I've had occasional disappointing results at every public company I've run (some more than others) and the experience is bruising for both you and the business. It will usually take two years of good results to get back on track, and you can forget about raising additional capital during that period, unless it's rescue capital – in which case a management change is generally a prerequisite.

If you arrive as a new CEO, the trick is to get all the bad news out as quickly as possible. This is called 'kitchen-sinking' and it means you can huck out and / or disclose all the bad news (and possibly more so that you can load up the larder for your new regime). You have about six months to identify and disclose all the FUFAs (foul-ups by the former administration) and this can get you off to a flying start. After then, it's all on you. I failed to do this once with disastrous consequences for everyone, most of all me.

As an incumbent CEO, you should be very familiar with all the forecasts in the market. Don't be relaxed about forecasts for the year after next – many leaders let their optimism and enthusiasm permeate through to future forecasts, which subsequently become rods for their own backs. Constantly monitor performance against what the market expects and look carefully for banana skins that might make you miss them.

Given how painful profit warnings are for all involved, you cannot issue them until you're more than, say, 75 per cent, certain you're going to miss your numbers. This leads to incredible concern the moment you receive any financial information whether it's daily sales figures or the monthly numbers from a small subsidiary. You're going to sleep very badly while this is going on. But once you've bitten the bullet, issued the warning and taken the flak, you generally feel better as you can get on with managing the business (assuming you're not removed) rather than worrying about what might save you.

The markets move up and down and you shouldn't get too upset when your shares fall alongside the market (but you should if they're underperforming a falling market). As part of this, I never like to issue shares at below market price if I can help it but it's also important not to demand the top price possible. If you want supportive shareholders it's always good for them to be holding shares above the price they paid. There's no point diluting existing shareholders unnecessarily, but if you overcook the pricing, you may find some new investors are resentful of overpaying.

Most CEOs believe their shares are undervalued and fail to see a reason for it. But a very shrewd investor once explained to me that you have to reflect on it – sometimes the market tells you something about your company that you have missed.

Finally, as a CEO, it is very unwise to tip your own shares, especially to friends and family. I thoughtlessly told a friend that I had seen a significant opportunity in the company I had joined. He bought shares and it cost him a lot of money. For a few years, he rather resented me – and not without reason. It's not worth it. You don't need the aggro of people buying your shares on your say-so and then losing money. Of course, if the shares go up, they usually view it as down to their stock-picking skills rather than your brilliant management.

The Indian Rope Trick

There are some strategies which can be particularly effective at a listed company. The 'Indian Rope Trick' is a slightly derogatory term which I think I picked up from someone. I can't be too critical of it, having been a proponent of it in various companies I've been involved with.

The underlying idea is to acquire companies on a lower multiple than your own listed multiple. You pay for the acquired companies using money generated raised from issuing your shares. The impact is an automatic increase in earnings per share (EPS) assuming the acquired company continues to contribute profits at its previous rates, and a bigger increase in EPS if it improves.

Let's take a very simple example. I am CEO of Bloggs plc which has 100 shares issued and trades on a P/E multiple of 10. I buy Smith Ltd on a multiple of five. In order to do so, I issue 10 more shares. Because Smith has been bought on a multiple of five, my extra 10 shares effectively pump my overall earnings up 20 per cent. Thus, my EPS (on all my shares) goes up by just over 9 per cent a share.

While some companies, particularly in the old days of the industrial conglomerate (older readers may remember GE in the US and Hanson Trust and BTR in the UK), buy broadly-related businesses, the IRT is most effective in a buy-and-build, where an operator is looking to consolidate a specific sector. In my case these have been tool hire, records management and, latterly as a non-exec director, compliance.

The key elements to the IRT and where it is most effective are:

- Small companies are generally worth much less than larger businesses (even on multiples of revenue).
- In most sectors, there are benefits of scale, particularly in administrative roles (you don't need two MDs, CFOs, etc.) and sales roles (particularly when both sales teams are competing against one another). You should also be able to buy better, not least by moving purchase prices down to the lower of the prices the acquiring and acquired companies pay.

- Often the acquiring company has better practices and can improve the acquired company's practices – and occasionally the acquirer can pick up some good ideas from the acquired.
- Being able to benchmark incoming companies against the main business and its components allows you to see where improvements can be made. Generally business costs conform to a certain model (e.g. on cost of goods sold, transport, labour, property costs, etc. and this will show you areas where cost can be reduced).
- Particularly in divestments from other companies, the business may have been neglected, the people may feel disillusioned, there may not have been much focus on the operation. The price may be low as the vendor wants to be seen to be undertaking strategic action and focusing their business. All these mean you have the opportunity to improve.

The keys to a good IRT are being in a pretty solid business yourself. Make sure you're in great shape when you start acquiring or you'll be building on weak foundations. I was lucky in two buy-and-builds where I came into companies with strong systems and reputation even if there were problems. In one case, the parent company was effectively bust, but the part of the company I was interested in had been originally established by a good operator who had built solid systems and a healthy business culture.

In another roll-up, this time from scratch (which briefly became a £1bn company), the initial business had weak systems and a poor culture and much of the first two years was spent firefighting and trying to work out the best industry practice.

Many attempted roll-ups including those using the IRT fail. This is most frequently down to:

- Having a poor initial business and believing that adding scale will reduce rather than increase problems.
- Failure to integrate businesses and simply enjoying the increase in EPS without working to harmonise combined businesses and achieve genuine cost synergies.
- Not appreciating that customers may not like a change of ownership and use this as an opportunity to change suppliers, resulting in lower revenues and lower profitability.
- Acquiring businesses from entrepreneurs looking to cash out in sectors where the barriers to entry are low. Once bored of the golf course, the entrepreneurs will start again and steal back the customers they sold to you two or three years previously.

- Poor people management post-acquisition where the stars will be the first to leave a business they no longer enjoy working in under new ownership.
- Focusing on the financial engineering side of the IRT rather than building a great business

The idea for the highly successful compliance business I was on the board of had been tried before but the poor execution and idle management in that effort led to failure in fairly short order.

Often the power of consolidation is huge and then the trick is not to share too much of that value with the vendors who may be happy with the price they receive and unaware or unconcerned of the value of their business to a consolidator. In one industry, the established valuation for a small private company was one times sales, which was about right for an industry making 15 per cent margins. However, with significant synergies and a more efficient operation, I believed I could increase that margin to over 30 per cent. It took several years by which time we had effectively become a duopolist in the UK (along with a major global operator). At that point the penny dropped with vendors and they realized they should be being paid more for their businesses.

You should be careful about showing too much of your hand. A roll-up opportunity I became involved in recently is likely to struggle because the acquiring company has pointed out to the fragmented marketplace how sensible it is for them to be consolidated. This means that potential vendors appreciate the value to the consolidator of their companies and want to take the lion's share of the benefits when they sell.

This is also reason why the bottom of the economic cycle is the best time to start a consolidation. This is the time owners may be fed-up and looking to sell out and the established valuations will be low. Moreover, this valuation model will remain in place for a while even when the economic cycle picks up.

There are many different styles of the IRT. The safety-equipment company Halma plc is perhaps the best example of the slow build. For at least 30 years, Halma has steadily grown its business primarily by acquiring smaller businesses at lower multiples than its own and integrating them brilliantly. It has taken time but it is now in the top 50 largest companies on the London Stock Exchange. Halma is also an exemplar of another facet of the IRT. It steadily moves into related markets often funded by its highly rated paper and consolidates those sectors both at home and abroad. And then, rinse and repeat. It is now considered a UK champion.

Investing in quoted roll-ups, particularly at an early stage, can generate huge returns, with very steep EPS growth leading to both a sharply higher rating alongside the increased earnings. This effectively turbocharges the shares and leads to a virtuous cycle of even higher EPS growth. I've seen this in a business I managed where the share price went up 20-fold in little more than five years.

At this point, a very smart thing to do is a variant on what Halma does, and move into more attractive related markets where the high rating will enable you to buy better quality businesses than your own and then grow them through consolidation, resulting in a long-term, highly valuable business. An example of this is a friend who merged his contracting business with a competitor, became quoted, bought some EPS-enhancing businesses and then used the resultant highly-rated paper to become a major player in a go-go sector with high quality of earnings and a valuation to reflect this.

11
WHEN IT ALL GOES WRONG

'We were carried off into a dark inane.'
ERSKINE CHILDERS, *THE RIDDLE OF THE SANDS*

The best way to learn what to do when bad things happen is for bad things to happen to you. How to quantify risk and how to deal with troubled companies – wipe, scrape and polish. The surreal and very lonely world of being in the middle of an epic corporate disaster – and what James Bond and the 70s stuntman Evel Knievel can teach us about failure and perseverance.

Shit happens

At our beach house on the Norfolk coast we have a sign on the fridge which says: 'Smooth seas never made a fair sailor'. The point is that 95 per cent of the time, only 10 per cent of your sailing knowledge and skills are required; the remaining 90 per cent are only needed 5 per cent of the time, when things get really tough. It's a saying you find in various forms everywhere.

As a CEO you may find yourself in trouble when times get tough and you don't have the right knowledge and skills to fall back on.

This points to a catch-22. It's difficult to acquire the knowledge needed to survive when things get very difficult, and yet the best lessons are learned when times are tough. Thus, the first time you find yourself in a really troubled business, chances are you won't make the right calls. But you will learn a lot. Failure is the best teacher and being in a troubled business will teach you far more about management than an MBA ever will.

Why shit happens

There are any number of reasons why companies end up in trouble. Sometimes these are external. It might be problems with the wider economy leading your customers to drastically cut their spending. It could be a sector specific issue (here, I always remember the effect of the smoking ban on dry cleaners – suddenly the number of stinking suits from nights in the pub plummeted. As CEO of the company which owned the largest chain of dry cleaners in the UK and was already in trouble, the collapse in revenues was immediate, huge and disastrous for the group). Or it could be disruption in the form of competition or technology – think of Amazon's impact on booksellers or the impact of streaming on music.

However, most external risks are (to a large extent) foreseeable and this points to the one thing that most troubled companies share: poor management. It's the people at the top not doing their jobs properly that causes nearly all company collapses. It might be failing to understand risk, it might be offering the wrong product or service, or it might be staying in a declining market too long. But the common thread is people doing stupid things.

It may be you who has done the stupid things or you may be picking up the pieces. Either way, the situation needs addressing. So how do you manage in a non-stupid way and ensure that you have the best chance of weathering any storms?

A good start is to quantify the risks you face. This can seem daunting but a comparatively recent and simple innovation here is the Risk Register. This attempts to address all the major risks an enterprise may face. It's a really good exercise if done intelligently and with regard to the specific business. However, you have to do it properly – too often it becomes an exercise in formulaic box-ticking rather than the outcome of a thoughtful, wide-ranging examination and understanding of the enterprise. And be aware that risk registers are never comprehensive – US Defence Secretary Donald Rumsfeld's 'unknown unknowns' are always out there.

Many years ago, when running a business in big trouble, I compiled an Immediate Risk Register. This was before anyone referred to them as this and, looking at it in retrospect, it makes very interesting reading for reasons that don't reflect very well on me.

What it shows is that I got it mostly wrong. I compiled the potential risks and ascribed likelihood of happening and scale of impact. I was way too optimistic about the risk percentages. In part, this was because as one area of the business unravelled it had a knock-on effect on the next. Every single risk I identified turned into reality. Basically, I had failed to recognize the full extent of the problems early on and the tendency towards contagion. In retrospect, the signs were all there. They included:

- Supposedly supportive shareholders selling shares whenever they could.
- Banks continually applying pressure.

- Several years of hitting the financial targets only through aggressive use of exceptional items.
- A thoughtful, decent customer making strong hints about corruption.
- A subsidiary company consistently hitting its numbers through a rapid increase in Work in Progress (essentially a balance sheet trick).
- A management team venting inexplicable fury on me when I delved into their business and started asking perfectly reasonable questions.
- The finance team crystallizing a profit on a currency hedge to improve monthly results. That was the last of the CFO's larder of understatements in the balance sheet being emptied and there was now only bad news left.
- A board that didn't want to know how wrong some of their historic decisions had been, to the point where they refused to discuss them
- At least two major capital projects where the Return on Capital was miscalculated and minuscule (or even negative).
- Skeletons falling out of every cupboard I opened.

Years of mismanagement had led to a terrible, near-terminal mess. So why didn't I recognize it? Because I was naive, dumb and hubristic. I'd arrived fresh from a big success – and that success had not taught me very much. I was only using 10 per cent of the sailing knowledge – and I couldn't use the other 90 per cent because I didn't know most of it.

So what should I have done? I should have moved much faster. I should have got to the bottom of the problems much more quickly and taken dramatic action. As it was, even as I was uncovering old problems, new ones were appearing. I should have recognized the mess for what it was and realized that the shares were worth much less than the company's debt. This meant the banks held the primary financial interest and effectively owned the business. I should have told the market that there were problems and that I was undertaking a review.

Having opened all the cupboards, identified all the skeletons, announced all the Foul-ups by the former administration and overprovided against the problems, I should have undertaken a financial restructuring. Then, finally, I should have worked on building a good business with some of the robust building blocks that were in place. But I didn't.

How to sort out a mess

Here it's worth looking at what the pros do, even if I have rather mixed feelings about them. There are specialists in restructuring, most of whom are exceptionally well paid. These include lawyers, banking advisers, accountants and management consultants. There is even an Institute of Turnaround Professionals.

Broadly, the specialists' approach is this. First they will discover who, if anyone, is going to pay their fees. Once they have established that they will be paid, they assume the absolute worst, throw expensive resources at uncovering the extent of all the problems, and sometimes take radical action. They will generally work for their paymaster, which is often the exposed banks, although it may sometimes be a parent company or a significant shareholder.

If the paymaster is the banks, the next calculation will be simple. Will more value, after expenses, be generated by putting the company into receivership or continuing to run it as a going concern? If they decide that the latter on is the best way forward, a capital restructuring is likely, again with big fees all round for all the professionals.

In the event of a receivership, there may still be a going business concern to be acquired. Here the business (but not the company) will live to fight another day, with much of the baggage that brought the original company down removed.

If a company is restructured, climbing out of the hole can take several years. The disastrous company I've just described did so after I left, with a CEO who had a great deal of experience in this area at the helm. Over a couple of years, he sold off the underperforming and non-core parts of the business. This allowed him to focus on a couple of the strongest parts which had always been excellent operations in their own right.

His approach contrasted with mine, which had been hopeful (yet hopeless). I was trying to panic-sell operations from a sinking ship while rearranging the managerial deck-chairs. My aims (inasmuch as I had any) were to raise desperately needed cash via exercises like sales-and-leasebacks of property, to line up alternative management teams to run what I feared was a corrupt division, to fend off the banks and to preserve as much value as I could for my shareholders. All these were made more difficult by the company being listed, which meant every finding, action and reaction had to be reported in real time to the stock market.

Some practical tips

Despite all this, troubled businesses can be a real opportunity for decent management, whether incumbent or newly arrived. Here, I offer some practical suggestions around what can be done to make things better. All of these are predicated on you having good management information – so ensuring this is the case should be your first priority.

- In a business with different types of operations or even different geographies, work out where the sweet spots are and where the real dogs lie. You need to protect and boost the former and get out of or crisis manage the latter.
- With the dogs, do a cost / benefit analysis on closure vs dramatic cost-cutting. Sometimes you have to keep a loss-making business going because the closure costs are too high. Here you should scale back as far as you can until closure costs are palatable.
- You'll be doing things like waiting for leases to fall in, for people to leave, for onerous customer contracts to end, and so on. While you do this, look around for potential buyers. These (as discussed in Chapter 3) will be companies that can generate synergies from your dogs which you can't. For example by achieving benefits of scale or having solid customers that you lack.
- Parkinson (him again) was famously scathing about large organizations which had succumbed to 'injellititis', where the corporate culture had gone sour with people focusing blindly on protecting their own position rather than trying to achieve anything. His solution was to break these organizations into smaller and smaller parts until managers had to take responsibility for outcomes rather than processes. Even in smaller entities, this is a sound approach.
- In a similar vein, *reculer pour mieux sauter* (draw back in order to make a better jump) is good advice. Don't try to grow yourself out of trouble – rather shrink back to what you're good at. If you do this, you will often end up with a robust operation which will grow without much effort once it's free of the laggards. Moreover, if you're shrinking, the pointless administrative functions which have grown and spread will reveal themselves and can be removed.
- Watch the cash obsessively. If necessary, set piddling authority levels so you can see every penny going out of the door.
- Make sure you have the right people. My experience is that in tough times, people tend to fall into three categories.

The first group are those who can see which way the wind is blowing and recognize that they will do better elsewhere. They will be looking around for the next opportunity and are probably smart enough to find one. The second group are agitators who become high maintenance and are a pain in the arse. They point out what's not right, ask for tools to put things right and worry about the future. The third group have seen this sort of thing before and get on with their job stoically.

You want lots of the second group in the key roles. They care about themselves but also about their people and the company. They may drive you nuts at times but they will help you realize weaknesses, not accept second best, and will be the people who will get you through tough times. People who are willing to tell you unpalatable truths are useful. I remember one colleague, a divisional MD, hissing at me, 'You have to sack him.' He was referring to another senior manager in a different division. He was right but, for various reasons, I couldn't. Nonetheless, I was grateful for his honesty. It wasn't self-interest either. He was in the trenches with me and really cared for the company. Many years later he became its CEO.

Most people fall into the third group and that's generally OK if they are not in leadership positions and haven't resorted to cynicism. I admire those stalwarts in businesses who may not find miraculous solutions but whose commitment to the cause is a source of steadiness and hope. One such person was an unambitious but excellent group financial controller. She was happy to replace the CFO in a troubled company when I asked her to, combined dispassionate process with a steely determination to keep things afloat in whatever state the business ended up. Given good leadership, she was key in helping the business plod out of its morass.

Counterintuitively, it is sometimes easiest to effect a turnaround when everyone else has given up hope (with the exception of the banks). At that point, all the stakeholders are used to bad news and most of the bad news is out in the open. Everyone has low expectations and if there is a decent business somewhere in there you will have free rein. It'll also be less stressful for you – anything positive you achieve will be a plus and anything negative will be par for the course. And, of course, you can make yourself some money (although probably not as much as the restructuring professionals will make).

Perhaps the best maxim for handling these turnarounds is best expressed as the 'Wipe, Scrape, Polish' maxim. Admittedly the first time I came across this was in the very different context of a primary school headmaster setting out hygiene principles to his pupils.

Failure is an orphan

In the right circumstances, taking over as CEO of a troubled company is a challenge but a good one. You want to roll up your sleeves and get cracking – there's work to be done. But often you will find it's harder than it looks – even if it looks awful.

As CEO, the buck stops with you – and rightly so. When things go wrong you will take the flak. Theoretically, the board should stand alongside you to support, advise, console and even deflect some of the flak. However, you will likely find yourself alone.

WHEN IT ALL GOES WRONG

The vultures, in the form of competitors, acquisitive bottom-fishers and the like, will be circling. What is more, many of those involved (co-directors, colleagues, advisers, etc.) who should support you and share some of the responsibility for the problems may not be behind you because they are looking after their own skins and wish to cover their own tracks. You are not a dead man walking – it's much worse than that. Some of the behaviour I have witnessed in troubled companies is jaw-dropping to the point where it feels like satire: the board pretending it was nothing to do with them; the divisional MDs scheming how they could buy their businesses as cheaply as possible; the advisers clocking up huge fees knowing that nobody would challenge these fees; the banks using brutal tactics to get their money back, as well as the additional fees they were now charging

Professional shareholders in these situations tend to behave more dispassionately. They can be pretty abrasive and unpleasant when you present them with disappointing results. But when confronted with a debacle, their stoicism kicks in. Some will have sold out at the first whiff of bad news and very few professional investors try to catch the falling knife which so frequently appeals to mug retail investors.

Those stuck with shares tend to act forensically. They are too emotionally feeble to take on the professionals who are pillaging the company, and are prepared to accept that a company going down the tubes is capitalism working. But they follow the process closely to work out whether a restructuring is likely or possible, and whether they want to play a part in refinancing what emerges from the wreckage.

There are few small-cap investors who deviate from this pattern. One I admire is a guy who is always up for a few ideas when a company gets into trouble and over the years has done very well by supporting restructurings. I think he partly does it as a bit of a risk-taker rather than as custodian for the widows and orphans he has looked after successfully for many years.

When things are looking tough the scavengers appear, too. I had never realized how many friends I had made in financial services – and at West London investment bankers' dinner parties – until I was running a sinking company. Generally it was the laziest operators, or those with brass necks, who suddenly remembered that I was somebody who needed a bit of their friendly help, in exchange for fees or the lowdown on where there might be a turn for them.

It's also interesting to see people's bloodlust appear. In a struggling business, I desperately needed to offload some assets. I knew these assets had value to other operators in this market and I knew they'd get a decent return, but naked greed is a funny thing. A logical trade-buyer reneged on a (admittedly rather generous) handshake deal. They decided they wanted to extract the most for their side to the point where it made no sense on my side to sell. Bottom-fishing 'recovery' private equity firms made offers and then hammered the terms down with no sense of decency. And has-been and wannabe corporate operators and financiers made encouraging offers on conditional funding that was totally imaginary.

Carry on Up the Khyber

Of course, while sharks are circling, as CEO, you have to keep up the pretence that the ship isn't sinking. Often this gets quite farcical and reminds me of my father's favourite film scene of all time. One for older UK readers, this is in *Carry on Up the Khyber*. The embassy is under attack and the British ambassador (Sid James) and his wife (the inimitable Joan Sims) have to pretend nothing is wrong as the edifice collapses. A few of these I endured were:

- Hosting dinner in Box No. 1 at Anfield football ground for the semi-final of the Champions League, knowing that it was wholly unaffordable and wincing every time champagne was ordered.
- Cutting the ribbon on a new head office opening knowing that it would be a close run thing as to whether I or the building was going to be closed out first.
- Bidding for (and unfortunately winning) the best lot at a subsidiary's charity auction, knowing that I didn't want a football signed by the England team and that the goodwill I would generate would shortly be worthless.
- Dutifully attending flamboyant networking events with my mind in chaos and knowing that I really didn't want the badge pinned to my chest, let alone the attentions of those ingénues who thought of me as a big cheese (albeit at the lower end).
- Trying to be jolly at a quiet but large Christmas party when all knew that I was no longer part of their working life.

It was an unenviable position to be in. Basically, as the CEO of a company and three months into the role, I realized that there was almost nobody else interested in the business's future except me. They all believed that the company was going down the tubes and were only concerned about saving their own skins.

Day to day, the company was eerily quiet with nobody expressing views about what I was doing right or wrong. It took me a month or two to realize that this was because a tsunami was on its way. All the birds had flown, the animals had run away and there was just me wandering on the beach alone with a few small fish flapping in the shallows for company. The wave duly arrived and, if I'm honest, I was probably the only major casualty. Everyone else had retreated to higher ground and was waiting to see what was going to be left once the floodwaters receded.

In that particular listed company, I reached the rare point of CEO denial – I couldn't face looking at the company's share price. I asked my secretary to ring a bell every time the shares dropped 5 per cent – one day when the chaos was at its peak, the bell rang four times.

As well as reminding me of waiting for a tsunami or a storm, the whole experience made me remember the second scene of the 1973 Bond film *Live and Let Die*. Here a funeral procession is playing a dirge while moving solemnly through the French Quarter in New Orleans. A British agent is watching and asks a sketchy looking bystander who sidles up to him, 'Whose funeral is it?'

The man replies, 'Yours' and knifes him in the gut, then the procession turns into a joyous Mardi Gras. Perhaps tellingly, the murdered man's dying expression suggests he can't believe he fell for such an obvious ruse.

What happens next?

When you're a CEO who has failed, things can look pretty bleak. You have gone from hero to zero. Do people want to work with you again? Will any bank or investor support your next project? Will you have lost your nerve? Do you really have any more appetite for running another company? Should you find a comfortable niche in a larger organization, (if anyone wants you)? The immediate aftermath and for quite a time afterwards can be the dark night of the soul.

However, there are upsides. It might sound trite but you learned more than you would have in something that went well. Most of the stuff which has helped me has been learned through failure. Failure is the best teacher – there really is no substitute.

Again, it seems obvious, but perhaps the single biggest thing you learn is to pick yourself up, learn from your mistakes and try again. It's a bit like Evel Knievel – the 1970s stuntman who was at least as famous for his crashes as his successes. He claimed to have broken 40 bones and suffered 433 fractures during his career. But he just kept going and in doing so he eventually jumped (among other things) the ornate fountain outside Caesars Palace, 14 Greyhound buses and a number of sharks.

Like Knievel, what differentiates a lot of successful businesspeople from also-rans is simply the ability to dust themselves off, learn from their mistakes and try again. You tried and you failed. Now try again. Don't be like Homer Simpson who once, very amusingly, said, 'You tried and you failed – the lesson is never try.' Continuing the self-help tone – never waste a crisis, particularly for yourself.

You should also behave well even when things are going badly. While I may not be proud of fouling up in a big way, I am proud that I behaved in a way that did not have ramifications for those I'd worked with. I suppose I would have liked to nail the real crooks and nasties, but as time goes on you need to let go of unsettled scores. You should also learn to accept your limits. Do not fart against thunder – but you won't be much of a CEO if you don't sometimes fart against high winds.

You should appreciate others too. Some people are surprisingly decent. A non-exec director on a board of a company I was running rang me a couple of days after a dismal board meeting to ask how I was feeling. As a former banker with little management experience apart from the dismal level of management that exists in the City, he didn't really have the art or practice of how to put his arm round someone, but I appreciated his humanity in trying.

But perhaps the single most important thing in business, as in life, is to remember that fortune's wheel turns. You'll be back on top again at some point if you stick with it – and make sure to enjoy it when you are.

ACKNOWLEDGEMENTS

With thanks to Rhymer Rigby, whose beautiful writing style makes this readable, and the lovely people at Bloomsbury.

QUOTE REFERENCES

Chapter 1. Seneca the Younger *Epistulae Morales ad Lucillum* Letters 71, Section 3. Loeb Classical Library (Harvard University Press) 1917, translated by Richard M. Gurnoe

Chapter 2. Adam Smith *The Wealth of Nations* Book 1 Chapter 2. W. Strahan and T. Cadell (1776)

Chapter 3. Sun Tzu *The Art of War*. Luzac and Company (1910), translated by Lionel Giles

Chapter 4. Anon

Chapter 5. William Shakespeare *Henry IV, Part II* Act 3, Scene 1. Bloomsbury (2016), edited by James C. Bulman

Chapter 6. Lord Bullock. *The Bullock Report Report of the Committee of Inquiry on Industrial Democracy* (1977)

Chapter 7. Joseph Conrad *The Mirror of the Sea*. Harper & Brothers (1906)

Chapter 8. James Sinegal, CEO Costco (1983-2011). Interview in *US News and World Report* (2009)

Chapter 9. Paul Wolfowitz, President of the World Bank (2005-2007). Attribution from QuotesCosmos - Paul Wolfowitz Quotes https://www.quotescosmos.com/people/Paul-Wolfowitz.html#google_vignette

Chapter 10. Fyodor Dostoevsky *The Idiot*. Barnes & Noble Classics (1913), translated by Constance Garnett.

Chapter 11. Erskine Childers *The Riddle of the Sands*. Smith Elder & Co (1903)

INDEX

acquisition strategy 19
age discrimination 116
Alternative Investment Market (AIM) 27
Amazon 73, 180
Ancient Greeks 12
angel investor 65, 66, 160
annual budget process 106
Apple 2, 73
The Art of War (Sun Tzu) 109
Aston Martin 149
audit committee 105
Augustus 127
Autonomy 35
AXA report 61

B2B (business to business) 10, 12, 36
B2C (business to consumer) 12, 36, 103
balance sheet 26, 31, 32, 42, 46, 49, 54, 70, 102, 181
Baldwin, Stanley 111
bankers 28, 95, 102, 128, 153, 154, 158
banking division 158
bank 28, 90, 103, 154, 156–9, 180–2
 balance 31, 87
 and CEO 154–5
 global banks 36
 investment banks 154
 lenders 71
 paymaster 182
Barbarians at the Gate 162
Beecham, Sinclair 62
benchmarking pay 105
Bezos, Jeff 73
big business 15
Big Four 91
Bigham, Charlie 2
Big Switch 92
BIMBOs (buy-in-management buyouts) 162
Blacker, Rohan 3
Bloggs plc 175
board 96–9, 104, 105, 107, 119, 144, 146, 158, 181
 good board 100–2
 meetings 85, 86, 98, 99, 102, 104, 106, 149
 roles 104–6
 room 100
Boden, Johnnie 3
Bond, Steven 92
Bond Helicopters 92
bonus 89, 128–35, 158, 164
Brandon Hire 3, 11, 16, 19, 21–2, 26, 30, 75, 79, 80, 84, 89
British Broadcasting company 74
British Business Bank 162
British Venture Capital Association 165
Buffett, Warren 22, 74

business   1, 3; *see also individual entries*
　　acquisition strategy   19
　　B2B (business to business)   12, 36
　　B2C (business to consumer)   12, 36
　　capital intensive business   13
　　contact making   17–18
　　cyclical business   14
　　emotional side   10–11
　　financial side   11
　　high fixed-cost base business   14
　　income stream   13
　　lifestyle side   10, 11
　　market cycle   15–16
　　market dynamics   14–15
　　networking   19
　　online information   16
　　owned by other people   12
　　owner-managed companies   12
　　polished-looking business   37
　　post-acquisition management   57–9
　　profitability   49, 50
　　profitable business   32
　　profit margin   34
　　small business   40, 67, 74
　　stable business   32
　　underlying business   17
　　virtual business   13
　　work-life balance   11
business management   109, 133
　　bullying dog-eat-dog style   110
　　hands off-approach   82, 84, 110
　　Management by Older Sibling   111
　　micro-management   110
　　over-friendly style   110
　　passive-aggressive style   110
　　Power and Responsibility Model   111–13
　　wheedling style   110

buyer   28, 30, 40, 43–9, 51–6, 66–9
buying business   63
　　balance sheet   42
　　freehold properties   42
　　post-acquisition management   41
　　price-earnings ratios   40
　　return on investment   40
　　rules of thumb   41
　　timing   42–3
　　turnover   42
　　valuations   41
　　working capital, company   42
Byzantine schemes   105, 146

CalPERS   164
Capita   9
capital asset   69
capital gains tax   70
capital intensive business   13
capital investment   65, 71, 132
capital projects   99, 181
Captain Mainwaring   157
Carillion's case   30, 156–7
Carry on Up the Khyber   186
cash flow   24–27, 31, 32, 102, 155
cash movements   31, 32, 156
cash profitability   27
CD   1, 2
centralization   113, 123
CEO   3, 9, 12, 13, 73, 100, 102, 104, 106, 107, 117, 126, 140, 143, 144, 146, 149, 155, 173, 175
　　believes bank   154–5, 159
　　big decisions   92–3
　　burden   74, 75
　　commitment   75
　　communication lines   82
　　day-to-day operations   81, 89
　　direct reports   82
　　hands-off approach   82
　　impact on business   75
　　leadership styles   93–4

INDEX

locking power and
   responsibility 81
managing adviser 90–1
matrix management 83
private equity-business 163
problems solving 89
public company 12, 23, 170–5
relationship with chairman 96
roles 19, 21
roll up 184
small business 74, 81
strengths 82
tasks and functions 87
tone of business 75–6
chairman 23, 26, 49, 86, 97
   bad chairman 97–100
   good chairman 96–7
   relationship with CEO 96, 97
Chief Financial Officer (CFO) 23, 26, 69, 82, 100, 104, 126, 143, 149, 155, 170, 173
Choe, David 135
Cleese, John 92
A Clockwork Orange (film) 159
Clooney, George 147
Cloud infrastructure 13
Companies House, London 16, 165
Conrad, Joseph 81, 140
consolidating market 15
contact making 17–18
contracts 27, 30, 35, 105, 149
Cook, Tim 74
cost / benefit analysis 183
cost-monitoring 120
COVID 74, 145
creative debt 155–6
crop-spraying business 92
cyclical business 14

Dad's Army (series) 157
damp-proofing business 68
Darwinian approach 88

deal-doers 34, 51
debt 23–6, 33, 65, 71, 103, 155, 156, 158
debt-to-equity ratio 155
defined benefit (DB) pension 26
Dennis, Felix 93
divisional MD 50, 78, 82, 99, 104, 106, 113, 125, 126, 142, 151, 185
Dostoyevsky 170
Dragons' Den 62, 82
drinks sector 44
due diligence (DD) 23, 27, 28, 30–1, 51, 52
Durrell, Lawrence 146

earnings per share (EPS) 45, 175, 177, 178
EBITDA margin 25
economic cycle 34, 177
EDITH (Estates Duties Inheritance Trust Holdings) 161
electronics business 169
Elsevier 92
entrepreneur 1, 2, 10, 38, 43–5, 55, 62, 65, 70, 73, 130, 135, 155, 160, 176
Entrepreneurship Through Acquisition (ETA) 4, 69
Europe 113, 142, 161

Facebook 75, 135
face-to-face meeting 53
family business 127–8
Far-Eastern bank 159
fast-moving technology 15
financial crisis 57, 154
financial DD 28
The First 100 Days 139
Flowers, Paul 77
FMCG (fast-moving consumer goods) businesses 44, 83

formal DD 28
freehold properties 33, 42
FTSE-100 company 78, 81
full-time job 65, 102
fund manager 18, 170, 171, 173

Gates, Bill 74
General Electric (GE) 88, 89
genuine bastard 148
German Field Marshal 78
Gladwell, Malcolm 39
global banks 36
global business 83
Goldman Sachs 91
good deal 46, 48
Green, Michael 74
Green, Philip 87
group debtor days 103
growth factors 129

Halma plc 177, 178
Hands Off, Eyes On 81, 106, 112
hands-off approach 82, 110
Hanson, James 77, 155
Hanson Trust 155
Harvard Business Review 109
Harvard Business School 129
Health & Safety (H&S) 58, 82, 106, 144
Heart of Darkness (Conrad) 140
Herzberg, Frederick 129
Hewlett Packard 35
high fixed-cost base business 14
high-margin contracts 35
Hold Harmless letters 28
How to Get Rich 94
HP 35
HR 83, 88, 147
  appointments and promotion 124
  recruitment 124
  role 123–4
  talent-spotting 124, 125
hurdle rate 163
Huston, Darren 77
HUT Group 167
hygiene factor 129, 132

The Idiot 170
immature business 88
immature market 14
Immediate Risk Register 180
immutable bastard 148, 150
incentive 91, 107, 130, 132, 133
income stream 13, 146
Indian Rope Trick 45, 175
integrity 77
Intel 77
internal rates of return (IRRs) 48
investment banks 154
investors in Industry (3i) 160–2
iPod 1, 2
IRT 175–7
IT recycler 4, 85
IT system 29, 58

Jack: Straight from the Gut 88
Jobs, Steve 73
Johnson, Boris 112
Johnson Service Group 17, 19, 21, 22, 24, 25, 79, 86, 90, 115

Kay, John 118
key performance indicators (KPIs) 50, 87, 88, 156
KISS (keep it simple, stupid) 80, 112, 132–3
Knievel, Evel 187
Krzanich, Brian 77

Laycock, John 2, 3
legal documentation 34, 56
lifestyle business 12, 74

INDEX

liquidity events 44, 168
liquidity moments 43, 44
Live and Let Die (film) 187
Liverpool Football Club 76
London Stock Exchange 177
long-term capital growth 131
long-term contracts 30, 35
long-term incentive plans (LTIPS) 107, 128
lower bonus 133–4
Lynch, Mike 35

MacArthur 58
Machiavelli 109
Macmillan Committee 160
Macmillan Gap 160
macro pitfall 43
management buy-in (MBI) 63, 64, 161
management buy-out (MBO) 63, 64, 162
Management by Older Sibling (MBOS) 111
Management Today 83
Marcus Aurelius 128
market cycle 15–16
market dynamics
    big business 15
    consolidating market 15
    developing market 15
    immature market 14
market knowledge 38
market sector 57
market value 49
marriage value 42, 46, 49
mass redundancy 14, 137, 138
matrix management 83, 113
Mavinwood 17, 18, 68
Maxwell, Robert 140
mergers and acquisitions (M&A) 39, 95
Meta 139

Metcalfe, Julian 62
micro-management 110
micro pitfall 43
Microsoft 74
mid-market PE firms 160
Miller, Martin 45
The Mirror of the Sea (Conrad) 81
momentum 56
Musk, Elon 138

narrative 78, 79, 144, 146
National Health Service 87
Nerva 127
networking 19
The New York Times 35
1992 *Cadbury Report* 95
nomination committee 105
non-executive directors (NEDs) 11, 23, 26, 73, 76, 90, 98, 101, 102, 105–7, 119, 126
non-lifestyle business 74

optimistic entrepreneur 155
Other People's Money (Kay) 118
other people's money (OPM) 118, 119, 121
over-friendly style 110
owner-managed companies 12, 66
owner-manager 18, 42, 125, 127, 162, 167
Oz (magazine) 93

Parkinson, Cyril Northcote 100, 183
Parkinson's law 100, 143
passive-aggressive style 110
Patton, George S. 78
pay 49, 55, 59, 68, 69, 71, 79, 91, 121, 135, 158, 163, 172, 173, 175
    benchmarking pay 105
    bonus 128, 130, 131, 133–5
    -controlled business 166

differentials, peers and near-peers 128
 in finance / marketing 129
 growth factors 129
 hygiene factor 129, 132
 incentive 130
 long-term incentive plans 128
 scales 37, 124
 share option scheme 128
paymaster 182
payroll 62, 156
pension fund 26
performance management 143, 145
Peter, Laurence J. 143
Peter Principle 143, 144
pharmaceutical industry 45
Pissing Money Up Against the Wall (PMUATW) 113
polished-looking business 37
post-acquisition management 40, 41, 57–9, 177
Post Office scandal 87
Power and Responsibility Model 82, 83, 111–13, 119, 129, 147
Power of One 74
Pret A Manger 62
price-earnings ratios 40, 45
Priceline 77
The Prince (Machiavelli) 109
private company 16, 32, 41, 43, 73, 167
private equity (PE) 25, 27, 28, 159, 160, 163, 165
 -backed CEO 166
 company / firm 27, 45, 46, 48, 64, 67, 156, 160, 162, 164, 167, 185
 -controlled business 163, 166
 cycle 162–4
 fund 160, 162, 164, 166

funding 63–4
 house 51, 64
 hurdle rate 163
 operators 164, 165
 owners 165
 traditional quick flip 163
private investor 62, 75
private sector 18, 70
private vendors 48
professional DD 29
professional investor 44, 67, 169, 170, 185
professional shareholders 185
profitability 13, 32, 49, 50
profit margin 15, 34, 150
property 33, 34, 42, 54, 63, 120
public company 18, 24, 32, 106, 166–9
 CEO 12, 23, 73, 170, 173
 investors 169–71
public market 40, 160, 167
purchaser 29, 44, 45, 50, 159

recruitment 124, 139
recycling business 38
redundancy 59, 62, 137–40
Reed Group 92
RELX plc 92
remuneration committee 105, 106
restaurant trade 44–5
Restore 18, 31, 67–9, 79, 83–5, 87, 93
retirement sales 16, 43, 160
return on capital employed (ROCE) 80, 92
return on investment (ROI) 40, 42, 45, 49
Risk Register 180
RJR Nabisco 162
Robinson, Gerry 92
Rod Aldridge 9
roll-ups 173, 176, 177, 184

INDEX

Rome 127, 128
Rucker, Chrissie 3
rules of thumb 41
Rumsfeld, Donald 180

Sale and Purchase Agreement 34
sale process 56
sales and purchase agreement (SPA) 59
SAYE (Save As You Earn) scheme 131
Schwed, Fred 153
Scottish company 161
Scoundrels In the C-Suite 77
search funds 65, 70
self-interest 133, 145
selling business 17, 22, 38, 46, 63, 67, 83, 97, 158
   earnings stream 43
   elements 52–3
   liquidity moments 43, 44
   private company 43
   public company 44
   retirement sales 43
senior management 58, 76, 106, 121, 125, 131, 134, 145, 148, 162
The Seven Pillars of Wisdom 114
S.G. Warburg 7, 9
shareholder 17, 18, 21, 22, 27, 37, 50, 52, 79, 80, 96, 101, 107, 117, 149, 167, 174
share option scheme 128, 130–2, 167
Silicon Valley 74
Simpson, Homer 187
Skinner, Keith 92
small business 40, 64, 67, 74
small-cap investors 185
small companies 5, 40, 52, 66, 67, 69, 123, 125, 175

small-to-medium sized enterprises (SMEs) 5, 81
Smith Ltd 175
stable business 32
stakeholder 38, 78, 95, 155, 164, 166, 184
Stanford University 77
stockbroker 169
strategy 78
success 21, 22, 48, 115, 130, 155, 181
succession 8, 127, 152
succession management 125–7
Sun Tzu 109
synergies 42, 50, 138, 177

talent-spotting 124, 125
Team Skinner 24
Thatcher, Margaret 113
timber treatment business 68
trade buyer 44, 45, 160, 164, 165, 167
trademark 29
turnover 30, 42
Tustain, Paul 3
Twain, Mark 80
Twitter 138
Two Factor Theory 129

ugly transactions 99
UK 87, 162, 177, 180
   1992 *Cadbury Report* 95
   entrepreneur 55
   family business 127
   Financial Services Authority 158
   Philip Green 87
   Post Office scandal 87
   public company 44
   recruitment 124
   RELX plc 92
   software business 35
   subsidiary 52

underlying business   17
Up in the Air (film)   147
US Glass-Steagall Act   154
US hedge-fund manager   171
US subsidiary   52

valuations   40–2, 45, 46, 48, 51, 53, 166, 167, 177
VAT payment   88, 156
vendor   29, 32, 40, 43–5, 47–57, 67, 70, 176, 177
   advantage   53–4
   deal   54
   information   56
   multiple earnings   70
   private vendors   48
   strategic approach   49
   trusts   69
Venn diagram   46, 49, 55, 57
Vietnam   87, 149

virtual business   13
von Moltke, Helmuth   78

warehouse manager   124
Weinstock, Arnold   110
Welch, Jack   88, 110
WePod   1, 2
wheedling style   110
Wheeler, Nick   3
Where Are the Customers' Yachts? (Schwed)   153
White, Gordon   77, 155
Wittgenstein   80
Wolseley   3, 21, 30
working capital   32, 33, 42, 69, 71, 157
work-life balance   11

Xenocrates   148

Yellow Pages   16

Zuckerberg, Mark   74, 139